Mickey Williams

SAMS
Teach Yourself
Visual C++® 6
in 24 Hours

SAMS

A Division of Macmillan Computer Publishing
201 West 103rd St., Indianapolis, Indiana, 46290 USA

Sams Teach Yourself Visual C++® 6 in 24 Hours

International Standard Book Number: 0-672-31303-0

Library of Congress Catalog Card Number: 98-84507

Printed in the United States of America

First Printing: August 1998

00   99   98   4   3   2   1

Trademarks

Warning and Disclaimer

EXECUTIVE EDITOR
Bradley L. Jones

ACQUISITIONS EDITOR
Matt Purcell

MANAGING EDITOR
Jodi Jensen

PROJECT/COPY EDITOR
Tonya Simpson

INDEXER
Greg Pearson

TECHNICAL EDITOR
Greg Guntle

PRODUCTION
Marcia Deboy
Michael Dietsch
Jennifer Earhart
Cynthia Fields
Susan Geiselman

Contents at a Glance

Contents

Dedication

For René, Alex, and Mackenzie.

Acknowledgments

As usual, a large number of people deserve my thanks for the help they provided me for the past few months.

First of all, thanks to all the people at Sams Publishing, especially Brad Jones, who seems to have several different jobs or is cloned into several realistic copies, and my acquisitions editor, Matt Purcell. Thanks also to Tonya Simpson, who did fantastic jobs editing my manuscript. Finally, thanks to Greg Guntle, who provided me with a great technical review and helped out during author review.

I'd also like to thank Bob O'Brien and all the folks at NuMega Technologies for their help.

Also thanks in no particular order to Simon Brown, Sanjay Gupta, and Rob Crandall, all of whom helped during the book writing process.

Last, but certainly not least, thanks to my wife, René. A wonderful wife, mother, and friend, she is much more patient than any author, especially me, deserves. And I still owe her a trip to Banff.

About the Author

Mickey Williams is the author of Sams Publishing's *Develop a Professional Visual C++ Application in 21 Days* and *Essential Visual C++ 4* and the coauthor of *Programming Windows NT Unleashed*. Mickey is a member of the ACM and IEEE Computer Society and the founder of Codev Technologies, a consulting and training company that specializes in 32-bit Windows development. Mickey can be reached at `mickey.williams@` `codevtech.com`.

Tell Us What You Think!

As the reader of this book, *you* are our most important critic and commentator. We value your opinion and want to know what we're doing right, what we could do better, what areas you'd like to see us publish in, and any other words of wisdom you're willing to pass our way.

As the Executive Editor for the Programming group at Macmillan Computer Publishing, I welcome your comments. You can fax, email, or write me directly to let me know what you did or didn't like about this book—as well as what we can do to make our books stronger.

Please note that I cannot help you with technical problems related to the topic of this book, and that due to the high volume of mail I receive, I might not be able to reply to every message.

When you write, please be sure to include this book's title and author as well as your name and phone or fax number. I will carefully review your comments and share them with the authors and editors who worked on the book.

Fax:	317-817-7070
Email:	prog@mcp.com
Mail:	Executive Editor
	Programming
	Macmillan Computer Publishing
	201 West 103rd Street
	Indianapolis, IN 46290 USA

Introduction

This book is written for programmers, beginning or experienced, who are new to Visual C++ and want to develop programs using Visual C++ 6. This book is a no-nonsense guide to programming for Windows, using plenty of short concise examples, without a lot of extraneous material or theory. Each hour includes short examples that illustrate how a different topic can be put to use. In most cases, the examples are limited to about one page of source code per chapter. This allows you to cover a great deal of material easily, even if you're not an expert typist.

What's New in Visual C++ 6.0?

Visual C++ 6.0 offers many new features and improvements over its predecessor, Visual C++ 5.0. Following is a summary of the new features that are covered in this book:

- The compiler has improved support for the ANSI C++ standard. Boolean types are now supported, and template support has been improved.
- The development system includes new enhancements to MFC, the Microsoft Foundation Class library. These enhancements include classes for Internet programming and support for new common controls introduced in Internet Explorer 4.0 and Windows 98.
- The Developer Studio editor is much improved, with features that allow the editor automatically to complete commonly used statements for you.
- The development environment is more tightly integrated with other visual tools installed on your computer, such as Visual J++ or the Microsoft Developer Network (MSDN) Library.
- An improved online help system puts the Microsoft Developer Network in easy reach, a mouse click away. The online help system will automatically use the latest version of the MSDN library if it's installed on your computer.

How This Book Is Structured

This book is divided into six sections, each of which focuses on a different aspect of using Visual C++:

- Part I, "Getting Started with Visual C++ 6," is a short tour of the Visual C++ compiler and its associated tools.

- Part II, "Dialog Boxes and Basic Controls," introduces the basic controls used in Windows programming, as well as the MFC classes used to interact with them.
- Part III, "Windows and MFC Architecture," includes coverage of the Document/View architecture used in Microsoft's MFC class library and event-driven programming.
- Part IV, "The Graphics Interface," introduces the Windows Graphics Device Interface and explains how it is used to draw shapes and fill objects in Windows.
- Part V, "Common Controls," covers the common controls first introduced in Windows 95 and Windows NT 3.51. These controls include the Tree View and List View controls, as well as the Slider and Progress controls.
- Part VI, "Advanced MFC Programming," includes important topics such as serialization, printing, and creating ActiveX controls.

Each chapter in the book is designed to take you about an hour to complete. The chapter begins with a list of teaching objectives and then dives right in to the first topic. In each hour, discussions are intertwined with hands-on examples that show you real-world applications for the lessons that you're learning. The end of the hour contains a Q&A section, a quiz, and exercises designed to test your knowledge and understanding of the hour's material. The answers to the quiz are found in Appendix A, "Quiz Answers."

What You'll Need

This book does not assume that you have any experience with the C or C++ programming languages, although some programming experience will be helpful. The first section of the book covers many basic parts of the C++ programming language, and other parts of the book discuss C++ language concepts as they are introduced.

The Visual C++ compiler comes in three different versions: the Learning Edition, the Professional Edition, and the Enterprise Edition. You can use this book with any version of the compiler.

To use the Visual C++ compiler, you'll need to use a recent version of Windows or Windows NT. You will need Windows 95, Windows 98 or Windows NT 3.51 or later. You'll also need at least 20MB of memory (24MB on Windows NT) and at least 50MB of disk space, although some installation options require over 500MB of disk storage. Like most Windows programs, Visual C++ will benefit from adding more memory; most serious programmers use 64MB of RAM or more.

That's all you'll need to get started. Now it's time to turn to Hour 1 for an introduction to the Visual C++ development system.

PART I

Getting Started with Visual C++ 6

Hour

HOUR 1

Using Visual C++ 6

Welcome to Hour 1 of *Sams Teach Yourself Visual C++ 6 in 24 Hours*!
Visual C++ is an exciting subject, and this first hour gets you right into the
basic features of the new Visual C++ 6 compiler and starts you off building
some basic programs.

These are the highlights of this hour:

- A short overview of the Visual C++ environment and how to work
  in it
- How to compile a simple console-mode program
- How to use AppWizard to create a Windows application

Exploring Visual C++ 6

Visual C++ 6 is the latest C++ compiler from Microsoft, continuing a long
line of Microsoft tools for Windows development. The Visual C++ package
contains more than a compiler; it also contains all the libraries, examples,
and documentation needed to create applications for Windows.

Windows development tools have certainly come a long way since the earliest
C and C++ compilers for Windows. By combining into a single tool all the

resources required to build Windows applications, Microsoft has made it much easier for you to learn to build applications.

The Visual C++ Integrated Development Environment

NEW TERM   An *IDE*, or *Integrated Development Environment*, is a program that hosts the compiler, debugger, and application-building tools. The central part of the Visual C++ package is Developer Studio, the Integrated Development Environment (IDE), shown in Figure 1.1. Developer Studio is used to integrate the development tools and the Visual C++ compiler. You can create a Windows program, scan through an impressive amount of online help, and debug a program without leaving Developer Studio.

FIGURE 1.1.

Using Developer Studio to create a Windows program.

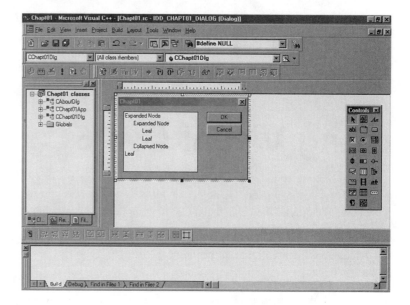

Visual C++ and Developer Studio make up a fully integrated environment that makes it very easy to create Windows programs. By using the tools and wizards provided as part of Developer Studio, along with the MFC class library, you can create a program in just a few minutes.

Many of the programs used as examples in this book require less than a page of additional source code. However, these programs use the thousands of lines of source code that are part of the MFC class library. They also take advantage of AppWizard and ClassWizard, two Developer Studio tools that manage your project for you.

Programming Tools Included with Developer Studio

Once upon a time, Windows programmers used simple text editors and tools that were hosted on MS-DOS to create their Windows programs. Developing a program under those conditions was tedious and error-prone. Times have definitely changed; Developer Studio includes several tools that you might once have paid extra to purchase.

- An integrated editor offers drag-and-drop and syntax highlighting as two of its major features. You can configure the Developer Studio editor to emulate the keystroke commands used by two popular programmer's editors, Brief and Epsilon.

- A resource editor is used to create Windows resources, such as bitmaps, icons, dialog boxes, and menus.

- An integrated debugger enables you to run programs and check for errors. Because the debugger is part of Developer Studio, it's easy to find and correct bugs. If you find a programming error while debugging, you can correct the source code and continue debugging without restarting your application.

Developer Studio also uses a special version of the Microsoft Developer Network (MSDN) Library as an online help system, which can be used to get context-sensitive help for all the tools included in Developer Studio, as well as detailed help on the C++ language, the Windows programming interface, and the MFC class library.

Generating Code with Developer Studio Wizards

NEW TERM A *wizard* is a tool that helps guide you through a series of steps. In addition to tools that are used for debugging, editing, and creating resources, Developer Studio includes several wizards that are used to simplify developing your Windows programs. The following are most commonly used ones:

- *AppWizard* (also referred to in some screens as MFC AppWizard) is used to create the basic outline of a Windows program. Three types of programs are supported by AppWizard: single- and multiple-document applications based on the Document/ View architecture and dialog box-based programs, in which a dialog box serves as the application's main window. Later in this hour you will use AppWizard to create a simple program.

- *ClassWizard* is used to define the classes in a program created with AppWizard. Using ClassWizard, you can add classes to your project. You can also add functions that control how messages received by each class are handled. ClassWizard also helps manage controls that are contained in dialog boxes by enabling you to associate an MFC object or class member variable with each control. You will learn more about ClassWizard in Hour 4, "Using Dialog Boxes."

- *ActiveX ControlWizard* is used to create the basic framework of an ActiveX control. An ActiveX control is a customized control that supports a defined set of interfaces and is used as a reusable component. ActiveX controls replace Visual Basic controls, or VBXs, which were used in 16-bit versions of Windows. ActiveX controls are used in Hour 19, "Using ActiveX Controls," and you will build an ActiveX control in Hour 24, "Creating ActiveX Controls."

MFC Libraries

New Term   A *library* is a collection of source code or compiled code that you can reuse in your programs. Libraries are available from compiler vendors such as Microsoft, as well as from third parties.

New Term   Visual C++ 6 includes Version 6.0 of MFC, the Microsoft Foundation Classes, a class library that makes programming for Windows much easier. By using the MFC classes when writing your programs for Windows, you can take advantage of a large amount of source code that has been written for you. This enables you to concentrate on the important parts of your code rather than worry about the details of Windows programming.

New Term   A recent addition to the C++ standard is the *standard C++ library*. This library includes a set of classes that were known as the standard template library (STL) during the standardization process. Unlike the MFC class library, which is used primarily for Windows programming, the standard C++ library is used for general-purpose programming.

> Now that the classes known as the Standard Template Library have been moved into the Standard C++ Library, the term STL is disappearing. The documentation for the classes used in the STL is under "Standard C++ Library" on the Visual Studio MSDN CD-ROM.

Starting Developer Studio

To start Developer Studio, click the Microsoft Visual C++ 6.0 icon located in the Microsoft Visual Studio 6.0 folder. To get to the Microsoft Visual Studio 6.0 folder, click the Start button on the taskbar and then select Programs. One of the items in the Programs folder is Microsoft Visual Studio 6.0.

Developer Studio initially displays two windows:

- A project workspace window located on the left side; this window will contain information about the project under development

- A Document window on the right side; this window will contain source files and project resources that make up your project

Developer Studio also includes a rich set of menus, toolbars, and other user interface features, as shown in Figure 1.2.

FIGURE 1.2.

Developer Studio as it appears when first started.

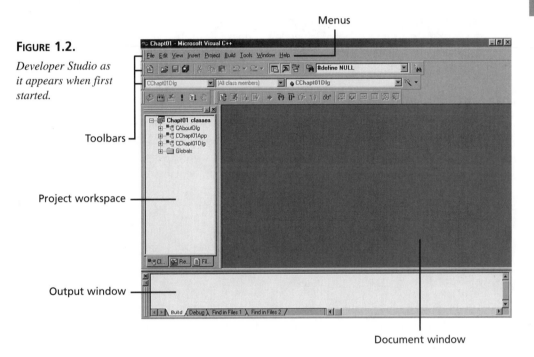

Menus

Toolbars

Project workspace

Output window

Document window

Exploring Online Help with the Microsoft Developer Network Library

Developer Studio uses the Microsoft Developer Network (MSDN) Library as its online help system. The MSDN Library included with Developer Studio will remain compatible with later versions of the MSDN Library. If you subscribe to the MSDN Library, this will allow you to search for help using the latest information.

Usually, the indexes used by the MSDN Library are copied to your hard disk and the actual database remains on the CD-ROM. If you would like to speed up the MSDN Library, run the MSDN Library setup again and install the entire library to the hard disk.

Using Dockable Windows in Developer Studio

NEW TERM   Many of the views displayed by Developer Studio are *dockable*, which means
            they can be attached to the edge of the Developer Studio workspace, where they
remain until undocked. The project workspace window shown in Figure 1.2 is an example of a dockable view. To "undock" a dockable window, double-click the window's
edge or drag it off the toolbar frame. To dock a floating window, move it to the edge of
the workspace. If it is a dockable window it docks itself. If you want to move a dockable
window close to the edge of a workspace without docking, press the Ctrl key on the keyboard when you move the window.

Getting Context-Sensitive Help

To get context-sensitive help from the MSDN Library, press F1. You select a topic based
on the current window and cursor position, and you see the MSDN Viewer window containing context-sensitive help. If you press F1 while editing a source file, help is provided for the word under the cursor. If there is more than one possible help topic you see a
list of choices.

The Visual C++ Editor

Developer Studio includes a sophisticated editor as one of its tools. The editor is integrated with the other parts of Developer Studio; files are edited in a Developer Studio
child window.

You use the Developer Studio editor to edit C++ source files that will be compiled into
Windows programs. The editor supplied with Developer Studio is similar to a word
processor, but instead of fancy text-formatting features, it has features that make it easy
to write source code.

You can use almost any editor to write C++ source code, but there are several reasons to
consider using the editor integrated with Developer Studio. The editor includes many
features that are found in specialized programming editors.

- Automatic syntax highlighting colors keywords, comments, and other source code
  in different colors.
- Automatic "smart" indenting helps line up your code into easy-to-read columns.
- Auto-Completion automatically displays a menu of items to help you finish C++
  statements.
- Parameter Help displays the parameters for Windows functions as you type.
- Emulation for keystrokes used by other editors helps if you are familiar with edi-
  tors such as Brief and Epsilon.

1

- Integrated keyword help enables you to get help on any keyword, MFC class, or Windows function just by pressing F1.
- Drag-and-drop editing enables you to move text easily by dragging it with the mouse.
- Integration with the compiler's error output helps you step through the list of errors reported by the compiler and positions the cursor at every error. This enables you to make corrections easily without leaving Developer Studio.

> If you choose to use another editor to create your source files, make sure the files are stored as ASCII, also known as "plain text" files. The Visual C++ compiler can't process files that have special formatting characters embedded in them, such as the files created by word-processing programs.

Using Editor Commands

A large set of editing commands are available from the keyboard. Although most editor commands are also available from the menu or toolbar, the following commands are frequently used from the keyboard:

- *Undo*, which reverses the previous editor action, is performed by pressing Ctrl+Z on the keyboard. The number of undo steps that can be performed is configurable in the Options dialog box.
- *Redo*, which is used to reverse an undo, is performed by pressing Ctrl+Y.
- *LineCut*, which removes or "cuts" the current line and places it on the Clipboard, is performed by pressing Ctrl+L.
- *Cut* removes any marked text from the editor and places it on the Clipboard. This command is performed by pressing Ctrl+X.
- *Copy* copies any marked text to the Clipboard but, unlike the Cut command, does not remove the text from the editor. If no text is marked, the current line is copied. This command is performed by pressing Ctrl+C.
- *Paste* copies the Clipboard contents into the editor at the insertion point. This command is performed by pressing Ctrl+V.

This is only a small list of the available keyboard commands. To see a complete list, select Keyboard Map from the Help menu. A list of the current keyboard command bindings is displayed, as shown in Figure 1.3.

FIGURE 1.3.

*An example of
keyboard command
bindings in Developer
Studio.*

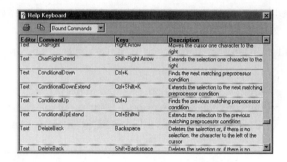

Creating Your First C++ Program

NEW TERM   A *console-mode* application is a character-based program that runs in a DOS
window. For your first Visual C++ program you will build a console-mode program that displays a Hello World greeting. Console-mode programs are often simpler to
build than Windows applications, and this example will take you through the steps of
building and running a program built with Visual C++.

Starting Your First Program

The first stage in writing your first Visual C++ program is to create a project. Follow
these steps:

1. Choose File | New from the main menu. The New dialog box is displayed.

2. Select the Projects tab, and then click the Win32 Console Application icon from
   the list box.

3. Specify Hello as the project name; a default location for your project will automatically be entered (see Figure 1.4).

FIGURE 1.4.

*Creating the Hello
console-mode project
in the New dialog box.*

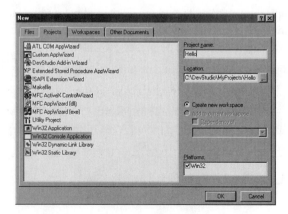

1

4. Click OK to continue.

5. A Win32 Application Wizard that asks for a project type will be displayed, as shown in Figure 1.5. Select the radio button labeled An Empty Project.

6. Click Finish to create the application.

FIGURE 1.5.

Selecting a console-mode project type in Visual Studio.

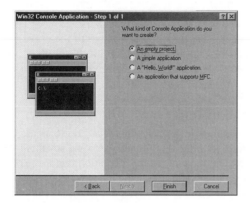

Editing Your First C++ Source File

The most important parts of any C++ program are the source files. Although the sample program provided in Listing 1.1 is very short, it contains many of the elements present in all C++ programs.

INPUT **LISTING 1.1.** A SIMPLE C++ CONSOLE-MODE PROGRAM.

```
// Hello world example
#include <iostream>
using namespace std;
int main()
{
    cout << "Hello World!" << endl;
    return 0;
}
```

Open a new source file document and type the program exactly as shown in Listing 1.1. As discussed earlier, there are two ways to open a new source file for editing:

- Click the New Text File icon on the toolbar.

- Select File | New from the main menu, and select C++ Source File from the New dialog box under the Files tab.

If you open a new file for editing while a project is open, you have the option of automatically adding the file to the currently open project. To take advantage of this option, make sure the Add to Project check box is checked, and provide a name for the file in the dialog box (in this case use `Hello.cpp`).

When you use C++ remember that capitalization is important. For example, `MAIN` and `main` are two different names to the compiler. Whitespace, such as the number of spaces before a word such as `cout`, is not significant to the compiler. Whitespace is often used to help make programs more readable.

If you used the toolbar's New Text File icon to create your new source file, you should save the file right away to take advantage of the Visual C++ syntax highlighting and auto-completion features. This is because the Developer Studio editor uses the file extension to determine the file type, and it does not know what type of file is being edited until you save the file.

Saving a Source File

After you have entered the program in Listing 1.1, save the source file in your project's directory as `Hello.cpp`. To save the contents of the editor, click the Save icon on the toolbar. The Save icon looks like a small floppy disk. You can also press Ctrl+S or select Save from the File menu.

When you save a previously saved source file, the existing file is updated using the current contents of the editor. If you save a new file you see the Save As dialog box, and you must choose a location and filename for the new source file.

To save a file under a new name, select Save As from the File menu. Enter the new path and filename using the Save As dialog box as described previously.

If you have not yet added the source file to the project, follow these steps:

1. Select Project | Add To Project | Files from the main menu. This will display the Insert Files into Project dialog box.
2. Select the `Hello.cpp` source file and then click OK.

Visual C++ requires that your C++ source files have a .cpp file extension. This helps Developer Studio properly compile your source code, as well as provide the proper syntax highlighting.

Other types of files also have standard extensions. For example, C source files must use the .c extension. Other file extensions will be discussed as they are introduced.

Building the Hello Project

NEW TERM   When you *build* your Visual C++ project, your program's files are compiled and linked into an executable program. Compile the Hello project by selecting Build | Build Hello.exe from the main menu (or press F7). If you entered Listing 1.1 correctly the project is built with no errors, and the last line in the status window reads as follows:

```
HELLO.exe - 0 error(s), 0 warning(s)
```

You can also build the Hello project by clicking the Build button on the toolbar. The toolbar was shown in Figure 1.2.

If errors or warnings are displayed in the Build status window, there is probably an error in the source file. Check your source file again for missing semicolons, quotes, or braces.

Running Your First C++ Program

To run the Hello program, open a DOS window and change the working directory to the project's directory. By default, this directory is

```
C:\Program Files\Microsoft Visual Studio\MyProjects\Hello
```

On some machines, filenames can be truncated, so the path on your machine might be something like this:

```
C:\progra~1\micros~1\myproj~1\hello
```

You'll see a subdirectory named DEBUG. The Visual C++ IDE puts all the executable and intermediate files into this directory by default. Change to the DEBUG directory and execute the Hello.exe program by typing the following at the DOS prompt:

```
HELLO
```

The program loads and then displays Hello World!. That's all there is to it.

All the console mode or DOS programs used as examples in this book should be compiled and executed just like Hello.exe. You'll always create a project, add files to it, and then build the project. After the application is built, you then go out to DOS and execute the program.

Creating a Windows Program Using AppWizard

AppWizard is a tool that generates an MFC project based on options that you select. AppWizard creates all the source files required to make a skeleton project that serves as a starting point for your program. You can use AppWizard to create single-document, multiple-document, or dialog box-based applications.

AppWizard creates all the source files required to build a skeleton Windows application. It also configures a project for you and enables you to specify the project directory. Although an AppWizard project is a skeleton of a future project, it uses the MFC class library to include the following functions:

- Automatic support for the common Windows dialog boxes, including Print, File Open, and File Save As
- Dockable toolbars
- Optional Internet Explorer-style toolbars, also known as ReBars
- A status bar
- Optional MAPI, ODBC, and OLE support

After answering a few questions using AppWizard, you can compile and run the first version of your application in a few minutes.

Building Windows Applications with AppWizard

In general, the following steps are used to build a program using AppWizard:

1. Create a program skeleton using AppWizard.
2. Create any additional resources used by the program.
3. Add any additional classes and message-handling functions using ClassWizard.
4. Add the functionality required by your program. You actually must write some code yourself for this part.
5. Compile and test your program, using the Visual C++ integrated debugger if needed.

1

To start AppWizard and create your first Windows program, follow these steps:

1. Select New from the File menu. The New dialog box is displayed.
2. Select the Projects tab. A list of project types is displayed.
3. To create an MFC-based project, select MFC AppWizard(exe) as the project type.
4. Specify HelloMFC as the project name; a default location for your project will automatically be entered (see Figure 1.6).

FIGURE 1.6.

Creating the HelloMFC project in the New dialog box.

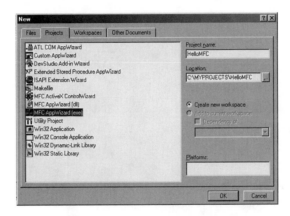

5. Make sure the Create New Workspace radio button is selected, and click OK to create the project.
6. The first MFC AppWizard screen asks for a project type, as shown in Figure 1.7. MFC AppWizard works similarly to the Developer Studio Setup Wizard, enabling you to move forward and backward using the Next and Back buttons. Select the radio button labeled Single Document and then click the Next button.

FIGURE 1.7.

The first MFC AppWizard screen for the HelloMFC project.

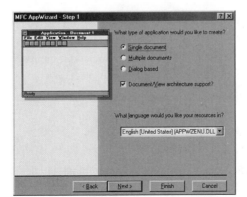

7. Move through all six MFC AppWizard screens. Each screen enables you to change a different option about the HelloMFC project. Although this example won't use any optional features, feel free to experiment with the options offered by MFC AppWizard.

8. The last MFC AppWizard screen presents a list of classes that is generated for the project. Click the button labeled Finish. MFC AppWizard displays a summary of the project, listing the classes and features you selected, as shown in Figure 1.8.

FIGURE **1.8.**

The New Project Information dialog box for the HelloMFC project.

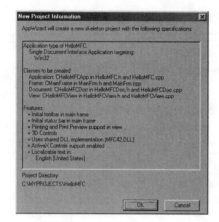

9. Click OK to start generating files required for the HelloMFC project.

Exploring the HelloMFC AppWizard Project

After you create the HelloMFC project using MFC AppWizard, the project workspace window opens. The project workspace window contains three tabs, each used to show a different view of the current project:

- The ClassView tab displays information about the C++ classes used in the HelloMFC project.

- The ResourceView tab displays information about the resources, such as bitmaps and dialog boxes, used in the HelloMFC project.

- The FileView tab displays information about the files used for the HelloMFC project.

Handling Output Using MFC

The HelloMFC project already contains a function that handles output. It's called OnDraw, and it can be found in the CHelloMFCView class. When your project is created by

AppWizard, the OnDraw function really doesn't do much useful work—it's up to you to supply a version of this function that does something meaningful.

To edit the CHelloMFCView class, follow these steps:

1. Click the ClassView tab in the project workspace window. A list of the classes used in the HelloMFC application will be displayed. Note that all the class names begin with the letter C. This is a Microsoft naming convention—all Microsoft's classes begin with C.

2. Expand the CHelloMFCView node of the tree control. A list of functions that are used in the CHelloMFCView class will be displayed.

3. Double-click the function named OnDraw. The editor will open to the OnDraw member function. Edit the CHelloMFCView::OnDraw function so that it looks like the function in Listing 1.2. You will need to remove a comment and two existing lines of code that were in the function already.

INPUT **LISTING 1.2.** THE OnDraw FUNCTION USED FOR HelloMFC.

```
void CHelloMFCView::OnDraw(CDC* pDC)
{
    pDC->TextOut(50,50,"Hello MFC!", 10);
}
```

Compile the HelloMFC project by selecting Build | Build HelloMFC.exe from the main menu (or press F7). The build window displays the progress of the build, which should look something like the following:

```
Compiling resources...
Compiling...
StdAfx.cpp
Compiling...
HelloMFCDoc.cpp
HelloMFC.cpp
MainFrm.cpp
HelloMFCView.cpp
Generating Code...
Linking...

HelloMFC.exe - 0 error(s), 0 warning(s)
```

Congratulations; you have created a simple Windows program! To execute the HelloMFC project, select Execute from the Build menu or press Ctrl+F5 on the keyboard. The most common way to launch a project from Developer Studio is to use the debugger. To start the debugger, click the Go button on the toolbar or press F5 on the keyboard.

Figure 1.9 shows an example of the HelloMFC application running under Windows 98.

FIGURE **1.9.**

The HelloMFC program displays a greeting in its main window.

One unusual aspect of the HelloMFC application is that the message is in a fixed location. If the window is resized, the text doesn't move. This is because the call to `DrawText` needs a fixed location for the message string in the first two parameters:

```
pDC->TextOut(50,50,"Hello MFC!", 10);
```

The third parameter is the actual message to be displayed, and the last parameter is the number of characters in the message.

In the next hour, you will learn how to display the message in the center of the main window.

Summary

In this chapter you were introduced to Developer Studio and Visual C++, as well as the main tools and wizards included in Developer Studio and the MFC class library.

You also created two small programs using Visual C++: a console-mode application that displayed Hello World! and a Windows application that was built with AppWizard.

Q&A

Q If I know C, how much effort is needed to learn C++?

A C++ is very close to C in several ways. Almost every legal C program is also a legal C++ program. C++ introduces the idea of classes, which are discussed in Hour 3, "Functions, Structures, and Classes." A C++ compiler also has a different standard library than a C compiler. As you will see, Visual C++ makes it very easy to develop Windows programs using C++, even if you have no experience in C or C++.

Q Can I replace the Developer Studio editor with my own favorite editor?

A No, but you can use your favorite editor to edit files, then use Developer Studio to build those files into a final executable. You will lose many of the integrated benefits of the integrated editor if you do this, however. You can change the Developer Studio editor to emulate Brief and Epsilon editors if you prefer their keyboard mappings.

1

Workshop

The Workshop is designed to help you anticipate possible questions, review what you've learned, and begin thinking ahead to putting your knowledge into practice. The answers to the quiz are in Appendix A, "Quiz Answers."

Quiz

1. What is a library?
2. How do you build a project using Developer Studio?
3. What is a wizard?
4. What are the three most commonly used wizards?
5. How do you invoke context-sensitive help inside the editor?
6. What are the four tab views inside the project workspace window?
7. What MFC function is used to display output?
8. What keyboard function is used to start the build process in Developer Studio?
9. What keyboard editor command is used for Undo?
10. What is the difference between Undo and Redo?

Exercises

1. Change the Hello World console-mode program to display your name.
2. The first two parameters in the TextOut function call are the position coordinates for the text message. Experiment with the HelloMFC application, and change the position of the output message.

HOUR 2

Writing Simple C++ Programs

In the previous hour you created and compiled some simple programs. Now it's time to learn some more details about how C++ programs work. Even simple C++ programs demonstrate basic concepts that are shared by all applications.

In this hour, you will learn

- The common elements of a C++ program
- Standard input and output in a C++ program
- The C++ preprocessor

In this hour you will build a simple C++ program that accepts input from the user and echoes it back on the screen.

The Common Elements of a C++ Program

NEW TERM Computer programs are composed of instructions and data. *Instructions* tell the computer to do things, such as add and subtract. *Data* is what the computer operates on, such as the numbers that are added and subtracted. In general, the instructions don't change as the program executes. Data, on the other hand, can and usually does change or vary as the program executes.

Fundamental C++ Data Types

The C++ language offers several fundamental data types. As in most other programming languages, these built-in types are used to store and calculate data used in your program. In later hours you use these fundamental types as a starting point for your own more complex data types.

C++ has a strong type system, which is used to make sure that your data variables are used consistently and correctly. This makes it easy for the compiler to detect errors in your program when it is compiled rather than when it is executing. Before a variable is used in C++, it must first be declared and defined as follows:

```
int     myAge;
```

This line declares and defines a variable named myAge as an integer. A declaration introduces the name myAge to the compiler and attaches a specific meaning to it. A definition like this also instructs the compiler to allocate memory and create the variable or other object.

When the Visual C++ compiler reads the myAge definition, it will do the following:

- Set aside enough memory storage for an integer and use the name myAge to refer to it
- Reserve the name myAge so that it isn't used by another variable
- Ensure that whenever myAge is used, it is used in a way that is consistent with the way an integer should be used

It's possible to define several variables on a single line, although as a style issue, many people prefer to declare one variable per line. If you want to make your source file more compact, you can separate your variables by a comma, as follows:

```
int     myAge, yourAge, maximumAge;
```

This line defines three integer variables. Declaring all three variables on one line of code doesn't make your code execute any faster, but it can sometimes help make your source code more compact.

Understanding Type Safety

Some languages enable you to use variables without declaring them. This often leads to problems that are difficult to trace or fix. When using C++, you must declare all variables before they are used. This gives the compiler the opportunity to catch most common errors. This capability to catch errors when your program is compiled is sometimes referred to as *type safety*.

You can think of type safety as a warranty that the compiler helps to enforce in your C++ program. For example, if you try to use an integer (int) when another type is expected, the compiler either complains or converts the variable into the expected type. If no conversion is possible, the compiler generates an error and you must correct the problem before the program can be compiled.

For example, character values are normally between 0 and 127 and are stored in variables of type char. In Visual C++, a char is a single-byte variable and is quite capable of storing all character values. If the compiler detects that you are attempting to store a number larger than 127 in a char, it will complain about it and issue a warning message. Listing 2.1 is an example of a program that tries to store a value that is too large in a char.

LISTING 2.1. AN EXAMPLE OF A PROBLEM THAT CAN BE CAUGHT BY THE COMPILER.

```
#include <iostream>
using namespace std;
// This program will generate a compiler warning
int main()
{
    char distance = 765;
    cout << "The distance is " << distance << endl;
    return 0;
}
```

To see an example of a type mismatch that is caught by the compiler, create a console mode project with Listing 2.1 as the only source file, following the steps used in Hour 1, "Using Visual C++ 6." The compiler flags line 6 with a warning; however, it still generates an executable program.

In order to get the program to compile with no warnings and run as expected, you must change line 6 so that the distance variable is defined as an integer:

```
int distance = 765;
```

Using Different Variable Types

So far, you've used integer (type `int`) variables, one of the fundamental types available in C++. They're called fundamental types because they are the basic data types that are a part of the language definition. In addition, you can define your own types that work just like the built-in types. The names of the built-in types used in C++ include the following:

- `bool` is a Boolean variable that can have the values `true` or `false`.

- `char` is a variable normally used for storing characters. In Visual C++, it can have any value from –128 to 127. If `char` is declared as `unsigned`, its range is from 0 to 255, and no negative values are allowed.

- A `short int` variable, sometimes just written as `short`, is similar to an `int`, but it can contain a smaller range of values. A `short` variable can store any scalar (whole) value between –32768 and 32767. If a `short` is declared as `unsigned`, its range is from 0 to 65535.

- `int` is an integer value used to store whole numbers. When using Visual C++, an `int` is a 32-bit value so it can store any value from –2,147,483,648 to 2,147,483,647. If an `int` is declared as `unsigned`, its range is from 0 to 4,294,967,295.

- A `long int`, usually just written as `long`, is a scalar variable like an `int`, only larger when using some compilers. In Visual C++, a `long int` can store the same values as an `int`.

- A `float` variable is the smallest variable type capable of storing floating-point values; that is, a value with a decimal point, like `3.14`. It is often an approximation of the value that was originally stored. In Visual C++, a `float` stores up to six decimal digits.

- A `double` variable stores floating-point values just like a `float` does. However, the compiler stores the value with more precision, meaning that a more accurate value can be stored. A `double` can store up to 15 decimal digits.

- A `long double` has the same characteristics as a `double` when using Visual C++. However, from the compiler's point of view they are different types.

Some of the variables in the preceding list can be declared as `unsigned`. When a variable is declared as `unsigned`, it can store only non-negative values.

An unsigned int can store a larger positive value because the computer must use one bit of data in the memory location to handle the sign. This sign indicates whether the variable is positive or negative. Because using the sign bit reduces the number of bits that are available for storage, the maximum value for the variable is reduced by about half. Figure 2.1 is an example of a variable that has been declared as int and another variable that has been declared as unsigned int.

FIGURE 2.1.

Most computers use a sign bit to determine whether a variable is positive or negative.

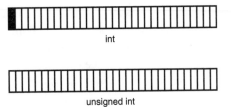

int

unsigned int

The fundamental variable types require different amounts of storage. As a rule, the char data type is large enough to contain all the characters in the machine's native language, or eight bits. The int type is usually the "natural" variable size for the target machine, so int variables are 32 bits in Visual C++. Table 2.1 lists the number of bytes required to store each of the fundamental types.

Earlier versions of Visual C++ that were used with Windows 3.1 were 16-bit compilers. The natural variable size under Windows 3.1 was 16 bits, so the int type was 16 bits. The last version of Visual C++ that used 16-bit integers was Visual C++ 1.5.

TABLE 2.1. STORAGE REQUIRED FOR FUNDAMENTAL C++ TYPES.

Type	Size (in Bytes)
bool	1
char	1
short	2
int	4
long	4
float	4
double	8
long double	8

Variable Naming

One important part of programming is the selection of names for your variables and other parts of your programs. The program listings you've seen so far have been very simple. As you become a more experienced user of Visual C++, you will need to establish some sort of naming convention for your identifiers.

When naming your variables, use names that are as long as necessary to indicate how the variable is used. A variable name in C++ is an example of an identifier. Identifiers in C++ are used to name variables and functions, among other things. In Visual C++, your identifiers can be literally hundreds of characters long and can include any combination of letters, numbers, and underscores, as long as the first character is a letter or underscore. Listing 2.2 is an example of several different variable declarations.

LISTING 2.2. SOME EXAMPLES OF GOOD AND BAD VARIABLE NAMES.

```
#include <iostream>
using namespace std;
int main()
{
    // Good declarations
    int     nEmployees;       // Number of employees
    char    chMiddleInitial;  // A middle initial

    // Declarations that could be improved
    int     i, n, k;          // What are these vars used for ?
    float   temp;             // May not be enough information
    char    ch;               // Should have more information

    return 0;
}
```

No matter which technique you use to name your variables, being consistent is important. For example, most of the sample programs and online help examples provided as part of Visual C++ use a naming convention known as Hungarian Notation.

When Hungarian is used properly, it's easy to tell the logical type of variable at a glance without searching for its declaration. For example, most scalar variables such as int, long, or short are prefixed with an n. Variables that are used to store characters are prefixed with ch, as in chEntry and chInitial. Most of the sample code available from Microsoft uses Hungarian Notation, which will be used for the remainder of the code listings in this book.

> It's a very good idea to use meaningful names for your variables. Using meaningful names makes it easy to read and understand your source code.

> Don't rely on capitalization to differentiate between variables. The Visual C++ compiler will treat xyz and Xyz as two different names, but it is easy to overlook the difference when you read your source code.

Assigning Values to Variables

In assigning values to variables you use the assignment operator. The assignment operator is just an equals sign used as follows:

```
int nFoo = 42;
```

This line assigns the integer value 42 to nFoo.

If a floating-point decimal value is assigned, the value is assumed by the compiler to be a double, as follows:

```
double dFoo = 42.4242;
```

You can assign to a variable of type char in two ways. If you are actually storing a character value, you can assign the letter using single quotes as shown here:

```
chInitial = 'Z';
```

The compiler converts the letter value into an ASCII value and stores it in the char variable. Small integer values can also be stored in a char, and the assignment is done just like an int variable.

```
chReallyAnInt = 47;
```

> The char variable type is sometimes used to store small integer values. This is useful if you are storing a large number of values because an int takes up four times the storage of a char.

A Simple C++ Program

In Hour 1, you created a C++ project named Hello that displayed a simple Hello World! message. In this hour you will make a simple modification to the Hello project—the Hello2 project will ask you for a name and then use the name in the greeting. Building this project will help demonstrate some common elements found in C++ programs.

Creating the Hello2 Project

The first step in writing any Visual C++ program is to create a project, as you did in the first hour. To review, these are the steps required to create a console-mode project:

1. Begin by selecting File | New from the Visual C++ main menu. This displays the New dialog box.

2. Select the Projects tab in the New dialog box. A list box containing different types of projects is displayed.

3. Select the icon labeled Win32 Console Application, as shown in Figure 2.2. You must also provide a name for the project—a default location will be provided for you automatically.

FIGURE 2.2.

The New Projects dialog box.

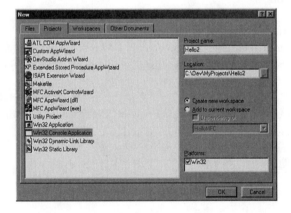

After you have selected the project type and the subdirectory, click Finish to close the Wizard, then click OK to create the project.

Creating the Source File for Your Program

The source file for the Hello2 project is shown in Listing 2.3. Unlike your first Hello program, this version collects input from the user and then outputs a greeting.

INPUT   **LISTING 2.3.** A CONSOLE MODE PROGRAM THAT ACCEPTS INPUT.

```cpp
#include <iostream>
#include <string>
using namespace std;

// Prompt the user to enter a name, collect the name,
// and display a message to the user that contains
// the name.
int main()
{
    string userName;

    cout << "What is your name? :";
    cin >> userName;
    cout << "Hello " << userName << "!" << endl;

    return 0;
}
```

Open a new C++ source file and type the code shown in Listing 2.3. Remember that C++ is case-sensitive. Save the file as Hello2.cpp in the project's directory. To review, these are the steps required to open a new C++ source file and add it to the project:

1. Select File I New from the main menu, and select the Files tab in the New dialog box.

2. Select the icon labeled C++ Source File.

3. Check the Add to Project check box, and enter the filename, Hello2.cpp.

4. Click OK to close the dialog box and open the file for editing.

Compile the Hello2 project by selecting Build I Build Hello2.exe from the main menu (or press F7). If the source code was entered correctly, the project will be built with no errors, and the last line in the status window will read

```
Hello2.exe - 0 error(s), 0 warning(s)
```

If there are errors or warnings, check the source code for typographical errors and build again.

Running the Hello2 Program

Open a DOS window and change to the DEBUG subdirectory under the Hello2 project directory. Run the Hello2 program by typing Hello2 at the DOS prompt. The program produces the following output:

```
What is your name? :Alex
Hello Alex!
```

The Hello2 program accepts any name as input and uses that name for its Hello World message.

Analyzing the Hello2 Program

Let's take a look at the Hello2 program because it has a lot in common with much larger C++ programs. Even though it is fairly short, it has many of the elements that you will see in more complicated Windows programs later in this book.

Include Statements

The first line of Hello2.cpp is a message to the compiler to include another file when compiling Hello2.cpp:

```
#include <iostream>
```

This include statement tells the compiler to look for the file named iostream and insert it into your source file. Actually, the #include statement is read by the preprocessor, a part of the compiler that scans the source file before the file is compiled.

Statements read by the preprocessor are known as *preprocessor directives* because they aren't actually used by the compiler. Preprocessor directives always begin with a # (pound symbol). You will learn more about preprocessor statements throughout the rest of the book.

The file iostream is an example of a *header file*. A header file contains declarations or other code used to compile your program. In order to perform common input and output operations, you must #include the iostream file.

Traditionally, C++ header files have an .h or .hpp file extension; the standard C++ library includes files such as iostream that have no extension. For backward compatibility, the Visual C++ compiler includes older versions of the include files that have the .h extension.

The `#include` preprocessor directive is seen in two basic forms:

- When including library files, the file to be included is surrounded by angled brackets, as shown in the `Hello2.cpp` file shown earlier. The preprocessor searches a predefined path for the file.
- When including header files that are specific to a certain application, the filename is surrounded by quotes, such as `#include "stdafx.h"`. The preprocessor will search for the file in the current source file directory. If the file is not found, the search will continue along the predefined include path.

The second line of `Hello2.cpp` is also an `#include` directive:

```
#include <string>
```

The string header file is part of the standard C++ library. Including the string header file enables a C++ source file to use the standard string class, which simplifies using text strings in a C++ application.

The `std` Namespace

NEW TERM   A collection of names and other identifiers in C++ is known as a *namespace*. By default, any name that is introduced in a C++ program is in the global namespace. All names found in the standard C++ library are located in the `std` namespace.

Namespaces make it easier to manage names in large C++ projects, especially when using libraries or code developed by different groups of people. Before namespaces were introduced to C++, it wasn't unusual to have two or more libraries that were incompatible with each other simply because they used conflicting names.

Namespaces allow libraries to place their names into a compartment that itself has a name. As shown in Figure 2.3, two namespaces can each use a common name, in this case `string`; because each namespace provides a compartment for the name `string`, the two names do not conflict with each other.

FIGURE 2.3.

Namespaces provide separate compartments for names used in a C++ program.

string

namespace std

string

namespace codev

When using a name from a namespace, the namespace must be prefixed, like
`std::string` or `codev::string`. Alternatively, a `using namespace` directive can be used
to tell the compiler that an identifier can be found in the global namespace, as in the next
line of the program, which tells the compiler that the names found in the program can be
found in the `std` namespace:

```
using namespace std;
```

Using Comments to Document Your Code

 A *comment* is a note provided to the person reading the source code. It has no
meaning to the compiler or computer.

Following the `using` statement, the next line begins with `//`, which is used to mark the
beginning of a single-line comment in a C++ program. By default, comments are colored
green by the Developer Studio editor. In contrast, `int` and `return` are colored blue to
indicate that they are C++ keywords.

 It's a good idea to use comments to document your code. After time has
passed, you can use your comments to help explain how your code was
intended to work.

The `main` Function

The next line of `Hello2.cpp` is the beginning of the `main` function.

```
int main()
```

The first line inside the `main` function is a variable declaration.

```
string userName;
```

Don't worry too much about what this means—for now, it's enough to know that
`userName` is a `string` variable. A `string` is not one of the fundamental data types;
instead, it's part of the standard library. The `string` type enables you to use strings of
text as though they are built-in fundamental types.

Following the declaration of `userName` is a statement that displays a message to the user
as a prompt for the user's name:

```
cout << "What is your name? :";
```

This particular statement in `Hello2.cpp` displays a line of characters to the console window by using the `iostream` object `cout`. The `iostream` library is included with every

C++ compiler, although it is not technically part of the C++ language definition; instead, it's part of the standard C++ library. Performing standard input and output for your console mode program is easy using the iostream library.

The iostream library uses the << symbol for output and the >> for input to and from IO streams. Think of a stream as a sequence of bytes, like a disk file, or the output to a printer or a character-mode screen.

2

One simple rule of thumb is that when you see the << symbol, the value to the right of the symbol will be output to the IO object on the left. When you see the >> symbol, data from the IO object on the left is stored in a variable to the right.

The iostream library provides the standard cin object. cin is an iostream object that manages the input of data into your program. The next line of Hello2.cpp accepts input from the user and stores it in userName:

```
cin >> userName;
```

The variable userName now contains whatever value was entered by the user.

The next line displays the Hello greeting and adds the contents of the userName variable. When using cout, several different components can be output one after another by separating them with the << symbol:

```
cout << "Hello " << userName << "!" << endl;
```

The last line of the main function is a return statement. When a return statement is executed, the function returns or stops executing, and the caller of the function is passed the value provided after the return keyword. Because this return statement is inside main, the value 0 is passed back to the operating system. The return keyword can appear almost anywhere in a function. However, as a matter of style, most people prefer to have a single return statement in a function if possible.

Summary

In this hour, you have learned more details about C++ programs. You wrote a simple console-mode program and analyzed its parts. You also learned about the C++ preprocessor, type safety, and variables.

Q&A

Q **When I compile the Hello2 project and enter my first and last name, only the first name is displayed. How can I display my first and last names?**

A When using `cin` to gather input as shown in the Hello2 project, whitespace such as the space between your first and last name will cause your names be parsed into two separate variables. You can use `cin` with multiple variables much like you use `cout` with multiple variables; just separate the variables with the >> operator. A new version of Hello2 that displays first and last names looks like this:

```
#include <iostream>
#include <string>
using namespace std;
int main()
{
    string strFirstName;
    string strLastName;

    cout << "Please enter your first and last name:";

    cin >> strFirstName >> strLastName;

    cout << "Hello " << strFirstName << strLastName << endl;
    return 0;
}
```

Q **When I declare a variable, sometimes I get strange error messages from the compiler in the Build window. This is the line that causes the error:**

```
int my age;
```

A In C++, all variables must be a single identifier. The compiler complains because after using the identifier as a variable name, it can't figure out what to do with the identifier name. One coding style is to separate the words that make up a variable name with an underscore, like this:

```
int my_age;
```

Workshop

The Workshop is designed to help you anticipate possible questions, review what you've learned, and begin thinking ahead to put your knowledge into practice. The answers to the quiz are in Appendix A, "Quiz Answers."

Quiz

1. What is the difference between the `cout` and `cin iostream` objects?
2. What are the two forms of the `#include` preprocessor directive?
3. What type of variable is used to store character values?
4. What is the purpose of a C++ namespace?
5. How can you declare more than one variable on a single line?
6. What is type safety?
7. What types of variable are used to store floating-point values?
8. How do you assign a value to a variable?
9. What type of variable is normally used to store integer values?
10. Why would you declare a variable as unsigned?

Exercises

1. Modify the Hello2 program to ask for your age in addition to your name; display the name and age in the Hello message.
2. Modify the Hello2 program so that it collects your name and address and displays it back to you in a message.

HOUR 3

Functions, Structures, and Classes

In the first two hours you've learned some of the basic concepts behind C++, and you have written some simple programs. In this hour you will be introduced to some more advanced Visual C++ programming topics. In particular, you will learn

- How to use expressions and statements in C++ programs
- How to use functions to provide small reusable chunks of code
- How to use structures and classes to create source code and data components

You will also build sample programs that illustrate the topics you learn in this hour.

What Are Statements and Expressions?

Statements and expressions are the elements defined by the C++ language that are converted into machine code by the compiler to build your C++

programs. Seems like a textbook-type definition, doesn't it? In reality, though, defining exactly what they are is difficult. When talking about a building, we can say that it is made of bricks, boards, and other things; we can define the brick or board very easily. In the case of the C++ programming language, it is much more difficult; here we are dealing with abstract concepts. The difference between a statement and expression is very subtle, as you will soon see. Although it appears to be confusing at first, the language will become understandable with practice. Eventually the C++ language will become as natural to you as your native language.

Just like the simple Hello programs, all C++ programs are made up of statements and expressions. Expressions and statements range from the simple statements that were shown in the Hello programs to very complex expressions that stretch across several lines.

Statements

All statements end with semicolons. In fact, the simplest statement is called the null statement, and it consists of only a single semicolon, as follows:

```
;
```

The null statement isn't used often; it's used only in situations in which the C++ syntax requires a statement, but no real work needs to be done.

You use a statement to tell the compiler to perform some type of specific action. For example, you know from the console mode programs you created that the following statement will display the characters Hello World! on your screen:

```
cout << "Hello World!" << endl;
```

Declarations

A declaration is another type of statement. A declaration introduces a variable to the compiler. The following line is an example of a simple declaration:

```
int myAge;
```

This tells the compiler that myAge is an integer.

Assignment

An assignment expression is used to assign a value to a variable, using the assignment operator, =, as follows:

```
int     myAge;
myAge = 135;
```

Every expression has a value. The value of an assignment expression is the value of the assignment. This means that the following statement assigns the value 42 to the variables yourAge and myAge:

```
myAge = yourAge = 42;
```

The program in Listing 3.1 demonstrates how to assign a value to a variable.

LISTING 3.1. A C++ PROGRAM THAT ASSIGNS A VALUE TO A VARIABLE.

```
#include <iostream>
using namespace std;
int main()
{
    int myAge;
    myAge = 42;
    cout << "Hello" << endl;
    cout << "My age is " << myAge << endl;
    return 0;
}
```

3

The assignment operator is just one example of the operators available in C++. More operators are discussed in the next section.

Other Common Expressions and Operators

The C++ language contains operators that you can use to write addition, subtraction, multiplication, and other expressions. Some common math operators are shown in Table 3.1.

TABLE 3.1. SOME COMMON MATH OPERATORS USED IN C++.

Operator	Description
+	Addition
-	Subtraction
/	Division
*	Multiplication

All math operators group from left to right. The multiplication and division operators have a higher precedence than the addition and subtraction operators. This means that the following expressions are equivalent:

a + 5 * 3

a + 15

You can use parentheses to force an expression to be evaluated in a preferred order. Note the grouping of the following expression:

(a + 5) * 3

This expression adds 5 to the value stored in a and then multiplies that value by 3. The math operators can also be combined with an assignment operator, as follows:

```
int myAge;
myAge = 40 + 2;
```

The expression 40 + 2 has a value of 42. After that value is calculated, the value of the expression is stored in the myAge variable.

Using Functions

NEW TERM A *function* is a group of computer instructions that performs a well-defined task inside a computer program. Functions are one of the primary building blocks of C and C++ applications. Functions provide a way to break up a large program into more manageable parts. At the same time, functions make it possible to perform the same task at various points within the program without repeating the code.

For example, if you buy a wagon you'll find that it comes with a full set of assembly instructions and has four identical wheels. Why should the instructions repeat the steps to assemble a wheel four times? It is much easier to describe the wheel assembly process once and indicate that you perform the process for each wheel. The wheel assembly instructions are a module (function) within the full set of assembly instructions (program) that is executed four times.

Every C++ program has at least one function; this function is usually called main. The main function is called by the operating system when your application starts; when main has finished executing, your program has finished.

Most Windows programs written in C++ have a similar function named WinMain that serves the same purpose as main in a console-mode program. In an MFC program the WinMain function is part of the MFC library code—you will rarely need to provide a WinMain function yourself.

Declaring Function Prototypes

Before you can use a function, you must declare it by supplying a function prototype to the compiler. To declare a function you specify the function's name, its return value, and a list of any parameters that are passed to it, as shown here:

```
int CalculateAge(int nYearBorn);
```

This line is a function prototype for the CalculateAge function, which takes a single integer as a parameter and returns an integer as its result. A function that returns no value is declared as returning the void type.

NEW TERM   The traditional way to provide function prototypes is to place them in *header files*, which are usually named with an .h extension. Header files that are part of the C++ standard library do not use the .h extension; two examples of standard header files are iostream and math. These header files contain all the prototypes and other declarations needed for IO streams and math functions to be compiled correctly.

Defining Functions

A function is defined the same way the main function is defined. All function definitions follow the same pattern; it's basically the function prototype with the function's body added to it. The function definition always consists of the following:

- The function's return value
- The function's name
- The function's parameter list
- The actual function body, enclosed in curly braces

Listing 3.2 shows how to use a function to display the Hello World! message. To run this project, create a new console-mode project named HelloFunc, using the steps described for the Hello and Hello2 projects in the first two hours.

INPUT   **LISTING 3.2.** THE HELLO WORLD! PROGRAM REWRITTEN TO USE A FUNCTION.

```
#include <iostream>
using namespace std;
// Function prototype
void DisplayAge(int nAge);

int main()
{
    DisplayAge(42);
    return 0;
}

void DisplayAge(int nAge)
{
    cout << "Hello World! I'm " << nAge << " years old." << endl;
}
```

Because the function doesn't return a value to the calling function, the return type is
defined as void.

Calling Functions

In the C++ language, the act of transferring control to a function is known as *calling* the
function. When a function is called, you supply a function name and a list of parameters,
if any. The following steps take place when a function is called:

1. The compiler makes a note of the location from which the function was called and
   makes a copy of the parameter list, if any.
2. Any storage required for the function to execute is temporarily created.
3. The called function starts executing, using copies of the data that was supplied in
   the parameter list.
4. After the function has finished executing, control is returned to the calling function
   and memory used by the function is released.

These steps are shown in Figure 3.1, which uses the function from Listing 3.1 as an
example.

FIGURE 3.1.

*Steps involved in
calling a function.*

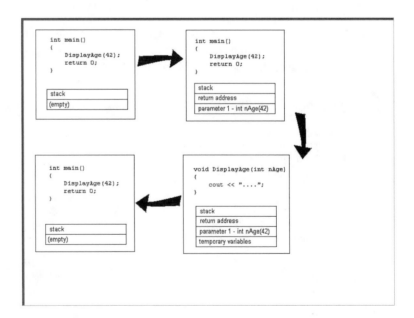

The requirement that you declare functions before using them is an extension of the C++ type system. Because function prototypes are required, the compiler can detect errors such as incorrect parameters used in a function call.

What Are Structures?

 A *structure* is a data type that contains other data types grouped together into a single user-defined type.

Structures are commonly used when it makes sense to associate two or more data variables.

3

An example of a structure is a payroll record, where the number of hours worked and the pay rate are combined in a structure, as shown in Figure 3.2.

FIGURE 3.2.

Structures are made up of member variables.

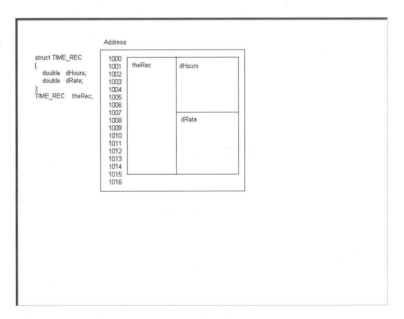

Declaring a structure introduces a new type of variable into your program. Variables of this new type can be defined just like int, char, or float variables are defined. Listing 3.3 is an example of how a structure is typically used.

LISTING 3.3. USING A STRUCTURE TO CALCULATE A WEEKLY SALARY.

```
#include <iostream>
using namespace std;
struct  TIME_REC
{
    double    dHours;
    double    dRate;
} ;

int main()
{
    TIME_REC    payrollRecord;
    payrollRecord.dHours = 40.0;
    payrollRecord.dRate = 3.75;

    cout << "This week's payroll information:" << endl;
    cout << "Hours worked : " << payrollRecord.dHours << endl;
    cout << "Rate         :$" << payrollRecord.dRate  << endl;

    double dSalary = payrollRecord.dRate * payrollRecord.dHours;
    cout << "Salary       :$" << dSalary  << endl;

    return 0;
}
```

What Are Classes?

NEW TERM   A *class* allows data and functions to be bundled together and used as if they were a single element. Classes typically model real-world concepts that have both data and some sort of behavior, although this is not a hard and fast rule.

NEW TERM   A function that is defined as part of a class is often called a *method*.

Classes are similar to structures; in fact, classes really are just structures with a different name. Classes have one feature that makes them very useful for object-oriented programming: Unless a member of a class is specifically declared as public, that member is generally not accessible from outside the class. This means that you can hide the implementation of methods behind the external interface.

Like functions, classes are an important part of the C++ programming language. In fact, one of the earliest names for C++ was *C with Classes*.

 An *instance* of a class, sometimes called an object, is an occurrence of a class. An instance of one of your classes can be used or manipulated inside your programs.

The Parts of a C++ Class

When using Visual C++, objects such as dialog boxes, window frames, menus, and buttons are controlled by C++ classes. A class is just a description of the object that can be created and the actions that can be performed on it.

A C++ class has two main parts:

- The *class declaration*. This contains the class interface and information about data members for the class. The class interface usually is located in a header file having a .H suffix. Any file in your program that uses the class must use the #include directive so that the preprocessor adds the class declaration to the source file.

- The *class implementation*. This includes all the member functions that have been declared as part of the class. The class implementation usually is located in a file that has a .CPP suffix.

The data that makes up an object, and the functions that are performed on that object, are combined to form a class, or a description of that object. Classes can inherit functionality from other objects, and you easily can add new classes that leverage existing classes.

Classes Versus Instances

Classes and instances of classes are not the same things. This can sometimes be a confusing concept if you are new to C++ or object-oriented programming. Think of a class as the description of an object; an instance of a class is a concrete occurrence of that class.

Constructors

 A *constructor* is a special member function that is created when an object of the class is created. A constructor always has the same name as the class and never has a return value, not even void. The purpose of the constructor is to place a newly created object into a known state. Typically, constructors can allocate system resources, clear or set variables, or perform some other type of initialization.

Destructors

NEW TERM   A *destructor* is a special member function that is called as an object is destroyed. The destructor is declared as having no return type and is never declared with a parameter list. The name of the destructor is the class name prefixed by a tilde (~) character.

Defining a destructor is not necessary unless specific tasks must be performed to clean up after an object, such as releasing system resources that might have been allocated.

An Example of a Simple C++ Class

As an example of a C++ class, let's look at a class that represents a weekly payroll record. The class must have two member variables:

- The number of hours worked
- The hourly salary

The class will also define three member functions that

- Set the hourly salary
- Set the number of hours worked
- Retrieve the calculated salary for the pay period

The definition of a class is similar to that of a structure, except that the keyword class is used instead of struct. Listing 3.4 provides a declaration for a CWeeklyPayRecord class.

LISTING 3.4. A DECLARATION FOR A WEEKLY PAY RECORD CLASS.

```
class CWeeklyPayRecord
{
    public:
        void    HoursWorked( double dHours );
        void    PayRate( double dRate );
        double GetSalary();

    private:
        double m_dHours;
        double m_dRate;
} ;
```

The keywords public and private are used to grant or deny access to members of the class. Any members of the class declared after the public keyword can be accessed from outside the class, just as though they were members of a structure. Any members of the class declared after the `private` keyword are not accessible outside the class. Any number of `public` or `private` access specifiers can be present in a class declaration. The closest access specifier, reading from top to bottom, is the one that is currently controlling a declaration.

Listing 3.5 is a complete example that uses the `CWeeklyPayRecord` class, with some typical member functions added.

LISTING 3.5. A COMPLETE EXAMPLE USING THE `CWeeklyPayRecord` CLASS.

```cpp
#include <iostream>
using namespace std;

class CWeeklyPayRecord
{
    public:
        void    HoursWorked( double dHours );
        void    PayRate( double dRate );
        double GetSalary();
    private:
        double m_dHours;
        double m_dRate;
} ;
//
// main - Create a weekly salary object, and calculate this
//         week's salary.
//
int main()
{
    CWeeklyPayRecord     weeklyPay;

    weeklyPay.HoursWorked( 40.0 );
    weeklyPay.PayRate( 3.75 );

    cout << "This week's payroll information:" << endl;
    cout << "Salary        :$" << weeklyPay.GetSalary() << endl;

    return 0;
}
//
// Member functions for the CWeeklyPayRecord class
//
void    CWeeklyPayRecord::HoursWorked( double dHours )
{
    m_dHours = dHours;
}
```

3

continues

LISTING 3.5. CONTINUED

```
void    CWeeklyPayRecord::PayRate( double dRate )
{
    m_dRate = dRate;
}

double CWeeklyPayRecord::GetSalary()
{
    return m_dHours * m_dRate;
}
```

Note that the member functions in Listing 3.5 are prefixed with CWeeklyPayRecord::
when they are defined. The names of all member functions are prefixed with their class
names; this is the only way the compiler can determine to which class the function
belongs. The only exception to this rule is a function that is defined inside the class
declaration.

Rectangles and Regions

The rectangle is a fundamental component of most Windows programs. Because most
windows and controls are rectangular, it isn't surprising that one of the most commonly
used data structures in Windows programming is used to represent a rectangle.

Rectangles are often used to represent the position or size of all types of windows: main
windows as well as controls, toolbars, and dialog boxes. There are two basic types of
rectangle coordinates:

- Screen rectangle coordinates, which place a rectangle in relationship to the entire
  screen
- Client rectangle coordinates, which always have their top and left values set to zero
  and provide the size of a rectangle that represents a window's client area

Screen rectangle coordinates are often used when moving a window in relation to the
entire screen. Client rectangles are most commonly used when positioning controls or
drawing inside a control or other window.

When requesting the dimensions of a rectangle, you must pass a CRect variable to one of
the Windows rectangle functions. The following two lines of code declare an instance of
CRect as a variable and pass it to the GetClientRect function:

```
CRect rcClient;
GetClientRect(rcClient);
```

The next example uses a client area rectangle to display a message to the user, just like the HelloMFC program in the first hour. The new example will draw the message in the center of the client area; if the window is resized, the message will be redrawn in the center of the new rectangle.

Create an MFC AppWizard application named HelloRect, following the steps presented in the first hour. Modify the OnDraw function found in the CHelloRectView class so that it looks like the function shown in Listing 3.6.

INPUT **LISTING 3.6.** USING A RECTANGLE TO CENTER A MESSAGE IN A WINDOW.

```
void CHelloRectView::OnDraw(CDC* pDC)
{
    CRect         rcClient;
    GetClientRect(rcClient);
    pDC->DrawText("Hello Client Rectangle!", -1, rcClient,
    DT_SINGLELINE | DT_CENTER | DT_VCENTER );
}
```

3

Build the HelloRect application and run it from Developer Studio. Note that if you resize the window, the message is redrawn so that it remains in the center of the client area.

Summary

In this hour you learned some of the more advanced building blocks that make up C++ programs: functions, structures, and classes. As an example of how C++ classes are used, a payroll class was created and used. The hour finished with a discussion about rectangles and regions in Windows programs.

Q&A

Q What is the difference between a rectangle that uses screen coordinates and a rectangle that uses client coordinates?

A Every window in a Windows application can be represented by a rectangle; this rectangle will typically use either screen or client coordinates. The rectangle that results from these coordinates is always the same, the difference is only in the point of reference that is used to measure the rectangle.

Q Can a structure have member functions?

A Absolutely. A class and a structure are exactly the same, except that all members of a structure are accessible by default, while class members are private (not accessible) by default. You will learn more about access restrictions in the next hour.

Q Why is no function prototype required for `main()`?

A The short answer: because the C++ standard says you don't need one. The purpose of function prototypes is to introduce new functions to the compiler; because every C++ program is required to have a main function, no function is necessary.

Workshop

The Workshop is designed to help you anticipate possible questions, review what you've learned, and begin thinking ahead to putting your knowledge into practice. The answers to the quiz are in Appendix A, "Quiz Answers."

Quiz

1. What is a function?
2. What are the four parts of a function definition?
3. How are classes different from structures?
4. What function is called when an instance of a class is created?
5. What function is called when an instance of a class is destroyed?
6. What is the value of the expression a = 42?
7. What symbol is used for multiplication?
8. What symbol is used for division?

Exercises

1. Write a console-mode program that asks for a distance in miles and converts the distance into feet. There are 5,280 feet in a mile.
2. Modify the HelloRect program to display different messages in different parts of the main window.
3. Modify the CWeeklyPayRecord class so that it calculates overtime pay.
4. Create a declaration for a class that tracks a screen location. The class should store an X and Y coordinate position and include member functions that set and retrieve the coordinates.

PART II
Dialog Boxes and Basic Controls

Hour

HOUR 4

Using Dialog Boxes

In this hour you will learn about a fundamental concept used when creating Windows programs: dialog boxes. The following topics are covered in this hour:

- Using dialog boxes in your Windows applications
- Creating dialog box–based projects
- Adding controls to dialog boxes
- Creating new classes using ClassWizard

Also during this hour you will create two sample projects that demonstrate how you can use dialog boxes in your applications.

What Is a Dialog Box?

NEW TERM A *dialog box* is a specialized window that is used to provide feedback or collect input from the user. Dialog boxes come in all shapes and sizes, ranging from simple message boxes that display single lines of text to large dialog boxes that contain sophisticated controls.

Dialog boxes are also used for one-way communication with a user, such as splash screens used to display copyright and startup information as a program is launched. The opening screen displayed by Developer Studio and Microsoft Word are two examples of dialog boxes used for one-way communication. Dialog boxes are sometimes used to notify the user about the progress of a lengthy operation.

> Dialog boxes provide a convenient way for users to interact with Windows programs. Users expect most interactions with a Windows program to take place through dialog boxes. All dialog boxes have certain things in common; these common characteristics make the user's life easier because users don't need to learn and relearn how dialog boxes work from program to program.

There are several different types of dialog boxes, and each has a specific purpose. This hour covers two main types of dialog boxes:

- Modal dialog boxes
- Modeless dialog boxes

Modal and Modeless Dialog Boxes

 The most commonly used type of dialog box is a *modal dialog box*. A modal dialog box prevents the user from performing any other activity with the program until the dialog box is dismissed.

 A dialog box that is *modeless* enables other activities to be carried out while the dialog box is still open.

An example of a modeless dialog box is the Find and Replace common dialog box used by Developer Studio. When the dialog box is open you can still make selections from the main menu, and even open other dialog boxes. In contrast, all other Developer Studio dialog boxes are modal. As long as they are open the user can't interact with the other parts of Developer Studio.

Using Dialog Boxes for Input

When most people think of dialog boxes, they think of the dialog boxes that collect input from a user. Dialog boxes are often used to contain controls that are used to handle user input. You can include in a dialog box a wide range of controls. In fact, a major portion of this book covers the various types of controls available in Windows.

Some dialog boxes are needed so often in Windows programs that they have been included as part of the operating system. These dialog boxes, known as *common dialog boxes*, are available by calling a function and don't require you to create a dialog box resource. There are common dialog boxes for opening and selecting files, choosing fonts and colors, and performing find and replace operations. Many of the common dialog boxes are covered later in the book. For example, in Hour 13, "Fonts," you will use a common dialog box to select a font.

Creating Dialog Boxes in Visual C++

Developer Studio makes using dialog boxes in a Windows program easy. All the necessary steps are automated, and the tools used to create the dialog box and include it in a project are all integrated.

Adding Message Boxes

The simplest type of dialog box is the message box, which is used to display information. This type of dialog box is so simple you can call it with just one line of code using the MFC class library. For example, to display a message box using default parameters supplied by MFC, just use this line:

```
AfxMessageBox( "Hello World" );
```

This line of code creates a message box with an exclamation mark inside a yellow triangle. You must supply at least a single parameter: the text that is displayed inside the dialog box. Optionally, you can also specify an icon style and a button arrangement pattern. The types of icons that are available for message boxes are shown in Figure 4.1.

FIGURE 4.1.

Icons that can appear on a message box.

Warning — ⚠ ⓘ — Information

Question — ⓠ ❌ — Error

Each icon in Figure 4.1 has a specific meaning. When most Windows programs display a message box, they use a standard icon for each message. When programs use the same icons consistently, users find it much easier to understand the meaning of information provided with message boxes. The meaning and style name for each icon is shown in Table 4.1.

TABLE 4.1. ICONS USED IN WINDOWS MESSAGE-BOX DIALOG BOXES.

Icon Displayed	Meaning	Message Box Style
Exclamation mark	Warning	MB_ICONEXCLAMATION
An "i" in a circle	Information	MB_ICONINFORMATION
Question mark	Question	MB_ICONQUESTION
Stop sign	Error	MB_ICONSTOP

In addition, you can specify a button arrangement to be used in the message box. By default, a single button labeled OK is included in the message box. However, sometimes it's convenient to ask a user a simple question and collect an answer. One use for these button arrangements is to ask the user what action to take during an error. For example, the following code displays a message box that contains a question mark icon and asks the user whether the current file should be deleted:

```
int nChoice = AfxMessageBox( "Overwrite existing file?",
                          MB_YESNOCANCEL ¦ MB_ICONQUESTION );
if( nChoice == IDYES )
{
    // Overwrite file
}
```

> The vertical bar used to separate two different options for the AfxMessageBox function is the bitwise OR operator, which is used to combine the bit patterns of two or more values.

When the preceding code fragment is used in a program, the user can choose between buttons marked Yes, No, and Cancel. Table 4.2 gives the additional button arrangements possible for a message box.

TABLE 4.2. BUTTON ARRANGEMENTS.

Message Box Style	Buttons Included in Dialog Box
MB_ABORTRETRYIGNORE	Abort, Retry, and Ignore
MB_OK	OK
MB_OKCANCEL	OK and Cancel
MB_RETRYCANCEL	Retry and Cancel
MB_YESNO	Yes and No
MB_YESNOCANCEL	Yes, No, and Cancel

The message-box return value indicates which button the user selected. Table 4.3 is a list of possible return values and the choice made by the user.

TABLE 4.3. MESSAGE-BOX RETURN VALUES.

Return Value	Button Pressed
IDABORT	Abort
IDCANCEL	Cancel
IDIGNORE	Ignore
IDNO	No
IDOK	OK
IDRETRY	Retry
IDYES	Yes

When using the bitwise OR operator with AfxMessageBox, you can combine one icon style and one button style. You can't combine two icon styles or two button styles. If no styles are provided, the message box will contain the exclamation-mark icon and an OK button.

4

Adding a Dialog Box

Adding a dialog box to a program usually takes four steps:

1. Design and create a dialog box resource using the Developer Studio resource tools.
2. Use ClassWizard to create a C++ class derived from CDialog that will manage the dialog box.
3. Add functions to handle messages sent to the dialog box, if needed.
4. If the dialog box is selected from the main menu, the menu resource must be modified and message-handling functions must be created using ClassWizard.

Each of these steps is covered in the following sections.

Understanding Resources

Dialog boxes are just specialized types of windows. However, because they commonly are used for short periods of time they usually are stored as program resources and loaded only when needed. You can see this behavior when you run a Windows program on a machine that has little free memory. Every time a dialog box is opened, the hard disk is accessed to load the dialog box resources from the EXE file.

Menus and accelerators, which are covered in Hour 10, "Menus," are two
types of resources. Other types of resources that are covered in later hours
include bitmaps, cursors, and icons.

Creating a Dialog Box Resource

Developer Studio enables you to create a dialog box and configure it visually. You can
add and size controls by using a mouse. You can set attributes for the dialog box and its
controls with a click of a mouse button.

Before using the following steps, create a single-document MFC AppWizard application
named HelloSDI, following the steps presented in Hour 1, "Using Visual C++ 6." Create
a new dialog box resource for the HelloSDI project using either of the following methods:

- Display the New Resource dialog box by selecting Resource from the Insert menu.
  Next, select Dialog as the resource type and click New.
- Right-click the Dialog folder in the Resource tree, and select Insert Dialog from
  the pop-up menu.

With either of these methods the dialog box editor is displayed, as shown in Figure 4.2.

FIGURE 4.2.

*The Developer Studio
dialog box editor.*

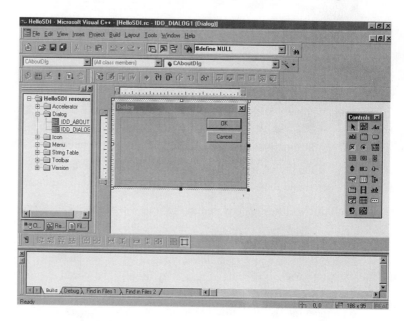

The dialog box that displays for editing initially contains two button controls, one labeled OK and another labeled Cancel. As you will learn in Hour 5, "Button Controls," these are two standard dialog box controls. The MFC class library usually handles the operation of these controls.

Customizing the Dialog Box's Properties

Every dialog box has properties that you can display by right-clicking and selecting Properties from the pop-up menu. Here are the dialog box properties under the General tab:

- *ID:* Normally set to something like `IDD_DIALOG1`. Naming dialog boxes with an identifier that begins with `IDD_` is an MFC convention, although you should try to name your dialog boxes with a more meaningful name; rename this dialog box `IDD_HELLO`.
- *Caption:* Normally set to a default of `Dialog`. You should change this to something more meaningful as well, such as `Hello` for the sample dialog box.
- *Menu:* Normally cleared because few dialog boxes use a menu.
- *X Pos:* Normally cleared to use the default positioning for the dialog box.
- *Y Pos:* Normally cleared to use the default positioning for the dialog box.
- *Font Name:* Contains the current font used by the dialog box.
- *Font Size:* Contains the current font size used by the dialog box.

> In most cases, you should keep the default font provided by Windows for your dialog box. There is also a pushbutton labeled Font that you can use to change the default font for the dialog box. However, just because you can doesn't mean you should. Windows enables users to set the font style used in dialog boxes; many users, such as the visually impaired, might need specific fonts to be able to use your dialog box.

Like all windows, a dialog box has several style attributes. You can display these attributes by selecting the Styles tab. Here are the default values for the following attributes:

- *Style:* Usually set to `Popup` for most dialog boxes. In the case of special dialog box templates used in form views or dialog bars, the style is set to `Child`.
- *Border:* Set to `Dialog Frame` for most dialog boxes.
- *Minimize Box:* Creates a minimize box for the dialog box. This check box is cleared for most dialog boxes, indicating that no minimize box is provided.

4

- *Maximize Box:* Used to create a maximize box for the dialog box. This check box is cleared for most dialog boxes, indicating that no maximize box is provided.
- *Title Bar:* Creates a title bar for the dialog box. This check box is almost always checked because most dialog boxes have a title bar.
- *System Menu:* Used to indicate that a system menu should be provided for the dialog box. This check box is normally checked.
- *Horizontal Scroll:* Used to create a scrollbar for the dialog box. This check box is almost always cleared because dialog boxes rarely use scrollbars.
- *Vertical Scroll:* Used to create a vertical scrollbar for the dialog box. Like the horizontal scrollbar, this attribute is rarely used.
- *Clip Siblings:* Used only with child windows. This check box is normally cleared.
- *Clip Children:* Used for parent windows. This check box is rarely checked for most dialog boxes.

The More Styles tab contains additional properties for the dialog box:

- *System Modal:* Creates a system-modal dialog box. If this option is enabled the user can't switch to another program.
- *Absolute Align:* Used to indicate how the dialog box is positioned when initially displayed. If this check box is checked, the dialog box is aligned with the screen instead of with the parent window.
- *No Idle Message:* Prevents a particular window message, WM_ENTERIDLE, from being sent when the dialog box's message queue is empty. This check box is normally cleared.
- *Local Edit:* Used to specify how an edit control's memory is allocated. This check box is normally cleared, which means edit controls use memory outside the program's data segment.
- *Visible:* Used to specify that the dialog box should be visible when first displayed. This check box is usually checked. In the case of form views, this check box is cleared. Form views are discussed in Hour 23, "Form Views."
- *Disabled:* Indicates that the dialog box should be disabled when initially displayed. This check box is usually cleared.
- *3D-Look:* Gives the dialog box a three-dimensional appearance. This check box is usually cleared.
- *Set Foreground:* Forces the dialog box to be placed into the foreground. This check box is usually cleared.

- *No Fail Create:* Tells Windows to create the dialog box even if an error occurs. This check box is usually cleared.
- *Control:* Creates a dialog box resource that can be used as a child control. This check box is usually cleared.
- *Center:* Causes the dialog box to be centered when it is initially displayed. This check box is usually cleared.
- *Center Mouse:* Places the mouse cursor in the center of the dialog box. This check box is usually cleared.
- *Context Help:* Adds a question mark icon for context-sensitive help in the title bar. This check box is usually cleared.

Advanced styles are located under the Extended Styles tab. These styles are rarely used and aren't discussed in this book.

Adding a Control to Your Dialog Box

A simple control that you can add to the dialog box is a static text control. The static text control requires no interaction with the dialog box; it is often used as a plain text label for other controls contained by the dialog box. To add a static text control, follow these steps:

1. Select the Static Text control icon on the control toolbar. The cursor changes shape to a plus sign when moved over the dialog box.
2. Center the cursor over the dialog box, and click the left mouse button. A static text control is created and contains the label Static.
3. Change the label of the static text control by right-clicking the control and selecting Properties from the shortcut menu; change the caption to Hello World.

The static text control is visible whenever the dialog box is displayed. Text controls are an excellent choice for labeling controls or messages that are not likely to change. Experiment with changing the size and position of the static text control by dragging its edges with the mouse.

Creating a Class for the Dialog Box

You can use the CDialog class to manage most of the interaction with a dialog box in your program. The CDialog class provides member functions that make a dialog box easy to use. You should use ClassWizard to derive a class from CDialog that is specifically tailored for your dialog box.

To start ClassWizard, use any of these methods:

- Press Ctrl+W almost any time in Developer Studio.
- Select ClassWizard from the View menu.
- Right-click anywhere in the dialog box editor, and select ClassWizard from the pop-up menu.

If ClassWizard knows that a new resource has been added, such as IDD_HELLO, a dialog box asks you to choose between two options for the new dialog box resource:

- Create a new class.
- Select an existing class.

You should almost always choose to create a new dialog box class unless you are reusing some existing code. A New Class dialog box is displayed, as shown in Figure 4.3.

FIGURE 4.3.

The New Class dialog box is used to add a new class to a Visual C++ project.

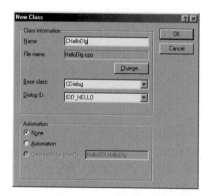

ClassWizard uses values you provide in the New Class dialog box to create a class that will manage the new dialog box resource. Use the values from Table 4.4 to fill in the values for the IDD_HELLO dialog box.

TABLE 4.4. SAMPLE VALUES FOR THE NEW CLASS DIALOG BOX.

Control	Value
Name	CHelloDlg
File Name	HelloDlg.cpp
Base Class	CDialog
Dialog ID	IDD_HELLO
Automation	None

Click the button labeled OK. The `CHelloDlg` class is generated, and two files will be added to your project:

- The `HelloDlg.h` file contains the class declaration.
- The `HelloDlg.cpp` file contains the class definitions.

Adding a Message Handler to Initialize the Dialog Box

Dialog boxes receive the `WM_INITDIALOG` message from the operating system when all the controls owned by the dialog box have been created. Most dialog boxes use the `WM_INITDIALOG` message to perform any initialization that is needed.

After you have added the `CHelloDlg` class to the HelloSDI project, you can use ClassWizard to add a message-handling function for messages such as `WM_INITDIALOG`.

To add a message handler for `WM_INITDIALOG`, follow these steps:

1. Open ClassWizard by pressing Ctrl+W or by right-clicking in a source code window and selecting ClassWizard from the menu.

2. Select the tab labeled Message Maps and select from the Class Name combo box the class that will handle the message—in this case, `CHelloDlg`.

3. Select the object that is generating the message from the Object ID list box—in this case, `CHelloDlg`. A list of messages sent to the dialog box will be displayed in the Messages list box.

4. Select the `WM_INITDIALOG` message from the Messages list box and click the Add Function button. ClassWizard will automatically add the `OnInitDialog` function to the `CHelloDlg` class.

5. Click OK to close ClassWizard.

The `CHelloDlg::OnInitDialog` function doesn't really need to initialize any variables, so you can display a message box instead. Edit `OnInitDialog` so that it looks like the function in Listing 4.1.

INPUT   **LISTING 4.1.** THE `CHelloDlg::OnInitDialog` FUNCTION.

```
BOOL CHelloDlg::OnInitDialog()
{
    CDialog::OnInitDialog();
    AfxMessageBox( "WM_INITDIALOG received" );
    return TRUE;
}
```

4

Adding a Menu Choice for the New Dialog Box

To add a menu item to the menu used by HelloSDI follow the steps in this section. Don't worry too much about what's going on here; you'll learn more about menus in Hour 10.

Menus are stored in your project as resources. To display the current menu resources, select the ResourceView tab in the project workspace window. Expand the resource tree to show the different resource types defined for the current project; one of the folders is labeled Menu.

Open the Menu folder to display the single menu named IDR_MAINFRAME. Open the menu resource by double-clicking the menu resource icon. The menu is displayed in the resource editor ready for editing. Clicking any top-level menu item displays the pop-up menu associated with that item, as shown in Figure 4.4.

FIGURE 4.4.

Using the Developer Studio resource editor to edit a menu resource.

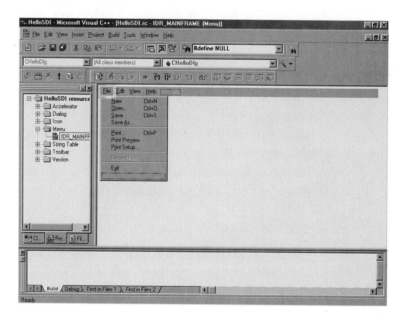

The last item of every menu is an empty box, which is used to add new menu items to the menu resource. All menu items are initially added to the end of a menu resource and then moved to their proper position. To add a new menu item, follow these steps:

1. Double-click the empty box on the File menu to display the Menu Properties dialog box.

2. To add a menu item, provide a menu ID and caption for the new menu item. For this example, enter ID_FILE_HELLO as the menu ID and &Hello as the menu caption.

3. Click anywhere outside the properties dialog box to return to the editor.

After adding a menu item, the next step is to add a message-handling function to handle the new menu item. To add a message-handling function for the ID_FILE_HELLO menu item, follow these steps:

1. Open ClassWizard by pressing Ctrl+W or by right-clicking in a source code window and selecting ClassWizard from the menu.

2. Select the tab labeled Message Maps and select from the Class Name combo box the class that will handle the message—in this case, CMainFrame.

3. Select the object that is generating the message from the Object ID list box—in this case, ID_FILE_HELLO. Two message-handling functions are displayed in the Messages list box.

4. Select the COMMAND message from the Messages list box and click the Add Function button. Accept the default name suggested by ClassWizard for the function name: OnFileHello.

5. Click OK to close ClassWizard.

Edit the CMainFrame::OnFileHello function so that it looks like the function provided in Listing 4.2.

INPUT   **LISTING 4.2.** THE MESSAGE-HANDLING FUNCTION FOR THE HELLO MENU ITEM.

```
void CMainFrame::OnFileHello()
{
    CHelloDlg    dlgHello;

    if( dlgHello.DoModal() == IDOK )
        AfxMessageBox( "OK button pressed" );
    else // IDCANCEL
        AfxMessageBox( "Cancel button pressed" );
}
```

Add an #include statement in MainFrm.cpp that includes the class definition for CHelloDlg, found in HelloDlg.h, by adding the following line just above the include statement for MainFrm.h:

```
#include "HelloDlg.h"
```

Compile and run the HelloSDI project. When the DoModal member function is called, the IDD_HELLO dialog box is displayed. The function call does not return until you close the dialog box by pressing one of the dialog box's buttons. If you press OK the return value is IDOK. If you press Cancel the return value is IDCANCEL.

Creating Dialog Box–Based Projects

NEW TERM A *dialog box–based project* uses a dialog box as the main window of a simple program. For example, many of the utilities found in the Windows Control Panel are dialog box–based.

A dialog box–based program has a menu that is accessed through the system menu at the upper-left corner of the dialog box's caption bar. A dialog box–based project is often used to build very small programs that interact with the user through a single dialog box. The program can be much smaller and easier to program because the number of classes created by AppWizard is reduced by about half.

 If your program must have sophisticated menus, it should not be dialog box–based.

A user can easily operate a dialog box–based program. There is only one dialog box window and all the available controls usually are initially visible. There are no hidden dialog boxes or menu items, and the user can usually see exactly which operations should be carried out.

AppWizard Support for Dialog Box–Based Projects

You can create a dialog box–based program using AppWizard, just like the SDI program you built earlier in this hour. Building a dialog box–based project is one of the initial options offered by AppWizard.

Because a dialog box–based project is much simpler than an SDI or MDI project, fewer steps are required when using AppWizard. Only four wizard pages are presented by AppWizard when building a dialog box–based project, versus the six pages required for an SDI or MDI project.

To create a dialog box–based project using AppWizard, follow these steps:

1. Open MFC AppWizard by creating a new project workspace, as you have in previous hours. For the purpose of building an example for this hour, use the name HelloDialog.

2. When the opening screen for AppWizard appears, select a dialog box–based project as the project type.

3. Accept the default project settings suggested by AppWizard and press the Finish button. You can also browse through the Wizard pages and change the default settings. AppWizard creates the dialog box–based project for you, just as it did earlier in the hour for the HelloSDI project.

Exploring the HelloDialog AppWizard Project

After you create the HelloDialog project, take some time to explore the project workspace. Much of the project workspace looks just as it does for an SDI project. There are four tabs for the different project workspace views, and several files and resources have been created for you.

There are several differences between a dialog box–based project and an SDI or MDI project:

- No menu resource is created for the project. Because the project uses a dialog box as its main window, there's no need for a menu in most cases.

- There are no document or view classes. Dialog box–based projects are intended to be very simple applications that don't require Document/View support.

- There are two dialog box resources. The main window for the project is a dialog box, as is the About box. The names of the two dialog box resources for the HelloDialog project are IDD_ABOUTBOX and IDD_HELLODIALOG_DIALOG.

Using the Dialog Box Editor

Open the dialog box editor by double-clicking the IDD_HELLODIALOG_DIALOG icon. The IDD_HELLODIALOG_DIALOG dialog box is displayed in the dialog box editor, along with a dockable control toolbar or palette. The dialog box will already contain a static text control. Modify the static text control so that it reads Hello Dialog Project, as shown in Figure 4.5.

FIGURE 4.5.

The main dialog box from the HelloDialog project.

4

Build and run the HelloDialog project. Because it is much smaller, the HelloDialog project will compile and launch faster than an SDI or MDI project. For that reason many of the examples in this book that deal with controls will use dialog box–based projects.

Summary

In this hour, you learned about dialog boxes and how they are used in programs written for Windows. This hour also covered the support provided by Developer Studio, including ClassWizard, the MFC class library, and the dialog box editor.

Q&A

Q When I display a modal dialog box no other part of the user interface can be used; does my application also stop functioning while the dialog box is displayed?

A A modal dialog box prevents the user from accessing other parts of your application; it does not prevent Windows from sending events to your message-handling procedures. Your application will continue to work normally while displaying a modal dialog box.

Q Why are C++ classes always split into two files? Wouldn't it be easier to have only a single file that defines the class as is done with Java?

A A key part of most languages that support object-oriented programming is the idea that the description of a class should be kept separate from its implementation. This fits in with the notion of information hiding, where unnecessary details are hidden whenever possible. In a well-designed C++ class, the implementation is considered a detail that the consumer doesn't need to be concerned with.

In Java, the class is always defined inside the class declaration, and they are never separated. This simplifies the work required for the compiler and runtime system. However, it also forces you to deal with implementation details when reading the class declaration.

If you prefer to define a class inside the class declaration, C++ supports that coding style; just include the function body after its declaration:

```
class CFoo
{
    int m_nBar;
public:
    CFoo(){
    m_nBar = 0;
}
```

```
void SetBar(int newVal){
    m_nBar = newVal;
}
int GetBar() const{
    return m_nBar;
}
};
```

Workshop

The Workshop is designed to help you anticipate possible questions, review what you've learned, and begin thinking ahead to putting your knowledge into practice. The answers to the quiz are in Appendix A, "Quiz Answers."

Quiz

1. What is the difference between a modal and modeless dialog box?

2. What message is sent to a dialog box for initialization purposes?

3. What is the file extension used for C++ class declaration files?

4. What is the file extension used for C++ class implementation files?

5. What message box style is provided by default when you use AfxMessageBox?

6. What message box style should be used when reporting an error to a user?

7. What MFC class is used to manage dialog boxes?

8. What member function is called to pop up a modal dialog box?

9. If the user presses the Yes button in a message box, what return value is provided to AfxMessageBox?

10. If the user presses the No button in a message box, what return value is provided to AfxMessageBox?

Exercises

1. Change the HelloSDI example so that the message box displayed for WM_INITDIALOG uses the information icon.

2. Add a second static text label to the HelloDialog project's main dialog box that displays your name.

Hour 5

Button Controls

Button controls are probably the most flexible controls available in Windows. Before learning about buttons, though, it's important to begin with a short lesson about conditional expressions in C++ programs. In this hour you will also learn about

- Using the different types of button controls provided by Windows
- Using the MFC CButton class that is used to manage button controls
- Using the MFC CWnd class to enable and disable controls

Later this hour you will add each type of button to a dialog box–based project. You will also use ClassWizard to add button events and member variables for the dialog box's button controls.

What Is a Button?

A button is a special type of window that contains a text or bitmap label, usually found in a dialog box, toolbar, or other window containing controls. Five different types of buttons are provided by Windows:

- Pushbuttons have a raised, three-dimensional appearance and seem to be depressed as they are clicked with the mouse. Pushbuttons normally have a text label on the face of the control.

- Radio buttons consist of a round button with a label adjacent to it.
- Check boxes are made up of a square box that contains a check mark when selected and a label next to the control.
- Owner-drawn buttons are painted by the button's owner instead of by Windows.
- Group boxes are rectangles that are used to surround other controls that have a common purpose.

In general, buttons are used to indicate a user selection. Buttons are used in Windows programs because they are convenient and easy for users to operate. Users have come to expect buttons to be presented in a large number of cases, especially when dialog boxes are present in a program.

What Are Pushbuttons?

Almost every dialog box has at least one pushbutton control to indicate actions that a user can invoke. Some common uses for pushbuttons include closing a dialog box, beginning a search, or asking for help.

What Are Radio Buttons?

Radio buttons are used when a selection must be made from several mutually exclusive options, such as a user's gender. Only one of the radio buttons, which usually are grouped together, is checked at any particular time.

What Are Check Boxes?

Check boxes are used as Boolean flags that indicate whether a particular condition is True or False. Unlike radio buttons, several check boxes in a group can be checked. Optionally, a check box can support a third state, disabled, meaning that the control is neither True nor False.

What Are Owner-Drawn Buttons?

Owner-drawn buttons are drawn by the owner of the button; usually a view or dialog box. This is unlike most controls, which are drawn by Windows. Owner-drawn buttons often add bitmaps, figures, or other visual effects, and sometimes offer additional functionality.

What Are Group Boxes?

A group box logically groups controls that are used for similar purposes. This helps the user understand the relationships between controls and makes a dialog box easier to use. Radio buttons are almost always enclosed in a group box so that it's obvious which controls are associated with each other.

MFC Support for Buttons

Button controls normally are created as part of a dialog box. After you add a button to a dialog box, you can use ClassWizard to add functions that can be used to handle events created when the button is pressed, checked, or selected. You also use ClassWizard to create CButton objects that are associated with individual button controls.

You can use the MFC class CButton to interact with button controls—both buttons that have been added to a dialog box resource and buttons that have been created dynamically. Use ClassWizard to associate a button control with a specific CButton object.

A Sample Project Using Buttons

In order to see how button controls can be used with dialog boxes, create a dialog box–based project named Button using AppWizard, following the steps provided in Hour 4, "Using Dialog Boxes." You will use this project for the rest of this hour as an example of how to use buttons in a dialog box.

When a dialog box–based project is created, the main dialog box is displayed in Developer Studio. If the main dialog box is not displayed, click the ResourceView tab in the project workspace. Open the dialog box editor by double-clicking the IDD_BUTTON_DIALOG icon in the Dialog resource folder.

The IDD_BUTTON_DIALOG dialog box is displayed in the dialog box editor, along with a dockable control toolbar or palette. The floating control palette contains all the controls available for a dialog box, as shown in Figure 5.1.

FIGURE 5.1.

The floating control palette, showing the button controls used to create dialog boxes.

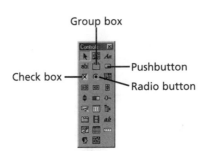

5

There are four different icons on the control palette for buttons, each used for a particular button type. Use one of the following steps to add a button control to a dialog box:

- Drag a button control from the palette to the dialog box by pressing the left mouse button while over the control button, then dragging the mouse cursor to the dialog box with the left mouse button still pressed. Release the mouse button when the cursor is over the desired spot in the dialog box.

- Select a button control by clicking a control in the control palette. Click the desired location for the control in the dialog box, and the dialog box editor creates a control for you in that location.

These steps apply for all controls in the control palette. After you've added a control to the dialog box, you can use the mouse to reposition and resize it.

As a demonstration, add several buttons to the main dialog box used in the Button project. You will use these controls later this hour to learn button events. Refer to Figure 5.2 for the location of the added buttons.

FIGURE 5.2.

The main dialog box used by the Button project.

Five buttons are added to IDD_BUTTON_DIALOG. Use the values from Table 5.1 to set the properties for each control. Except for the ID and caption, all controls use the default set of properties.

TABLE 5.1. VALUES USED FOR CONTROLS IN IDD_BUTTON_DIALOG.

Control ID	Button Type	Caption
IDC_BTN_TEST	Pushbutton	&Test
IDC_RADIO_HIGH	Radio button	&High
IDC_RADIO_LOW	Radio button	&Low
IDC_GROUP_VOLUME	Group control	&Volume
IDC_CHECK_AMP	Check box	&Amplify

Button Control Properties

Like all controls, buttons have a set of properties that define the behavior of each control. Although there are five different types of button controls, they share a common set of properties. You can display the properties for a particular control by selecting Properties from the menu displayed when you right-click the control. The following properties are available for button controls:

- ID: Used for the button's resource ID. A default resource ID, such as IDC_BUTTON1, is supplied by Developer Studio. Using IDC_ as a prefix for control resource IDs is a Microsoft naming convention.

- Caption: Indicates the text that appears as the button's label. Developer Studio supplies a default name, such as Button. To make one of the letters in the caption of a control the mnemonic key, precede it with an ampersand (&).

- Visible: Indicates that the button is initially visible. This check box is normally checked.

- Disabled: Indicates that the button should be initially disabled. This check box is normally cleared.

- Group: Marks the first control in a group. All controls following a control with this attribute are considered part of the same group if this check box is cleared. A user can move between controls in the same group using the arrow keys.

- Tab Stop: Indicates that this control can be reached by pressing Tab on the keyboard. This check box is normally checked.

- Default Button: Marks this control as the dialog box's default button. There can be only one default button in a dialog box, and it is executed if the user presses Enter without using any other controls in the dialog box. This property is available only for pushbutton controls. This check box is normally cleared.

- Owner Draw: Indicates that the button will be drawn by the button's owner; in this case, the dialog box. This property is available only for pushbutton controls. In most cases, this check box is cleared.

- Help ID: Creates a context-sensitive help ID for this control. This option is normally cleared.

- Icon: Specifies that this control displays an icon instead of text. The icon is assigned to the button using the `SetIcon` function. This option is normally cleared.

- Bitmap: Specifies that this control displays a bitmap instead of text. The bitmap is assigned to the button using the `SetBitmap` function. This option is normally cleared.

- Notify: Specifies that notification messages should be sent to the control's owner. Button click messages will be sent to the control's owner even if this option is not selected. This check box is normally cleared.

- Horizontal Alignment: Specifies how the text should be aligned horizontally. Possible selections are Default, Left, Right, and Center. This selection is normally set to Default.

- Multiline: Allows the button text to be placed on multiple lines if the text is too long to fit on one line. This property is not available for group boxes. This check box is normally cleared.

5

- Flat: Specifies that the button should be drawn without 3-dimensional effects. This style is not available for group boxes. This check box is normally cleared.

- Vertical Alignment: Specifies how the text should be aligned vertically. Possible selections are Default, Top, Bottom, and Center. This selection is normally set to Default.

- Auto: Specifies that the control should change its state when selected rather than when clicked. You select a control without clicking it by using the Tab key. This property is available only for check boxes and radio buttons. This check box is normally cleared.

- Left Text: Specifies that the text should be placed on the left side of the control. This property is available only for check boxes and radio buttons. This check box is normally cleared.

- Push-Like: Specifies that a radio button or check box is drawn like a pushbutton. The control is drawn in the down state when the control is checked or selected.

- Tri-State: Specifies that a check box can have three states instead of two. In addition to `True` and `False`, the control can be disabled, which means that the value is neither `True` nor `False`.

In addition, all controls have a property page labeled Extended Styles. These styles are rarely used, and aren't discussed in this book.

Using Standard Pushbutton Layouts in Your Dialog Boxes

Several pushbuttons are commonly used in dialog boxes that contain controls. Because each of these pushbuttons carries a specific meaning, you should try to use the standard terminology whenever possible because it minimizes the amount of work required for users of your programs. Here are the standard meanings for these buttons:

- OK: Used to close and accept any information that is present in the dialog box. Any user-supplied information in the dialog box is used by the program. Note that the OK pushbutton is the only button spelled with all capital letters.

- Cancel: Used to close the dialog box and remove any changes that might have been performed while the dialog box was open. If there are changes that cannot be reversed, the label for this button should be changed to read Close. Changing the label for a button is discussed later in the section, "Changing a Button's Label."

- Close: Used to close the dialog box. It does not necessarily imply that any action is taken by the program. Close is most often used when a Cancel button can't be used to remove changes made while the dialog box is open. Many programs change a Cancel button into a Close button.

- Help: Used to request context-sensitive help for the open dialog box.
- Apply: Used to perform changes based on data that has been entered in the dialog box. Unlike the OK button, the dialog box should remain open after the Apply button is pressed.

Associating Member Variables with a Button Control

The easiest way to set or retrieve the value of a control is to associate it with a class-member variable using ClassWizard. When associating a member variable with a control, you can associate the member variable either with the control or with the control's value. Member variables representing buttons are rarely associated by value; instead, the CButton class is used to represent most button controls. You learn about associating member variables by value with dialog box controls in Hour 6, "Using Edit Controls."

To add a member variable to a CDialog-derived class, follow these steps:

1. Open ClassWizard.
2. Select the tab labeled Member Variables.
3. Select the CDialog-derived class that manages the dialog box; in this case, CButtonDlg.
4. Select the control ID representing the control associated with the new member variable.
5. Press the button labeled Add Variable. An Add Member Variable dialog box appears. Enter the control's name, category, and variable type, then press OK.
6. Close ClassWizard.

Follow these steps for all controls added to the IDD_BUTTON_DIALOG earlier. Use the values from Table 5.2 for each new member variable added to CButtonDlg.

TABLE 5.2. VALUES USED TO ADD MEMBER VARIABLES FOR CButtonDlg.

Control ID	Variable Name	Category	Type
IDC_BTN_TEST	m_btnTest	Control	CButton
IDC_GROUP_VOLUME	m_btnVolume	Control	CButton
IDC_CHECK_AMP	m_btnAmp	Control	CButton

5

ClassWizard automatically adds the member variables to the CButtonDlg class declaration for you.

Adding Button Events to a Dialog Box Class

Although the buttons are part of the dialog box resource and appear whenever the dialog box is displayed, nothing happens when the buttons are used because no button events are handled by the dialog box class.

Pushbuttons are normally associated with button events in a dialog box class. To add a button event for the Test button, IDC_BTN_TEST, follow these steps:

1. Open ClassWizard.
2. Select the tab labeled Message Maps.
3. Select CButtonDlg as the class name.
4. Select IDC_BTN_TEST as the object ID.
5. Select BN_CLICKED from the Messages list box.
6. Press the button labeled Add Function and accept the default name for the member function.
7. Close ClassWizard.

Check boxes and radio buttons sometimes use BN_CLICKED messages, but not as often as pushbuttons. Add the source code from Listing 5.1 to the CButtonDlg::OnBtnTest function, then compile and run the project.

INPUT   **LISTING 5.1.** THE CButtonDlg::OnBtnTest MEMBER FUNCTION.

```
void CButtonDlg::OnBtnTest()
{
    AfxMessageBox( "Test button pressed" );
}
```

Changing a Button's Label

Like all controls, a button is just a special type of window. For that reason, the MFC class library uses the CWnd class as a base class for all control classes. To change the label for a button, you can use the SetWindowText function.

This function commonly is used to change the label for buttons after the dialog box has been created. You can use the SetWindowText function to change the Amplify button from the earlier example into a Record button. To do so, replace the CButtonDlg::OnBtnTest function with the function provided in Listing 5.2.

INPUT LISTING **5.2.** CHANGING THE LABEL FOR SEVERAL BUTTONS.

```
void CButtonDlg::OnBtnTest()
{
    static BOOL bSetWaterLevel = TRUE;
    if( bSetWaterLevel == TRUE )
    {
        m_btnVolume.SetWindowText( "&Water Level" );
        m_btnAmp.SetWindowText( "&Record" );
        bSetWaterLevel = FALSE;
    }
    else
    {
        m_btnVolume.SetWindowText( "&Volume" );
        m_btnAmp.SetWindowText( "&Amplify" );
        bSetWaterLevel = TRUE;
    }
}
```

After you build the Button example using the code from Listing 5.2, the radio button group will alternate between Volume and Water Level.

Controlling Your Program with Conditional Expressions

NEW TERM Listing 5.2 uses *conditional expressions* to determine the labels for buttons in the dialog box. A conditional expression is an expression that results in a True or False value.

Most programs exercise some type of control over their execution flow using conditional expressions. They perform different actions based on varying conditions as the execution progresses.

Using the `if` Statement

The `if` statement enables one or more statements to be executed only if an expression inside the parentheses is True. If necessary, values inside the parentheses are converted into Boolean values, with zero being converted to False and all nonzero values converted to True.

Listing 5.3 provides a function that shows how the `if` statement is used. If the parameter passed to the function is greater than zero, the function returns a value of True.

5

LISTING 5.3. A FUNCTION THAT RETURNS True IF A POSITIVE NUMBER IS PASSED TO IT.

```
bool IsPositive( int nCheckValue )
{
    bool bReturn = false;
    if( nCheckValue > 0 )
        bReturn = true;
    return bReturn;}
```

Using Compound Statements

The statement controlled by an if statement is executed only when the test condition is True. If more than one statement must be executed, group the statements together to form a compound statement. Compound statements are often called *blocks* because they group statements into blocks of code.

A compound statement begins and ends with curly braces, just like a function body. All the statements within a compound statement that follows an if statement are executed when the test condition is true, as shown earlier in Listing 5.2.

A common mistake made with the if statement is to use =, which is the assignment operator, instead of ==, which is used to test for equality.

A standard code-formatting convention is to visually nest each conditional "level" of your source code by indenting statements, as in Listings 5.2 and 5.3. Indentation helps make your code more readable because it helps make the flow of control in your source code easy to see.

Using else with if Statements

You can couple an else statement with an if statement to create an either/or selection. When the expression tested by the if statement is True, the first statement (or block statement) is executed. When the expression is False, the statements grouped with the else statement are executed instead.

Using the switch Statement

Sometimes you must choose between more than just one or two alternatives. Suppose you are implementing a simple menu function with many choices. One way to implement the menu selection code is to use a large number of if statements that repeatedly test the same variable.

C++ also includes the switch statement, which is used to easily replace large numbers of if statements that choose among several alternative paths. A switch statement evaluates an expression and then chooses from a list of choices, as shown in Listing 5.4.

LISTING 5.4. USING THE switch STATEMENT.

```
bool HandleMenuSelection( char chSelection )
{
    bool bValidSelection = true;
    switch( chSelection )
    {
        case 'F':
            OpenNewFile();
            break;
        case 'P':
            PrintDocument();
            break;
        case 'S':
            SaveFile();
            break;
        default:
            bValidSelection = false;
    }
    return bValidSelection;
}
```

As Listing 5.4 shows, the switch statement has several different parts. Here are the major features of a switch statement:

- The switch() expression. The expression contained inside the switch parentheses is evaluated, and its value is used as the basis for making the selection.

- One or more case labels. Each case label includes a value. Every case label must be unique. If a case label's value matches the switch expression, the statements after the case label are executed.

- One or more break statements. The break statement is used to stop execution inside a switch statement. A break statement is normally placed between every case. If a break statement is removed, statements in the next case are executed until a break is reached or until no more statements remain inside the switch.

- A default label. The default label is selected when no case labels match the switch expression.

5

Enabling and Disabling Buttons

Most controls are enabled by default, although a control can be initially disabled by setting that attribute in its property list. A control can be selected only if it is enabled. The
CWnd class includes the EnableWindow member function that allows a CWnd object to be
enabled or disabled. Because CButton and all other control classes are derived from
CWnd, they include all the member data and member functions from the CWnd class, and
you can disable a button like this:

```
pButton->EnableWindow( FALSE );  // Disables control
```

The parameter for EnableWindow is True if the window or control should be enabled and
False if it should be disabled. The default parameter for EnableWindow sets the parameter to True because no parameter is needed to enable the control:

```
pButton->EnableWindow();  // Enables control
```

It is common practice for buttons and other controls to be enabled or disabled based on
events that are received by the dialog box. As an example, pressing one button can cause
another button to be disabled or enabled. To disable a dialog box control, replace the
CButtonDlg::OnBtnTest function with the source code provided in Listing 5.5.

INPUT   LISTING 5.5. USING CWnd::EnableWindow TO DISABLE A DIALOG BOX CONTROL.

```
void CButtonDlg::OnBtnTest()
{
    static BOOL bEnableControl = FALSE;
    m_btnAmp.EnableWindow( bEnableControl );
    if( bEnableControl == TRUE )
        bEnableControl = FALSE;
    else
        bEnableControl = TRUE;
}
```

Now when you click the Test button the Amplify check box is disabled. When you click
the Test button again the check box is enabled.

Hiding a Button

It's not unusual to need to hide a button that is located in a dialog box. Often, a button
has its properties set to be hidden by default. Once again, the CWnd class has a member
function that can be used to hide or display a window as needed. Use the
CWnd::ShowWindow member function like this:

```
pButton->ShowWindow( SW_HIDE );  // Hide control
```

This code hides the pButton window, which is a button control in this case. To display a hidden window, the ShowWindow function is used with the SW_SHOW parameter:

```
pButton->ShowWindow( SW_SHOW );   // Display control
```

Listing 5.6 provides a function that uses CWnd::ShowWindow to alternately hide and display some of the other buttons in the main dialog box.

LISTING 5.6. USING CWnd::ShowWindow TO HIDE A DIALOG BOX CONTROL.

```
void CButtonDlg::OnBtnTest()
{
    static int nShowControl = SW_HIDE;
    m_btnAmp.ShowWindow( nShowControl );
    if( nShowControl == SW_SHOW )
        nShowControl = SW_HIDE;
    else
        nShowControl = SW_SHOW;}
```

Defining and Setting Tab Order

When a dialog box is presented to the user, one control will have the keyboard focus, sometimes just called the focus. The control that has the focus receives all input from the keyboard. When a control has the focus a dotted focus rectangle is drawn around it.

A user can change the focus to a new control by pressing the Tab key on the keyboard. Each time the Tab key is pressed, a new control receives the focus. If you aren't familiar with how this works, you might want to experiment with a few dialog boxes from Developer Studio.

The controls are always selected in a fixed order, known as the *tab order*. Tab order lets users select controls without using the mouse. Although almost all Windows users have access to a mouse, using the keyboard sometimes is more convenient. Also, because tabbing between controls is a standard feature in Windows dialog boxes, you should use it correctly.

The tab order should follow a logical pattern through the dialog box. If the tab order follows a predictable pattern, users will find it much easier to navigate using the Tab key. Usually, the first editable control receives the focus when the dialog box is opened. After that, the focus should be passed to the next logical control in the dialog box. The buttons that control the dialog box—OK, Cancel, and Apply—should receive the focus last.

5

In a dialog box, the tab order follows the sequence in which controls were defined in the resource script. As new controls are added they are placed at the end of the tab order. You can use the resource tools included in the Developer Studio to change this sequence, thereby altering the tab order.

> To prevent a user from selecting a control using the Tab key, clear the Tab Stop property for the control.

With the dialog box displayed in the Developer Studio, select Tab Order from the Layout menu, or press Ctrl+D. Each control in the dialog box that has the `tabstop` attribute is tagged with a number, as shown in Figure 5.3.

FIGURE 5.3.

Displaying the tab order for dialog box controls.

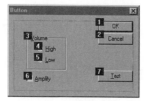

To change the tab order, just click the control that should be in tab position 1; the tag associated with that control changes to reflect its new tab order. Repeat the process of clicking controls until the displayed tab order is correct.

Summary

In this hour you learned about the different types of button controls provided by Windows and used the controls in a variety of ways. You also built a dialog box–based project. Finally, you learned about control tab order and conditional expressions.

Q&A

Q What is the difference between BOOL and bool?

A The bool type is defined by the C++ standard, whereas the BOOL type is defined deep inside the Windows header files. In practice they work very much alike, and you can interchange them without any problem. The reason for the BOOL type is historical; bool was only recently added to the C++ standard, and the BOOL type has been used for Windows programming for many years. In fact, BOOL was used for Windows programming before C++ was invented.

Q When is it more appropriate to hide a control instead of disable it?

A If a control is unavailable or doesn't make sense for a temporary period, it should be disabled. If the control is unavailable for a long period of time, it should be hidden. In general, the user should be presented with as few options as possible, especially if those options can't be selected.

Workshop

The Workshop is designed to help you anticipate possible questions, review what you've learned, and begin thinking ahead to putting your knowledge into practice. The answers to the quiz are in Appendix A, "Quiz Answers."

Quiz

1. What is the difference between the Cancel and Close buttons?
2. What is the difference between the OK and Apply buttons?
3. What MFC class is used to manage button controls?
4. What are the five types of button controls?
5. How do you prevent the Tab key from being used to select a control?
6. What function is used to disable a control at runtime?
7. What function is used to hide a control at runtime?
8. What is the `default` label used for in a `switch` statement?
9. What is the difference between the = and == operators?
10. What function is used to change the label on a button?

Exercises

1. Modify the Button project so that the Amplify check box is removed from the tab order.
2. Modify the Button project so that the source code from Listing 5.2 is used, except that the Amplify check box is hidden when the group box caption is set to Water Level.

5

HOUR **6**

Using Edit Controls

In Windows programs, user input is often collected using edit controls. In this hour you will also learn about

- Using edit controls to collect and display free-form text supplied by the user
- Associating an edit control with CEdit and CString objects using ClassWizard
- Using DDV and DDX routines for data validation and verification

You will also create an SDI project and use it to learn how data is transferred in and out of edit controls used in dialog boxes.

Understanding Edit Controls

 An *edit control* is a window used to store free-form text input by a user.

 A *single-line edit control* is an edit control that enables a single line of text to be entered.

NEW TERM A *multiple-line edit control*, sometimes called an *MLE*, is an edit control that enables multiple lines of text to be entered.

Edit controls are usually found in dialog boxes. You can usually find an edit control almost anywhere user input is required.

Why Use an Edit Control?

You use single-line edit controls when text must be collected. For example, when a name or address must be entered in a dialog box, an edit control is used to collect that information. Multiple-line edit controls often use scrollbars that enable more text to be entered than can be displayed.

A prompt in the form of default text can be provided for an edit control. In some situations this can reduce the amount of typing required. All edit controls also support a limited amount of editing, without any need for extra programming on your part. For example, the standard cut-and-paste commands work as expected in an edit control. Table 6.1 lists the editing commands available in an edit control.

TABLE 6.1. EDITING COMMANDS AVAILABLE IN AN EDIT CONTROL.

Command	Keystroke
Cut	Ctrl+X
Paste	Ctrl+V
Copy	Ctrl+C
Undo	Ctrl+Z

 Because of the built-in editing capabilities of the edit control, it's possible to create a simple text editor using a multiple-line edit control. Although a multiple-line edit control can't replace a real text editor, it does provide a simple way to collect multiple lines of text from a user.

One difference between edit controls and the pushbutton controls you saw in Hour 5, "Button Controls," is that a button control is normally used to generate events. An edit control can generate events also, but it usually is used to actually store data.

MFC Support for Edit Controls

You normally add edit controls to a dialog box just as you added buttons in Hour 5. After you add the control to a dialog box, use ClassWizard to configure the control for use in the program.

The MFC class CEdit is often used to interact with edit controls. As you will see in the next section, you can use ClassWizard to associate an edit control with a specific CEdit object. An edit control can also be associated with a CString object, which can simplify the use of edit controls in dialog boxes. You will learn about using edit controls associated with CString objects in detail beginning with the section "Passing Parameters to Dialog Boxes Using DDV and DDX Routines," later in this hour.

Building an SDI Test Project

Some of the sample programs in this book require you to build an SDI project and add a test dialog box. You can use the following steps to build a test project that includes a test dialog box:

1. Create an SDI project named EditTest using MFC AppWizard, as discussed in Hour 1, "Using Visual C++ 6." Feel free to add or remove any of the optional features suggested by AppWizard, because they aren't used in this hour. *Pg. 17*

2. As discussed in Hour 4, "Using Dialog Boxes," add a dialog box resource to the program. Name the dialog box IDD_TEST, and set the caption to Test Dialog. Using *Pg. 60* ClassWizard, create a dialog box class called CTestDlg for the new dialog box.

3. Add to the View menu a menu choice ID_VIEW_TEST with a caption of Test.... Add a message-handling function for the new menu item using ClassWizard. The steps required to add a message-handling function that uses a CDialog-based object *Pg 67* were discussed in Hour 4. Use the source code provided in Listing 6.1 for the CMainFrame message-handling function.

4. Include the class declaration for CTestDlg in the MainFrm.cpp file by adding the following line after all the #include directives in MainFrm.cpp:

   ```
   #include "testdlg.h"
   ```

5. Add to the dialog box a pushbutton control called IDC_TEST and labeled Test, as was done in Hour 5. Using ClassWizard, add a function that handles the BN_CLICKED message, which will be used in later examples.

6. After following these steps, make sure the project compiles properly by pressing the Build icon on the toolbar or by selecting Build | Build EditTest.exe from the main menu. Try the menu item to make sure the IDC_TEST dialog box is displayed when View | Test is selected.

6

INPUT   **LISTING 6.1.** HANDLING A MENU-ITEM SELECTION FOR EDITTEST.

```
void CMainFrame::OnViewTest()
{
    CTestDlg    dlg;
    dlg.DoModal();
}
```

Adding an Edit Control to a Dialog Box

You add an edit control to a dialog box just as you added a button control in Hour 5, using either of these two basic methods:

- Using drag-and-drop, drag an edit control from the control palette and drop at a desirable location in the dialog box.
- Select an edit control by clicking the Edit Control icon in the tool palette, and click over the location in the dialog box where the edit control should be located.

Arrange the edit control so that the dialog box resembles the one in Figure 6.1.

FIGURE 6.1.

The dialog box used in the edit control examples.

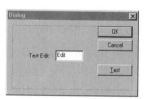

In Figure 6.1, a static text control is located immediately to the left of the edit control. Edit controls are usually labeled with static text so a user can determine the type of input needed. Static text controls were discussed in Hour 4.

Edit Control Properties

You can examine the properties for an edit control, just as with other resources, by right-clicking over the control and selecting Properties from the pop-up menu. These general properties are available for an edit control:

- ID: Used for the edit control's resource ID. Like other controls, a default resource ID is supplied by Developer Studio.
- Visible: Indicates that the edit control is initially visible. This option is normally selected.

- Disabled: Indicates that the edit control should be initially disabled. This option is not normally selected.

- Group: Used to mark the first control in a group. All controls following a control with this attribute are considered part of the same group if the attribute is cleared. A user can move between controls in the same group using the arrow keys.

- Help ID: Creates a context-sensitive help ID for this control.

- Tab Stop: Indicates that this control can be reached by pressing the Tab key. This option is normally selected.

There also is a group of properties that apply specifically to edit controls. The following properties are displayed by clicking the Styles tab in the Properties dialog box:

- Align Text: A drop-down list box that is enabled if the edit control is an MLE. The text can be aligned to the left, center, or right, with left as the default.

- Multiline: Defines the control as a multiple-line edit control. This option is not selected by default.

- Number: Restricts the edit control to digits only.

- Horizontal Scroll: Enabled only for an MLE and provides a horizontal scrollbar. The option is not selected by default.

- Auto HScroll: Scrolls text to the right if needed. This option is normally selected.

- Vertical Scroll: Enabled only for an MLE and provides a vertical scrollbar. The option is not selected by default.

- Auto VScroll: Enabled only for an MLE and provides automatic scrolling when the user presses Return on the last line. The option is not selected by default.

- Password: Hides the user's input by displaying an asterisk instead of each character. This option is available only in single-line controls and is not selected by default.

- No Hide Selection: Changes the way an edit control handles the focus. When this option is enabled, text appears to be selected at all times. This option is not selected by default.

- OEM Convert: Performs conversions on the user's input so that the `AnsiToOem` function works correctly if called by your program. This option is not selected by default.

- Want Return: Applies to MLE controls. This option allows an edit control to accept an Enter keypress, so that an Enter keypress doesn't affect the dialog box's default pushbutton.

- Border: Creates a border around the control. This option is selected by default.

6

- Uppercase: Converts all input to uppercase characters. This option is not selected by default.

- Lowercase: Converts all input to lowercase characters. This option is not selected by default.

- Read-only: Prevents the user from typing or editing text in the edit control. This option is not selected by default.

The ID for the new edit control is set by default to IDC_EDIT1 or a similar name. For the sample program, change the ID to IDC_EDIT_TEST, leaving the other properties set to their default values.

Binding a CEdit Object to an Edit Control

As discussed earlier, one way to interact with an edit control is through a CEdit object attached to the control. To attach a CEdit object to an edit control, you use ClassWizard much as you did for button controls in the previous hour:

1. Open ClassWizard.
2. Select the CDialog-derived class that manages the dialog box; in this case, CTestDlg.
3. Select the tab labeled Member Variables.
4. Select the control ID representing the control associated with the new member variable; in this case, IDC_EDIT_TEST.
5. Click the button labeled Add Variable. An Add Member Variable dialog box appears. Enter the control's name, category, and variable type, then click OK. For this example, use the values from Table 6.2.

TABLE 6.2. VALUES USED TO ADD A CEdit MEMBER VARIABLE FOR CTestDlg.

Control ID	Variable Name	Category	Type
IDC_EDIT_TEST	m_editTest	Control	CEdit

The default value displayed in the Category control is Value. The Value category is used for some member variables later this hour, when you learn about DDV and DDX routines.

Collecting Entered Text from an Edit Control

The primary reason for using an edit control, of course, is to collect information from a user. To do that, you must get the information from the edit control. Using the CEdit class simplifies this process.

Using CEdit Member Functions to Retrieve Text

Several CEdit member functions are useful when you are collecting information from an edit control, such as the GetWindowText and LineLength member functions. As an example, add the source code in Listing 6.2 to the CTestDlg::OnTest member function created earlier.

INPUT   **LISTING 6.2.** COLLECTING INPUT FROM AN EDIT CONTROL USING CEdit.

```
void CTestDlg::OnTest()
{
    CString szEdit;
    CString szResult;
    int nLength = m_editTest.LineLength();
    m_editTest.GetWindowText( szEdit );
    szResult.Format( "%s has %d chars", szEdit, nLength );
    AfxMessageBox( szResult );
}
```

When the Test button is clicked, the text entered in the edit control is retrieved by using the m_editTest object. The text is placed in a CString object called szEdit.

The CString Format member function is used to format the string's contents, using a pattern that is passed as the first parameter. You can use symbols such as %s and %d as placeholders for additional parameters that are combined to create the contents of the CString. The %s symbol is used as a placeholder for a string. The %d symbol is used as a placeholder for an int.

Normally, you are interested only in data contained in an edit control if OK is clicked. If the Cancel button is clicked, the dialog box should be closed and, usually, any entered information is simply discarded.

6

Passing Parameters to Dialog Boxes Using DDV and DDX Routines

The DDV and DDX routines are helper functions that help manage data for dialog boxes. DDV (Dialog Data Validation) routines are used for data validation. DDX (Dialog Data Exchange) routines are used to exchange data to and from the controls in a dialog box.

> You should rely on ClassWizard to add DDV and DDX routines instead of trying to hand-code the necessary function calls. Although you can use the DDV and DDX routines in your dialog boxes directly, ClassWizard adds the code for you at the click of a button.

Why Are DDV and DDX Routines Used?

The DDV routines are useful when collecting data from an edit control. In general, you have little control over how a user enters data in an edit control. A DDV enables you to perform some simple validation based on range or string length.

For example, if an edit control is used to collect an abbreviated state name, you want to limit the entered text to two characters. Using a DDV routine, making sure two characters have been entered is easy.

DDX functions link member variables from the dialog box class to controls that are contained in the dialog box. DDX routines enable data to be transferred to and from the controls much easier than is otherwise possible. As discussed in Hour 4, a dialog box is normally used something like this:

```
CMyDialog    dlgMine;
dlgMine.DoModal();
```

In this example, the dialog box is created when DoModal is called, and the function does not return until the user closes the dialog box. This presents a problem if data must be passed to or from the dialog box. Because none of the controls exist until the dialog box is created, using SetWindowText, GetWindowText, or other functions to interact directly with controls contained in the dialog box is not possible. After the dialog box has been dismissed, it is too late to use those functions to collect user input.

When DDX routines are used to exchange information with a dialog box, the dialog box can be used like this:

```
CMyDialog    dlgMine;
dlgMine.m_szTest = "Hello World";
dlgMine.DoModal();
```

The DDX routines enable you to have access to the dialog box's controls before and after the dialog box has been created. This simplifies dialog box programming because it is a much more flexible method than adding code in the InitDialog member function.

Using DDV and DDX Routines

The easiest and most useful way to add DDV and DDX routines to your dialog box class is by using ClassWizard. Member variables associated with dialog box controls by value automatically use the DDV and DDX routines provided by MFC. For example, CString member variables are often associated with edit controls. ClassWizard adds source code to handle the exchange and validation of data in two places:

- In the dialog box's constructor, source code is added to initialize the member variable.
- In the dialog box's DoDataExchange member function, ClassWizard adds DDV and DDX routines for each member variable associated with a control's value.

DoDataExchange is a virtual function that is called by the MFC framework to move data between the control and the dialog box's member data. You never call the DoDataExchange member function directly; instead, you call UpdateData, and the MFC framework will call DoDataExchange for you.

UpdateData takes a single parameter, either TRUE or FALSE, with TRUE as the default parameter. When UpdateData(FALSE) [TRUE/FALSE] is called, data is moved from the member variable to the control. When UpdateData(FALSE) is called, data is copied from the control to the member variable. [TRUE]

When the dialog box is initially displayed during CDialog::OnInitDialog, UpdateData(FALSE) [TRUE/FALSE] is called to transfer data from the member variables to the dialog box's controls. Later, during CDialog::OnOk, UpdateData() is called to transfer data from the dialog box's controls to member variables.

As shown in Figure 6.2, UpdateData has a single parameter that controls the direction in which data, in this case m_szTest, is copied.

6

FIGURE 6.2.

*DDV and DDX
routines used to handle
dialog box data.*

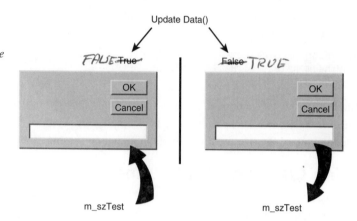

Associating a Control's Value with a Member Variable

You add member variables that are associated with a control's value almost exactly the way you added control-type variables earlier in this hour. For example, to create a member variable associated with the IDD_EDIT_TEST edit control, follow these steps:

1. Open ClassWizard.
2. Select the CDialog-derived class that manages the dialog box; in this case, CTestDlg.
3. Select the Member Variables tab.
4. Select the control ID representing the control associated with the new member variable; in this case, IDC_EDIT_TEST.
5. Click the Add Variable button. An Add Member Variable dialog box appears. Enter the control's name, category, and variable type; then click OK. For this example, use the values from Table 6.3.

TABLE 6.3. VALUES USED TO ASSOCIATE A CString MEMBER VARIABLE WITH AN EDIT CONTROL.

Control ID	Variable Name	Category	Type
IDC_EDIT_TEST	m_szTest	Value	CString

The preceding steps are exactly like the steps used to add a control-type variable earlier in this hour, except that the control type is set to Value. A member variable associated by value with an edit control can be an int or any other data type, although it is most commonly a CString.

After closing the Add Member Variable dialog box, ClassWizard displays an edit control that you can use to specify the type of validation to be performed on the member variable. If a CString object is associated with an edit control, the maximum string length can be specified. If a numeric variable is used, the allowed range can be defined.

Exchanging Edit-Control Information Using DDX Functions

The member variables associated with dialog box controls by ClassWizard are added to the dialog box class as public variables. This allows the member variables to be easily accessed and used. For example, to use the m_szTest variable that was added in the previous section, edit the CMainFrame::OnViewTest member function so it looks like the function in Listing 6.3.

INPUT

LISTING 6.3. USING MEMBER VARIABLES TO EXCHANGE INFORMATION WITH AN EDIT CONTROL.

```
void CMainFrame::OnViewTest()
{
    CTestDlg    dlg;
    dlg.m_szTest = "DDX Test";
    if( dlg.DoModal() == IDOK )
    {
        AfxMessageBox( dlg.m_szTest );
    }
}
```

Listing 6.3 sets the value of m_szTest before the dialog box is displayed to the user. CDialog::OnInitDialog calls the CWnd::UpdateData function, which calls UpdateData. Because UpdateData is a virtual function, the proper version of the function is called— the version that is part of the CDialog-derived class that handles the dialog box.

After the dialog box closes, the CMainFrame::OnViewTest function checks the return value of DoModal. If IDOK was returned, the dialog box was closed using the OK button, and the value of m_szTest is displayed.

6

Summary

In this hour, you learned about the Windows edit control and how it usually is used in a dialog box. You saw how to associate an edit control with a CEdit object using ClassWizard and used data exchange and validation to pass parameters to and from dialog boxes.

Q&A

Q I would like to use the DDV routines for all my dialog box data, but what if I have a complex data type, such as a credit card number? How can I use the DDV and DDX mechanism?

A You have two options. You can perform the validation yourself when accepting user input by testing for valid data before the user is allowed to close the dialog box. You can also write your own custom DDV routine. Technical Note 26 describes how to write such a routine. You can find this technical note by searching for TN026 in the Developer Studio online help.

Q Can I call UpdateData at any time? I would like to implement an Undo feature in my dialog box.

A Normally, UpdateData is called when the dialog box is initialized and when the user closes the dialog box by clicking OK. However, if you must call UpdateData at other times, it's perfectly okay.

Workshop

The Workshop is designed to help you anticipate possible questions, review what you've learned, and begin thinking ahead to putting your knowledge into practice. The answers to the quiz are in Appendix A, "Quiz Answers."

Quiz

1. What MFC class is used to manage edit controls?
2. What is the difference between a multiple-line edit control and an single-line edit control?
3. How are DDV and DDX routines used?
4. What member function do you call to transfer data to and from your dialog box controls?
5. What function is used to retrieve text from an edit control?
6. What function is used to set text in an edit control?
7. What property is used to hide user input in an edit control by replacing it with asterisks?
8. What keystroke is used to paste text into an edit control?
9. What keystroke is used to copy text from an edit control?
10. What keystroke is used to cut text from an edit control?

Exercises

1. Set the maximum length for the text entered in the edit control in the Test project to five characters.

2. Change the Test project so that the edit control is used to store an integer value instead of a string.

6

HOUR 7

Using List Box and Combo Box Controls

List boxes and combo boxes are two types of controls that are used often in Windows programming. The list box often is used to enable a user to select from a large number of possible choices, whereas the combo box is a combination of the list box and edit controls. In this hour, you will learn about these controls and use them in simple examples.

What Are List Boxes?

NEW TERM *List box* controls are used to contain a list of items available for selection. The user can select items by using the keyboard or by clicking an individual item using a mouse.

NEW TERM A *single-selection list box* enables one item to be selected at a time. This is the default style for a list box.

NEW TERM A *multiple-selection list box* enables multiple items to be selected at one time.

A list box normally is found in a dialog box, control bar, or other window that contains controls. List boxes often are used to contain a large number of items. If some items can't be displayed, a scrollbar displays to help the user navigate through the list.

Why Use a List Box?

List boxes are the simplest control that enables an arbitrary number of items to be displayed to a user. List boxes are often used to display lists of information that are extracted from databases or reports. Because the list box doesn't have to be sized, it is well-suited for this type of data. When a sorted list box is used, it's easy for a user to search through a large number of text items and make a selection.

List boxes are also extremely easy to program. If you have created a list box object, you can add an item to the list box with just one line of code, like this:

```
listBox.AddString("Gwen");
```

No other control is as flexible and easy to use for both the programmer and the user.

> The list box is also the first control you have seen that uses indexes.
> Whenever an item is selected, inserted, or deleted, a zero-based index is
> used to identify the item. This index can be synchronized with a database
> index or used to identify the item in other ways.

MFC Support for List Boxes

You normally add list boxes to a dialog box resource just as you added buttons and edit controls in the previous two hours. After you have added the control, use ClassWizard to add message-handling functions and associate the control with a CListBox object.

You can use the MFC CListBox class to manage and interact with the list box control. Like other control classes, CListBox is derived from CWnd, and most CWnd functions can be used with CListBox objects. You will see more details about the CListBox later, in the section, "Using the CListBox Class."

Adding a List Box to a Dialog Box

For demonstration purposes, create a dialog box-based project named ListBox using AppWizard, following the steps presented in Hour 4, "Using Dialog Boxes." Click the ResourceView tab in the project workspace. Open the dialog box editor by double-clicking the IDD_LISTBOX_DIALOG icon in the Dialog resource folder.

Adding a list box to IDD_LISTBOX_DIALOG, the main dialog box, is just like adding a button or edit control. Either drag and drop a list box control from the control palette to the main dialog box, or select the list box control on the tool palette using the mouse, and click the desired position in the main dialog box. Figure 7.1 shows the IDD_LISTBOX_DIALOG with a list box control.

FIGURE 7.1.

The main dialog box used in the ListBox program.

Open the Properties dialog box for the list box by right-clicking the control and selecting Properties from the shortcut menu. Change the resource ID to IDC_LIST. Set all other properties to their default values.

List Box Properties

Just like other controls, list boxes have properties that you can configure using the Developer Studio resource editor. Some of these properties are available in other controls, and some are unique to list boxes. These properties are available for a list box control:

- ID: Used for the list box resource ID. Developer Studio supplies a default resource ID, such as IDC_LIST.

- Visible: Indicates that the list is initially visible. This check box is normally checked.

- Disabled: Indicates the list should be initially disabled. This check box is normally cleared.

- Group: Marks the first control in a group. This check box is normally cleared.

- Tab Stop: Indicates that this control can be reached by pressing the Tab key. This check box is normally checked.

- Help ID: Creates a context-sensitive help ID for this control.

- Selection: Determines how items in a list box can be selected. A single-selection list box enables one item to be selected at any given time. Multiple-selection list boxes enable several selections at once, but ignore the Shift and Control keys. Extended selection list boxes use the Shift and Control keys during selection.

- Owner Draw: Indicates that the button will be drawn by the button's owner, in this case the dialog box. In most cases, this option is set to No.

7

- Has Strings: Specifies that an owner-drawn list box contains strings. All other list boxes contain strings by default.
- Border: Specifies a border for the list box. This option is enabled by default.
- Sort: Indicates that the list box contents should be sorted. This option is normally selected.
- Notify: Indicates that notification messages should be sent to the dialog box. This option is normally selected.
- Multi-Column: Creates a multicolumn list box. This option is normally cleared.
- Horizontal Scroll: Creates a list box with a horizontal scrollbar. This option is normally cleared.
- Vertical Scroll: Creates a list box with a vertical scrollbar. This option is normally selected.
- No Redraw: Indicates that the list box should not update its appearance when its contents are changed. This option is rarely selected and is cleared by default.
- Use Tabstops: Specifies that text items displayed in the list box can contain tabs. This option is normally cleared.
- Want Key Input: Indicates that the list box owner should receive WM_VKEYTOITEM or WM_CHARTOITEM messages when keys are pressed while the list box has the input focus. This option is normally cleared.
- Disable No Scroll: Displays a vertical scrollbar even if it's not needed. This option is normally cleared.
- No Integral Height: Indicates that Windows should display the list box exactly as specified in the resource description, displaying partial items if needed. This option is normally selected.

Using the CListBox Class

Like control classes used in previous hours, the MFC CListBox class makes your life much easier by providing a C++ class that hides control messages and provides an easy-to-use interface. To attach a CListBox object to a list box control, use ClassWizard as you have for controls in previous hours:

1. Open ClassWizard.
2. Select the CDialog-derived class that manages the dialog box; in this case, CListBoxDlg.
3. Select the Member Variables tab.
4. Select the control ID representing the control associated with the new member variable; in this case, IDC_LIST.

5. Click the button labeled Add Variable. An Add Member Variable dialog box appears. Enter the control's name, category, and variable type; then click OK. For this example, use the values from Table 7.1.

TABLE 7.1. VALUES USED TO ADD A `CListBox` MEMBER VARIABLE FOR `CListBoxDlg`.

Control ID	Variable Name	Category	Type
IDC_LIST	m_listBox	Control	CListBox

Adding an Item to a List Box

There are two ways to add a text string to a list box:

- To add a string to a list box, the `AddString` member function can be called:

  ```
  m_listBox.AddString( "Rene'" );
  ```

  Any strings added to a sorted list box are sorted as they are added. If the list box is not sorted, the item is added after the last item in the list.

- To add an item at a specified position in a list box, use the `InsertString` member function:

  ```
  m_listBox.InsertString( 0, "Alex" );
  ```

  All positions in a list box are numbered beginning with zero. Any existing list box items are shifted down, if needed, to make room for the new item.

Both the `InsertString` and `AddString` functions return the position of the new item. If an error occurs when adding an item, `LB_ERR` is returned from the `AddString` or `InsertString` functions. If the list box is full, `LB_ERRSPACE` is returned. Using the source code from Listing 7.1, add three strings to the `IDC_LIST` list box during the `CListBoxDlg::OnInitDialog` member function. There already are several lines of code in `CListBoxDlg::OnInitDialog`; add the three `AddString` statements after the `//TODO` comment supplied by AppWizard.

INPUT   **LISTING 7.1.** USING `AddString` TO ADD STRINGS TO A LIST BOX.

```
// TODO: Add extra initialization here
m_listBox.AddString( "Foo" );
m_listBox.AddString( "Bar" );
m_listBox.AddString( "Baz" );
```

7

To determine the number of items currently in a list box, use the GetCount member function:

```
nItems = listBox.GetCount();
```

The GetCount function returns the total number of items in a list box, not the value of the last valid index. If a list box contains five items, GetCount returns five, but the last valid index is four.

Removing Items from a List Box

To remove items from a list box, specify the item position to be removed in a call to the DeleteString member function:

```
listBox.DeleteString(8);
```

This line removes the item in the ninth position of the list box. Remember, all list box position indexes start from zero. The return value from the DeleteString member function is the number of items remaining in the list box, or LB_ERR if any errors occur. The return value can be used like this:

```
int nItems = listBox.GetCount();
while(nItems > 3 && nItems != LB_ERR )
nItems = listBox.DeleteString(nItems - 1);
```

This code removes the contents of a list box, except for the first three items. To clear a list box completely, use the ResetContent function:

```
listBox.ResetContent();
```

The ResetContent function returns void.

Receiving List Box Messages

Several messages are sent to the parent of a list box for notification purposes when certain events occur. All these messages are prefixed with LBN_, for List Box Notification. For these messages to be sent, the list box must have the Notify property enabled. The following messages are sent from the list box to its parent:

- LBN_DBLCLK is sent when a user double-clicks a list-box item.
- LBN_ERRSPACE indicates that an action could not be performed due to a lack of memory.
- LBN_KILLFOCUS is sent just before the list box loses the input focus.

- LBN_SELCANCEL is sent when a user cancels a list box selection.
- LBN_SELCHANGE is sent when the selection state in a list box is about to change.
- LBN_SETFOCUS is sent when a list box receives the input focus.

The LBN_DBLCLK message is the most frequently used notification message. Most users expect some sort of default action to take place when a list box item is double-clicked. For example, when a list of filenames is displayed, double-clicking a particular filename might be expected to open that file for editing.

The steps to add message-handling functions for any of the controls used in Windows are very similar. To create a message-handling function for the LBN_DBLCLK notification message, follow these steps:

1. Open ClassWizard and click the Message Maps tab.
2. Select the CListBoxDlg class and the IDC_LIST Object ID.
3. Select LBN_DBLCLK, and click the Add Function button.
4. Accept the suggested function name CListBoxDlg::OnDblclkList.
5. Click the button labeled Edit Code.
6. Add the source code from Listing 7.2 to the CListBoxDlg::OnDblclkList function.

INPUT   **LISTING 7.2.** HANDLING A LIST BOX NOTIFICATION MESSAGE.

```
void CListBoxDlg::OnDblclkList()
{
    int nSelection = m_listBox.GetCurSel();
    if( nSelection != LB_ERR )
    {
        CString szSelection;
        m_listBox.GetText( nSelection, szSelection );
        AfxMessageBox( szSelection );
    }
}
```

Compile and run the ListBox project and then double-click any of the list box items. The LBN_DBLCLK message is sent to the CListBoxDlg::OnDblclkList function, and a message box is displayed with information about the selected item.

You can determine the currently selected item in the list box by using the CListbox::GetCurSel member function, as shown in Listing 7.2. The GetCurSel member function

7

returns the position of the currently selected item, with the first item position starting at zero. If no item is selected, or if the list box has the multiple-selection property, LB_ERR is returned.

What Are Combo Boxes?

A combo box control is a single control that combines an edit control with a list box. A combo box enables a user to enter data either by entering text like an edit control or by selecting an item from several choices like a list box.

Combo boxes are quite useful when a user is not limited to selecting only the items presented in a list box. The list box portion of the combo box can be used to display recent selections, giving the user the freedom to enter a new selection in the edit control.

There are three types of combo boxes:

- Simple combo boxes display an edit control and list box. Unlike the other combo box types, the list box is always visible. When the list box contains more items than can be displayed, a scrollbar is used to scroll through the list box.
- Drop-down combo boxes hide the list box until the user opens it. With this type of combo box, the list uses much less room in a dialog box than that used by the simple combo box.
- Drop-down list boxes are similar to drop-down combo boxes in that they display the list box only when opened by the user. However, a static-text control is used to display the selection instead of an edit control. Therefore, the user is limited to selecting items from the list box.

Combo boxes also are used when space in a dialog box is at a premium. A large number of choices in a combo box can be hidden until the combo box is opened, enabling more controls to be placed in a smaller area than that required for a list box.

Combo Box Properties

A combo box has a large number of properties because it combines an edit control and a list box. Most edit-control and list-box styles have similar properties that can be applied to combo boxes. These combo box properties are identical to the list box properties discussed earlier:

- ID
- Visible
- Disabled
- Group
- Tab Stop
- Owner Draw
- Has Strings
- Sort
- Vertical Scroll
- No Integral Height
- Help ID
- Disable No Scroll

The following combo box properties are identical to properties offered for edit controls (discussed in Hour 6, "Using Edit Controls"):

- Auto HScroll
- Uppercase
- Lowercase
- OEM Convert

These two properties are unique to combo box controls:

- List Choices: Used to list items that appear by default when the dialog box is created. Press Ctrl+Enter after each entry.
- Type: Used to specify the type of the combo box. You can choose between Simple, Dropdown, and Drop List. Dropdown is the default choice.

MFC Support for Combo Boxes

Just like list boxes and other controls, you normally add combo boxes to dialog box resources using the Developer Studio dialog box editor. After you add the control, use ClassWizard to add message-handling functions and associate the control with a `CComboBox` object.

You use the MFC `CComboBox` class to manage and interact with the combo box control, and it contains many of the member functions that are available in the `CListBox` and `CEdit` classes. For example, you can use `GetCurSel` to get the currently selected item from the list box part of a combo box.

7

Adding Items to a Combo Box

You add strings to combo boxes just as you add them to list boxes. Just like `CListBox`, the `CComboBox` class contains `AddString` and `InsertString` member functions:

```
comboBox.AddString( "Riley" );
```

or

```
comboBox.InsertString( 0, "Mitch" );
```

All positions in a combo box are numbered beginning with zero, just like list boxes. However, if an error occurs, `CB_ERR` is returned instead of `LB_ERR`. If an item can't be added due to insufficient space, `CB_ERRSPACE` is returned.

To determine the number of items currently in a combo box, `CComboBox` includes the `GetCount` member function:

```
nItems = comboBox.GetCount();
```

Unlike list boxes, combo boxes return `CB_ERR` when an error occurs.

Collecting Input from a Combo Box

You can collect input from a combo box by using the `GetWindowText` member function, just like an edit control. For simple combo boxes and drop-down combo boxes, this is the easiest way to get the current selection. You can also use the `GetCurSel` member function to determine the current selection position from the list box.

To retrieve the text string from a given position in the list box, use the `GetLBText` member function. `GetLBText` has two parameters: the list index and a `CString` member variable that will receive the text string.

```
m_combo.GetLBText( 1, szChoice );
```

Searching for an Item in a Combo Box

You can search for a particular string in a combo box by using the `FindString` and `FindStringExact` member functions. `FindString` searches for an item in the combo box that begins with a search string:

```
int index = m_combo.FindString( -1, szSearch );
```

`FindString` has two parameters: an index where the search should start and a string that contains the prefix to search for. The search index specifies the index before the first item that is searched, so to start at the beginning you must pass –1 as the search index.

FindStringExact searches for an item in the combo box that matches the search string exactly, using the same parameters used for FindString:

```
int index = m_combo.FindStringExact( -1, szSearch );
```

The FindString and FindStringExact functions return the index of the first item that matches the search string, or CB_ERR if no item is found.

A Combo Box Example

To create a sample project using a combo box and the CComboBox class, follow these steps:

1. Create a dialog box-based project named ComboList using AppWizard, as described in previous examples.

2. Add a drop-down combo list to the IDD_COMBOLIST_DIALOG resource, as you did for the list box earlier in this hour.

3. Give the combo box the resource ID IDC_COMBO. Use the default values for all other properties.

4. Add a static text control to the dialog box, and give it the resource ID IDC_RESULT. This text control will be used to display information about messages received from the combo box.

5. Using ClassWizard, add a member variable to the CComboListDlg class named m_comboList. Set the Category to Control.

6. Using ClassWizard, add message-handling functions for IDC_COMBO control messages to the CComboListDlg class. Add functions to handle CBN_CLOSEUP and CBN_EDITUPDATE messages.

Adding Strings to a Combo Box

After completing these steps, add the source code in Listing 7.3 to the CComboListDlg::OnInitDialog member function. This code adds three entries to the combo box. There are already several lines of code in the function; don't remove them. Just add the code from Listing 7.3 after the //TODO comment provided by AppWizard.

INPUT

LISTING 7.3. SOURCE CODE ADDED TO THE CComboListDlg::OnInitDialog FUNCTION.

7

```
// In OnInitDialog...
// TODO: Add extra initialization here
m_comboList.AddString( "Foo" );
m_comboList.AddString( "Bar" );
m_comboList.AddString( "Baz" );
```

Detecting Combo Box Events

Add the source code provided in Listing 7.4 to the `CComboListDlg::OnCloseupCombo`
function. When the `CBN_CLOSEUP` message is received, a message is displayed on the
static text control `IDC_RESULT`.

LISTING 7.4. SOURCE CODE ADDED TO THE `CComboListDlg::OnCloseupCombo`
FUNCTION.

INPUT

```
void CComboListDlg::OnCloseupCombo()
{
    CString     szChoice;
    CString     szResult;
    int         nChoice;
    // Get current selections from edit and list-box controls
    m_comboList.GetWindowText( szChoice );
    nChoice = m_comboList.GetCurSel();
    if( nChoice != CB_ERR )
    {
        // If a valid choice was made from the list box, fetch
        // the item's text string.
        m_comboList.GetLBText( nChoice, szChoice );
        szResult = "Closing after selecting " + szChoice;
    }
    else if( szChoice.IsEmpty() == TRUE )
    {
        // No choice was made from the list box, and the edit
        // control was empty.
        szResult = "No choice selected";
    }
    else if( m_comboList.FindStringExact(-1, szChoice) != CB_ERR )
    {
        // The string from the edit control was found in the
        // list box.
        szResult = "Closing after selecting " + szChoice;
    }
    else
    {
        // The edit control contains a new string, not currently
        // in the list box. Add the string.
        m_comboList.AddString( szChoice );
        szResult = "Adding " + szChoice + " to list";
    }
    // Get a pointer to the static-text control, and display an
    // appropriate result message.
    CWnd* pWnd = GetDlgItem( IDC_RESULT );
    ASSERT( pWnd );
    if( pWnd )
        pWnd->SetWindowText( szResult );}
```

The `CComboListDlg::OnCloseupCombo` function collects the contents from the edit control section of the combo box and the selected item from the list box section of the combo box. If a selection has been made in the list box, the item's string is retrieved and displayed. Otherwise, if a string was entered in the edit control, it is displayed. The string is not currently in the list box; it is added to it.

Add the source code provided in Listing 7.5 to the `CComboListDlg::OnEditupdateCombo` member function. `CBN_EDITUPDATE` is received when the user types inside the edit control. When the `CBN_EDITUPDATE` message is received, the contents of the edit control are displayed on the `IDC_RESULT` text control.

LISTING 7.5. SOURCE CODE ADDED TO THE
INPUT `CComboListDlg::OnEditupdateCombo` FUNCTION.

```
void CComboListDlg::OnEditupdateCombo()
{
    CString     szChoice;
    CString     szResult;
    m_comboList.GetWindowText( szChoice );
    szResult = "Choice changed to " + szChoice;
    CWnd* pWnd = GetDlgItem( IDC_RESULT );
    ASSERT( pWnd );
    if( pWnd )
        pWnd->SetWindowText( szResult );
}
```

Compile and run the ComboList project. Experiment by adding new entries to the combo box and by expanding and closing the combo box. Other messages sent to the combo box can be trapped and displayed just as `CBN_EDITUPDATE` was handled in Listing 7.5.

Using Loops

In Hour 5, "Button Controls," you learned about using conditional expressions to control the flow of execution in C++ programs. Another way to control the flow of execution in your program is to execute sequences, also known as loops or iterations. Popular uses for loops include waiting for user input, printing a certain number of reports, or reading input from a file until an End Of File (EOF) mark is detected. Three different loop statements are used in C++:

- The `while` loop
- The `do-while` loop
- The `for` loop

7

Using the while Loop

The while loop is used to execute a statement as long as a test expression evaluates as True. Listing 7.6 shows an example of a while loop.

LISTING 7.6. EXECUTING A while LOOP 10 TIMES.

```
CString szMsg;
szMsg.Format("This is loop number %d", nLoopCounter);
int nLoopCounter = 0;
while(nLoopCounter < 10)
{
    nLoopCounter++;
    AfxMessageBox(szMsg);
}
AfxMessageBox("The loop is finished");
```

In Listing 7.6, the compound statement following the while loop is executed as long as nLoopCounter is less than 10. When nLoopCounter is equal to 10, the condition tested by while becomes False, and the next statement following the block controlled by while is executed. In this example, a compound statement is executed; however, a single statement can also be executed.

Using a do-while Loop

A relative of the while loop is the do-while loop. The do-while loop is used when a statement or series of statements must be executed at least once. Listing 7.7 is an example of a do-while loop used to check an input character for Q.

LISTING 7.7. USING THE do-while LOOP TO TEST FOR USER INPUT IN A CONSOLE MODE PROGRAM.

```
#include <iostream>
using namespace std;

int main()
{
    char ch;
    do{
        cout << "\nPress 'Q' to exit ->";
        cin >> ch;
        // Ignore input until a carriage return.
        cin.ignore( 120, '\n');
    }while( ch != 'Q' );
    cout << "Goodbye" << endl;

    return 0;}
```

Using the for Loop

The for loop is often used in C++ programs to write a very compact loop statement. The for loop enables you to write loops in a more compact style than is possible using while loops. Listing 7.8 is equivalent to Listing 7.6, except that it has been rewritten using the for loop.

LISTING 7.8. USING A for LOOP TO DISPLAY A MESSAGE 10 TIMES.

```
CString szMsg;
szMsg.Format("This is loop number %d", nLoopCounter);
for(int nLoopCounter = 0; nLoopCounter < 10; nLoopCounter++)
{
    AfxMessageBox(szMsg);
}
AfxMessageBox("The loop is finished");
```

There are four components to every for statement:

```
for( expression1; expression2; expression3 )
    statement1
```

When the for loop begins, *expression1* is executed. This is usually where you declare loop counters. As long as *expression2* is true, the statement controlled by the loop is executed. After the controlled statement (*statement1*) has been performed, *expression3* is executed. Loop counters are usually incremented in *expression3*.

In the example in Listing 7.8, the expression nLoopCounter++ was used as a way to increment the value of nLoopCounter by one. To decrement the value, you can use nLoopCounter--.

As a rule, if the loop is executed a fixed number of times, it's usually easier to use for instead of while. However, if you are waiting for an event to occur, or if the number of loops isn't easily predicted, it's better to use while.

7

Summary

In this hour, you learned about list box and combo box controls and how they are used in Windows programs. You also learned how to associate these controls with `CListBox` and `CComboBox` objects.

Q&A

Q What is the easiest way to create a list box that has a bitmap image next to each item?

A The only way to display a bitmap in a list box is to create an owner-drawn list box, where you take responsibility for drawing each item in the list box. You can easily achieve a similar effect by using a list view control, which is discussed in Hour 17, "List View Controls."

Q When should I use a combo box drop list, and when is a list box more appropriate?

A A drop list is appropriate when space on your dialog box is at a premium. A list box is more appropriate when the user must see more than one item without clicking on the control.

Q I've added a combo box to my project, but the drop-down list isn't large enough. How can I extend the drop-down list so that it shows more items?

A To change the size of the drop-down portion of a combo-box, click the combo box's down arrow while editing the dialog box resource. An outline that represents the drop-down list boundary will be displayed. Drag the drop-down list to the desired size, and you're all set.

Workshop

The Workshop is designed to help you anticipate possible questions, review what you've learned, and begin thinking ahead to putting your knowledge into practice. The answers to the quiz are in Appendix A, "Quiz Answers."

Quiz

1. Which MFC class is used to manage list box controls?
2. What message is sent to your dialog box when a user double-clicks a dialog box?
3. What functions are used to add items to a list box control?
4. What function is used to retrieve the number of items in a list box control?

5. What function is used to retrieve the currently selected index in a list box?

6. What are the three styles used for list box controls?

7. What are the three types of loops used in C++ programs?

8. Which MFC class is used to manage combo boxes?

9. What function is used to add an item to a combo box at a specific index?

10. What are the three styles used for combo boxes?

Exercises

1. Modify the ListBox project by adding a new button labeled Loop. When a user clicks the Loop button, display each item in the list box in a message box, one item at a time.

2. Modify the ComboList project so that the currently selected combo box item is displayed in a message box when the user clicks OK.

7

PART III

Windows and MFC Architecture

Hour

Hour **8**

Messages and Event-Driven Programming

Messages are at the heart of every Windows program. A good understanding of how the Windows operating system sends messages will be a great help to you as you write your own programs.

In this hour, you will learn

- How Windows applications use messages to communicate with the operating system and window objects in the application
- How messages are managed using the MFC framework
- MFC base classes that are used in every MFC application

In this hour, you will also create a small sample program to learn how messages are passed to applications by the Windows operating system.

Understanding the Windows Programming Model

Programs written for Windows differ from most console-mode programs. The console-mode programs that you created in Hours 1 and 2 consisted of short listings that created small sequential programs that assumed complete control over a console-mode window.

Although sequential programs work well for explaining simple concepts like the basics of the C++ language, they don't work well in a multitasking environment like Microsoft Windows. In the Windows environment everything is shared: the screen, the keyboard, the mouse—even the user. Programs written for Windows must cooperate with Windows and with other programs that might be running at the same time.

In a cooperative environment like Windows, messages are sent to a program when an event that affects the program occurs. Every message sent to a program has a specific purpose. For example, messages are sent when a program should be initialized, when menu selections are made, and when a window should be redrawn. Responding to event messages is a key part of most Windows programs.

Another characteristic of Windows programs is that they must share resources. Many resources must be requested from the operating system before they are used and, after they are used, must be returned to the operating system so that they can be used by other programs. This is one way Windows controls access to resources like the screen and other physical devices.

In short, a program that runs in a window must be a good citizen. It can't assume that it has complete control over the computer on which it is running; it must ask permission before taking control of any central resource, and it must be ready to react to events that are sent to it.

What Are Messages?

Programs written for Microsoft Windows react to events that are sent to a program's main window. Examples of events include moving the mouse pointer, clicking a button, or pressing a key. These events are sent to the window in the form of messages. Each message has a specific purpose: redraw the window, resize the window, close the window, and so on.

NEW TERM   The *default window procedure* is a special message-handling function supplied by Windows that handles the message if no special processing is required. For many messages, the application can just pass the message to the default window procedure.

8

A Windows program can also send messages to other windows. Because every control used in a Windows program is also a window, messages are also often used to communicate with controls.

Two different types of messages are handled by a Windows program:

- Messages sent from the operating system
- Messages sent to and from controls that deal with user input

Examples of messages sent from the operating system include messages used to tell the program that it should start or close or to tell a window that it is being resized or moved. Messages sent to controls can be used to change the font used by a window or its title. Messages received from a control include notifications that a button has been pressed or that a character has been entered in an edit control.

There are two reasons why messages are used so heavily in Windows programs:

- Unlike a function call, a message is a physical chunk of data, so it can be easily queued and prioritized.
- A message is not dependent on a particular language or processor type, so a message-based program can easily be ported to other CPUs, as is often done with Windows NT.

Queues work well for event-driven programming. When an event occurs, a message can be created and quickly queued to the appropriate window or program. Each message that is queued can then be handled in an orderly manner.

The fact that messages are language independent has enabled Windows to grow over the years. Today, you can write a Windows program using diverse languages such as Visual Basic, Delphi, Visual C++, or PowerBuilder. Because messages are language independent, they can easily be sent between these programs. The message interface enables you to add new features to the programs you write and also enables Windows to grow in the future.

When using an event-driven programming model such as Microsoft Windows, you can't always be certain about message order. A subtle difference in the way different users use a program can cause messages to be received in a different sequence. This means that every time you handle an event, you should handle only that particular event and not assume that any other activity has taken place.

A Program to Test for Mouse Clicks

As an example, you're about to create a program that actually shows how messages are used to notify your application about events. This program, MouseTst, will be an application that displays a message whenever the mouse is clicked inside the client area. The first step in creating MouseTst is to use AppWizard to create an SDI application. Feel free to select or remove any options offered by AppWizard, because none of the options have any bearing on the demonstration. Name the application MouseTst.

What Are Message Queues?

Messages are delivered to all windows that must receive events. For example, the simple act of moving the mouse cursor across the main window of a Windows program generates a large number of messages. Messages sent to a window are placed in a queue, and a program must examine each message in turn. Typically, a program examines messages that are sent to it and responds only to messages that are of interest, as shown in Figure 8.1.

FIGURE 8.1.

Messages are queued and handled in order by an application.

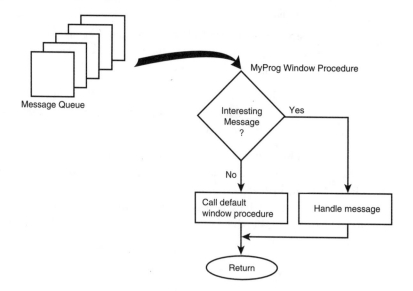

As shown in Figure 8.1, messages sent to a program are handled by a window procedure that is defined for the program.

How Are Messages Handled?

When a user moves the mouse over a program's main window, two messages are sent to the program's window procedure.

- WM_NCMOUSEMOVE is sent when the mouse is moved over the menu or caption bar.
- WM_MOUSEMOVE is sent when the mouse is over the window's client area.

Another type of mouse message is the WM_LBUTTONDOWN message, sent when the primary mouse button is pressed. Because this is the left button for most mouse users, the message is named WM_LBUTTONDOWN. A similar message is WM_RBUTTONDOWN, sent when the secondary, usually right, mouse button is pressed.

These and other messages are sent to a window's window procedure. When a window procedure receives the message, the parameters passed along with the message are used to help decide how the message should be handled.

Handling Messages with ClassWizard

ClassWizard (also called MFC ClassWizard) adds code that typically is used for a particular message-handling function. This commonly reused, or "boilerplate," code can help reduce the number of errors still further because it's guaranteed to be correct. Listing 8.1 is an example of a function created by ClassWizard to handle the WM_LBUTTONDOWN message.

LISTING 8.1. THE OnLButtonDown FUNCTION CREATED BY CLASSWIZARD.

```
void CMyView::OnLButtonDown(UINT nFlags, CPoint point)
{
    //TODO: Add your message handler code here and/or call default
    CView::OnLButtonDown(nFlags, point);
}
```

NEW TERM   A *message map* connects messages sent to a program with the functions that are meant to handle those messages.

When AppWizard or ClassWizard adds a message-handling function, an entry is added to the class message map. Listing 8.2 shows an example of a message map.

LISTING 8.2. A MESSAGE MAP FOR THE CMyView CLASS.

```
BEGIN_MESSAGE_MAP(CMyView, CView)
    //{{AFX_MSG_MAP(CMyView)
    ON_WM_LBUTTONDOWN()
    //}}AFX_MSG_MAP
    // Standard printing commands
    ON_COMMAND(ID_FILE_PRINT, CView::OnFilePrint)
    ON_COMMAND(ID_FILE_PRINT_DIRECT, CView::OnFilePrint)
    ON_COMMAND(ID_FILE_PRINT_PREVIEW, CView::OnFilePrintPreview)
END_MESSAGE_MAP()
```

> The message map begins with the BEGIN_MESSAGE_MAP macro and ends with the END_MESSAGE_MAP macro. The lines reserved for use by ClassWizard start with //{{AFX_MSG_MAP and end with //}}AFX_MSG_MAP. If you make manual changes to the message map, do not change the entries reserved for ClassWizard; they are maintained automatically.

Messages Handled by MouseTst

The MouseTst program must handle four messages used to collect mouse events. The messages used by MouseTst are listed in Table 8.1.

TABLE 8.1. MESSAGES HANDLED BY MOUSETST.

Message	Function	Description
WM_LBUTTONDOWN	OnLButtonDown	Left mouse button clicked
WM_LBUTTONDBLCLK	OnLButtonDblClk	Left mouse button double-clicked
WM_RBUTTONDOWN	OnRButtonDown	Right mouse button clicked
WM_RBUTTONDBLCLK	OnRButtonDblClk	Right mouse button double-clicked

In addition, when the WM_PAINT message is received the MFC framework calls the OnDraw member function. MouseTst will use OnDraw to update the display with the current mouse position and last message.

Updating the MouseTst View Class

All the work that keeps track of the mouse events will be done in the CMouseTstView class. There are two steps to displaying the mouse event information in the MouseTst program:

8

1. When one of the four mouse events occurs, the event type and mouse position are recorded and the view's rectangle is invalidated. This causes a WM_PAINT message to be generated by Windows and sent to the MouseTst application.

2. When a WM_PAINT message is received by MouseTst, the CMouseTstView::OnDraw member function is called, and the mouse event and position are displayed.

> All output is done in response to a WM_PAINT message. WM_PAINT is sent when a window's client area is invalidated. This often is due to the window being uncovered or reopened. Because the window must be redrawn in response to a WM_PAINT message, most programs written for Windows do all their drawing in response to WM_PAINT and just invalidate their display window or view when the window should be updated.

To keep track of the mouse event and position, you must add two member variables to the CMouseTstView class. Add the three lines from Listing 8.3 as the last three lines before the closing curly brace in MouseTstView.h.

INPUT LISTING 8.3. NEW MEMBER VARIABLES FOR THE CMouseTstView CLASS.

```
private:
    CPoint   m_ptMouse;
    CString  m_szDescription;
```

Adding Message-Handling Functions

Using ClassWizard, add message-handling functions for the four mouse events that you're handling in the MouseTst program. Open ClassWizard by pressing Ctrl+W, or by right-clicking in a source-code window and selecting ClassWizard from the menu. After ClassWizard appears, follow these steps:

1. Select the CMouseTstView class in the Object ID list box; a list of messages sent to the CMouseTstView class displays in the Message list box.

2. Select the WM_LBUTTONDOWN message from the Message list box, and click the Add Function button.

3. Repeat step 2 for the WM_RBUTTONDOWN, WM_LBUTTONDBLCLK, and WM_RBUTTONDBLCLK messages.

4. Click OK to close ClassWizard.

Edit the message-handling functions so they look like the function provided in Listing 8.4.
You must remove some source code provided by ClassWizard in each function.

INPUT **LISTING 8.4.** THE FOUR MOUSE-HANDLING FUNCTIONS FOR CMouseTstView.

```
void CMouseTstView::OnLButtonDblClk(UINT nFlags, CPoint point)
{
    m_ptMouse = point;
    m_szDescription = "Left Button Double Click";
    InvalidateRect( NULL );
}
void CMouseTstView::OnLButtonDown(UINT nFlags, CPoint point)
{
    m_ptMouse = point;
    m_szDescription = "Left Button Down";
    InvalidateRect( NULL );
}

void CMouseTstView::OnRButtonDblClk(UINT nFlags, CPoint point)
{
    m_ptMouse = point;
    m_szDescription = "Right Button Double Click";
    InvalidateRect( NULL );
}

void CMouseTstView::OnRButtonDown(UINT nFlags, CPoint point)
{
    m_ptMouse = point;
    m_szDescription = "Right Button Down";
    InvalidateRect( NULL );
}
```

Each message-handling function in Listing 8.4 stores the position of both the mouse
event and a text string that describes the event. Each function then invalidates the view
rectangle.

Displaying the Event in the MouseTst Program

The next step is to use the CMouseTstView::OnDraw function to display the event. Edit
CMouseTstView::OnDraw so it contains the source code in Listing 8.5. Remove any existing source code provided by AppWizard.

INPUT   **LISTING 8.5.** THE OnDraw MEMBER FUNCTION FOR CMouseTstView.

```
void CMouseTstView::OnDraw(CDC* pDC)
{
    pDC->TextOut( m_ptMouse.x, m_ptMouse.y, m_szDescription );
}
```

The OnDraw member function uses TextOut to display the previously saved event message. The CPoint object, m_ptMouse, was used to store the mouse event's position. A CPoint object has two member variables, x and y, which are used to plot a point in a window.

Running MouseTst

Build and run MouseTst, then click the main window's client area. A message is displayed whenever you click the left or right mouse button. Figure 8.2 shows the MouseTst program after a mouse button has been clicked.

FIGURE 8.2.

The MouseTst program displaying a mouse event.

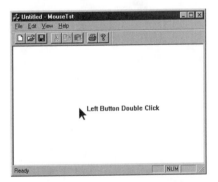

What Are MFC Base Classes?

The MFC class library includes a large number of classes well suited for Windows programming. Most of these classes are derived from CObject, a class that is at the root of the MFC class hierarchy. In addition, any class that represents a window or control is derived from the CWnd class, which handles basic functions that are common to all windows.

The CObject and CWnd classes use virtual functions, which enable your program to access general-purpose functions through a base pointer. This enables you to easily use any object that is derived from CObject or CWnd when interacting with the MFC framework.

The CObject Base Class

Almost every class used in an MFC program is derived from CObject. The CObject class provides four types of services:

- Diagnostic memory management provides diagnostic messages when memory leaks are detected. These leaks are often caused by failing to free objects that have been dynamically created.
- Dynamic creation support uses the CRuntimeClass to enable objects to be created at runtime. This is different from creating objects dynamically using the new operator.
- Serialization support enables an object to be stored and loaded in an object-oriented fashion. Serialization is discussed in Hour 22, "Using MFC to Save Program Data."
- The MFC class library uses runtime class information to provide diagnostic information when errors are discovered in your program. Runtime class information is also used when you're serializing objects to or from storage.

The CWnd Base Class

The CWnd class is derived from CObject and adds a great deal of functionality that is shared by all windows in an MFC program. This also includes dialog boxes and controls, which are just specialized versions of windows. Figure 8.3 shows some of the major MFC classes derived from CWnd.

FIGURE 8.3.

Some of the major MFC classes derived from CWnd.

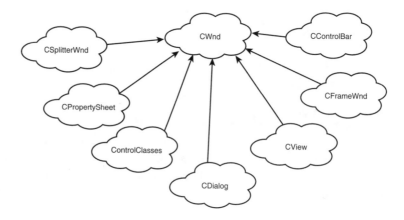

The CWnd class defines functions that can be applied to any CWnd object, including objects that are instances of classes derived from CWnd. As first shown in Hour 5, "Button Controls," to set the caption or title for any window, including controls, you can use the CWnd::SetWindowText function.

8

Almost every significant object in an MFC program is a CObject instance. This enables you to take advantage of the MFC support for discovering many common memory leaks and other types of programming errors. The CObject class also declares functions that can be used to provide diagnostic dumps during runtime and support for serialization. Serialization is discussed in Hour 22.

Every window in an MFC program is a CWnd object. CWnd is derived from CObject so it has all the CObject functionality built in. Using the CWnd class to handle all controls and windows in your program enables you to take advantage of polymorphism; the CWnd class provides all the general window functions for all types of windows. This means you don't need to know exactly what type of control or window is accessed through a CWnd pointer in many cases.

An Example Using the CObject and CWnd Base Classes

The CObject and CWnd classes are used in different ways. The CObject class is normally used as a base class when you create your own classes. The CWnd class is often passed as a function parameter or return value and is used as a generic pointer to any type of window in an MFC program.

In this section, you create a sample console mode project that demonstrates how the CObject class is used. To start the sample, create a new console mode project named Runtime. When the wizard page prompts you for the type of console-mode application to be created, select An Application That Supports MFC.

Using CObject as a Base Class

The CObject class is always used as a base class; not much can be done with a plain CObject. When used as a base class, the CObject class provides a great deal of basic functionality to a class. You can control the amount of functionality provided by CObject by using macros in the derived class's declaration and definition files.

Four different levels of support are offered by CObject to its derived classes:

- Basic support with memory leak detection requires no macros.
- Support for runtime class identification requires the use of the DECLARE_DYNAMIC macro in the class declaration and the IMPLEMENT_DYNAMIC macro in the class definition.
- Support for dynamic object creation requires the use of the DECLARE_DYNCREATE macro in the class declaration and the IMPLEMENT_DYNCREATE macro in the class definition. The use of dynamic object creation is discussed later in this hour.

- Serialization support requires the use of the DECLARE_SERIAL macro in the class declaration and the IMPLEMENT_SERIAL macro in the class definition. The use of serialization is discussed in Hour 22.

Each CObject macro is used in a similar way. All DECLARE macros have one parameter—the name of the class. The IMPLEMENT macros generally take two parameters—the name of the class and the name of the immediate base class. IMPLEMENT_SERIAL is an exception because it requires three parameters, as discussed in Hour 22.

Listing 8.6 is the class declaration for CMyObject, a simple class that is derived from CObject. The CMyObject class supports dynamic creation, so it includes the DECLARE_DYNCREATE macro.

LISTING 8.6. THE CMyObject CLASS DECLARATION, USING CObject AS A BASE CLASS.

```
class CMyObject : public CObject
{
    DECLARE_DYNCREATE( CMyObject );
// Constructor
public:
    CMyObject();
//Attributes
public:
    void Set( const CString& szName );
    CString Get() const;
//Implementation
private:
    CString m_szName;
};
```

Save the source code from Listing 8.6 in the Runtime project directory as MyObj.h. It's just an include file, so don't add it to the project.

The source code for the CMyObject member functions is provided in Listing 8.7. Save this source code as MyObj.cpp and add it to the Runtime project. This source file contains the IMPLEMENT_DYNCREATE macro that matches the DECLARE_DYNCREATE macro from the class declaration.

8

LISTING 8.7. MEMBER FUNCTIONS FOR THE CMyObject CLASS.

```
#include "stdafx.h"
#include "MyObj.h"
IMPLEMENT_DYNCREATE( CMyObject, CObject );
CMyObject::CMyObject()
{
}
void CMyObject::Set( const CString& szName )
{
    m_szName = szName;
}
CString CMyObject::Get() const
{
    return m_szName;
}
```

It's important to remember that the DECLARE and IMPLEMENT macros are used in two different places. A DECLARE macro, such as DECLARE_DYNCREATE, is used in the class declaration. An IMPLEMENT macro, such as IMPLEMENT_DYN-CREATE, is used only in the class definition.

Creating an Object at Runtime

There are two ways to create objects dynamically. The first method uses the C++ operator new to dynamically allocate an object from free storage.

```
CMyObject* pObject = new CMyObject;
```

The second method is used primarily by the MFC framework and uses a special class, CRuntimeClass, and the RUNTIME_CLASS macro. You can use CRuntimeClass to determine the type of an object or to create a new object. Listing 8.8 creates a CMyObject instance using the CRuntimeClass::CreateObject function.

LISTING 8.8. CREATING AN OBJECT AT RUNTIME USING CRuntimeClass.

```
int _tmain(int argc, TCHAR* argv[], TCHAR* envp[])
{
    if(AfxWinInit(GetModuleHandle(NULL),
                NULL, GetCommandLine(), 0) == FALSE)
    {
        return -1;
    }
```

continues

LISTING 8.8. CONTINUED

```
    CRuntimeClass* pRuntime = RUNTIME_CLASS( CMyObject );
    CObject* pObj = pRuntime->CreateObject();
    ASSERT( pObj->IsKindOf(RUNTIME_CLASS(CMyObject)) );
    CMyObject* pFoo = (CMyObject*)pObj;
    pFoo->Set( "FooBar" );
    CString szReturn = pFoo->Get();
    cout << szReturn.GetBuffer(0) << endl;
    delete pFoo;

    return 0;
}
```

Open the `Runtime.cpp` file, and replace the current `_tmain` function with the one provided in Listing 8.8. Add an include directive to the top of the `Runtime.cpp` file, just after the existing include directives:

```
#include "MyObj.h"
```

Compile the Runtime project and if there are no errors, run the project in a DOS window by following these steps:

1. Open a DOS window from the Start button's Programs menu.

2. Change the current directory to the project directory.

3. Type `Debug\Runtime` in the DOS window. The program executes and outputs `FooBar`.

Testing for a Valid Object

The MFC class library offers several diagnostic features. Most of these features are in the form of macros that are used only in a debug version of your program. This gives you the best of both worlds. When you are developing and testing your program, you can use the MFC diagnostic functions to help ensure that your program has as few errors as possible, although it runs with the additional overhead required by the diagnostics. Later, when your program is compiled in a release version, the diagnostic checks are removed and your program executes at top speed.

Three macros are commonly used in an MFC program:

- `ASSERT` brings up an error message dialog box when an expression that evaluates to `FALSE` is passed to it. This macro is compiled only in debug builds.

- `VERIFY` works exactly like `ASSERT` except that the evaluated expression is always compiled, even for non-debug builds, although the expression is not tested in release builds.

- ASSERT_VALID tests a pointer to a CObject instance and verifies that the object is a valid pointer in a valid state. A class derived from CObject can override the AssertValid function to enable testing of the state of an object.

The ASSERT and VERIFY macros are used with all expressions, not just those involving CObject. Although they both test to make sure that the evaluated expression is TRUE, there is an important difference in the way these two macros work. When compiled for a release build, the ASSERT macro and the expression it evaluates are completely ignored during compilation. The VERIFY macro is also ignored, but the expression is compiled and used in the release build.

A common source of errors in MFC programs is placing important code inside an ASSERT macro instead of a VERIFY macro. If the expression is needed for the program to work correctly, it belongs in a VERIFY macro, not an ASSERT macro. These functions are used in examples throughout the rest of the book to test for error conditions.

Summary

In this hour, you looked at how messages are handled by a program written for Windows, and you wrote a sample program that handles and displays some commonly used mouse event messages. You also looked at the CObject and CWnd base classes and learned how to add diagnostic features to your classes.

Q&A

Q I want to have runtime class identification support for my class, and I also want to be able to create objects dynamically. I tried using the DECLARE_DYNAMIC and DECLARE_DYNCREATE macros together in my header file and the IMPLEMENT_DYNAMIC and IMPLEMENT_DYNCREATE macros in my source file, but I got lots of errors. What happened?

A The macros are cumulative; The xxx_DYNCREATE macros also include work done by the xxx_DYNAMIC macros. The xxx_SERIAL macros also include xxx_DYNCREATE. You must use only one set of macros for your application.

Q **Why does the MouseTst program go to the trouble of invalidating part of the view, then updating the window in OnDraw? Wouldn't it be easier to just draw directly on the screen when a mouse click is received?**

A When the MouseTst window is overlapped by another window then uncovered, the view must redraw itself; this code will be located in OnDraw. It's much easier to use this code in the general case to update the display rather than try to draw the output in multiple places in the source code.

Workshop

The Workshop is designed to help you anticipate possible questions, review what you've learned, and begin thinking ahead to putting your knowledge into practice. The answers to the quiz are in Appendix A, "Quiz Answers."

Quiz

1. What is the default window procedure?
2. Why are messages used to pass information in Windows programs?
3. How is an application notified that the mouse is passing over one of its windows?
4. What is a message map used for?
5. What is the base class for most MFC classes?
6. What is the difference between the ASSERT and VERIFY macros?
7. What message is sent to an application when the user presses the primary mouse button?
8. How can you determine which source code lines in a message map are reserved for use by ClassWizard?

Exercises

1. Modify the MouseTst program to display the current mouse position as the mouse is moved over the view.
2. Add an ASSERT macro to ensure that pObj is not NULL after it is created in Runtime.cpp.

HOUR 9

The Document/View Architecture

The main topic for this hour is Document/View, the architecture used by programs written using AppWizard and the MFC class library. In this hour, you will learn

- The support offered for Document/View by the MFC class library and tools such as AppWizard and ClassWizard
- The MFC classes used to implement Document/View
- Using pointers and references and the role they play in Document/View

Also in this hour you will build DVTest, a sample program that will help illustrate how documents and views interact with each other in an MFC program.

Visual C++ Support for Document/View

MFC and AppWizard use the Document/View architecture to organize programs written for Windows. Document/View separates the program into four main classes:

- A document class derived from CDocument
- A view class derived from CView
- A frame class derived from CFrameWnd
- An application class derived from CWinApp

Each of these classes has a specific role to play in an MFC Document/View application. The document class is responsible for the program's data. The view class handles interaction between the document and the user. The frame class contains the view and other user interface elements, such as the menu and toolbars. The application class is responsible for actually starting the program and handling some general-purpose interaction with Windows. Figure 9.1 shows the four main parts of a Document/View program.

FIGURE 9.1.

The Document/View architecture.

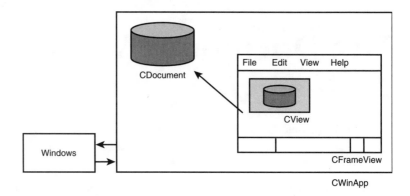

Although the name "Document/View" might seem to limit you to only word-processing applications, the architecture can be used in a wide variety of program types. There is no limitation as to the data managed by CDocument; it can be a word processing file, a spreadsheet, or a server at the other end of a network connection providing information to your program. Likewise, there are many types of views. A view can be a simple window, as used in the simple SDI applications presented so far, or it can be derived from CFormView, with all the capabilities of a dialog box. You will learn about form views in Hour 23, "Form Views."

SDI and MDI Applications

There are two basic types of Document/View programs:

- SDI, or single document interface
- MDI, or multiple document interface

An SDI program supports a single type of document and almost always supports only a single view. Only one document can be open at a time. An SDI application focuses on a particular task and usually is fairly straightforward.

Several different types of documents can be used in an MDI program, with each document having one or more views. Several documents can be open at a time, and the open document often uses a customized toolbar and menus that fit the needs of that particular document.

Why Use Document/View?

The first reason to use Document/View is because it provides a large amount of application code for free. You should always try to write as little new source code as possible, and that means using MFC classes and letting AppWizard and ClassWizard do a lot of the work for you. A large amount of the code that is written for you in the form of MFC classes and AppWizard code uses the Document/View architecture.

The Document/View architecture defines several main categories for classes used in a Windows program. Document/View provides a flexible framework that you can use to create almost any type of Windows program. One of the big advantages of the Document/View architecture is that it divides the work in a Windows program into well-defined categories. Most classes fall into one of the four main class categories:

- Controls and other user-interface elements related to a specific view
- Data and data-handling classes, which belong to a document
- Work that involves handling the toolbar, status bar, and menus, usually belonging to the frame class
- Interaction between the application and Windows occurring in the class derived from CWinApp

Dividing work done by your program helps you manage the design of your program more effectively. Extending programs that use the Document/View architecture is fairly simple because the four main Document/View classes communicate with each other through well-defined interfaces. For example, to change an SDI program to an MDI program, you must write little new code. Changing the user interface for a Document/View program impacts only the view class or classes; no changes are needed for the document, frame, or application classes.

Using MFC AppWizard

Use MFC AppWizard to create SDI and MDI applications. In earlier chapters, you used MFC AppWizard to create the SDI programs used as examples. Although doing so is more complicated, you can use MFC AppWizard to create an MDI application almost as easily as an SDI.

The basic difference between an SDI application and an MDI application is that an MDI application must manage multiple documents and, usually, multiple views. The SDI application uses only a single document, and normally only a single view.

Using ClassWizard

You have used ClassWizard in previous hours to add member variables to dialog box classes, add new classes to a project, and handle messages sent to view windows and dialog boxes. You also use ClassWizard to add interfaces defined as part of the Document/View architecture. In most cases, default behavior provided by the MFC framework is enough for simple programs.

You will learn about the interfaces used by the document and view classes in the next section. However, you add almost all these interfaces using ClassWizard.

For the examples in this hour, you will create an MDI project named DVTest. To create the DVTest example, use AppWizard to create a default MDI program. Name the program DVTest. Feel free to accept or change any of the default parameters offered by AppWizard because they have no impact on these examples. When finished, DVTest displays a collection of names stored by the document class.

Pointers and References

Pointers are important topics in C++ programming. A good understanding of the ways in which pointers are used will help you write programs that are more flexible and reliable. C++, and MFC in particular, relies very heavily on proper understanding and use of pointers.

NEW TERM   A *pointer* is simply a numeric variable. This numeric variable is an address, or location in memory where the actual data resides. Pointers must also follow the same rules that are applied to other variables. They must have unique names, and they must be declared before they can be used.

Every object or variable used in an application takes up a location or multiple locations in memory. This memory location is accessed via an address (see Figure 9.2).

FIGURE 9.2.

The text Hello *stored beginning at address 1000.*

1000	1001	1002	1003	1004	1005
H	e	l	l	o	\0

9

In this figure, the text Hello is stored in memory beginning at address 1000. Each character takes up a unique address space in memory. Pointers provide a method for holding and getting to these addresses in memory. Pointers make manipulating the data easier because they hold the address of another variable or data location.

> Pointers give flexibility to C++ programs and enable the programs to grow dynamically. By using a pointer to a block of memory that is allocated at runtime, a program can be much more flexible than one that allocates all its memory at once.

A pointer is also easier to store than a large structure or class object. Because a pointer just stores an address, it can easily be passed to a function. However, if an object is passed to a function the object must be constructed, copied, and destroyed, which can be costly for large objects.

The Indirection and Address Operators

Two operators are used when working with addresses in a C++ program: the *address-of operator* (&) and the *indirection operator* (*). These operators are different from operators seen previously because they are *unary*, meaning that they work with only one operand.

The address-of operator, &, returns the address of a variable or object. This operator is associated with the object to its right, like this:

```
&myAge;
```

This line returns the address of the myAge variable.

The indirection operator, *, works like the address-of operator in reverse. It also is associated with the object to its right, and it takes an address and returns the object contained at that address. For example, the following line determines the address of the myAge variable; then it uses the indirection operator to access the variable and give it a value of 42:

```
*(&myAge) = 42;
```

Using the Indirection Operator

You can use a pointer with the indirection operator to change the value of the other variable, as shown in the console-mode program in Listing 9.1.

LISTING 9.1. USING A POINTER VARIABLE WITH THE INDIRECTION OPERATOR.

```
#include <iostream>
using namespace std;
int main()
{
    int   nVar;
    int* pVar;
    // Store a value in nVar, and display it. Also
    // display nVar's address.
    nVar = 5;
    cout << "nVar's value is " << nVar << "." << endl;
    cout << "nVar's address is " << &nVar << "." << endl;

    // Store the address of nVar in pointer pVar. Display
    // information about pVar and the address it points to.
    pVar = &nVar;
    cout << "pVar's value is " << pVar << "." << endl;
    cout << "*pVar's value is " << *pVar << "." << endl;

    // Change the value of the variable pointed to by pVar.
    *pVar = 7;
    cout << "nVar's value is " << nVar << "." << endl;
    cout << "pVar's value is " << pVar << "." << endl;
    cout << "*pVar's value is " << *pVar << "." << endl;
    return 0;
}
```

It's important to remember that the pointer does not contain a variable's value, only its address. The indirection operator enables you to refer to the value stored at the address instead of to the address itself.

As shown in Listing 9.1, a pointer variable is declared using the indirection operator, like this:

```
int*     pVar;  // declare a pointer to int
```

If you are in the habit of declaring several variables on one line, look out for pointer declarations. The indirection operator applies only to the object to its immediate right, not to the whole line. The declaration

```
int* pFoo, pBar;
```

declares and defines two variables: a pointer to an int named pFoo, and an int named pBar. The pBar variable is not a pointer. If you insist on declaring more than one pointer per line, use this style:

```
int *pFoo, *pBar;
```

Using Pointers as Function Parameters

Pointers are useful when you must change a parameter inside a function. Because parameters are always passed by value, the only way to change the value of a parameter inside a function is to send the address of the variable to the function, as Listing 9.2 does.

LISTING 9.2. USING A POINTER AND A FUNCTION TO CHANGE A VARIABLE'S VALUE.

```
#include <iostream>
using namespace std;
void IncrementVar( int* pVar );

int main()
{
    int   nVar = 0;
    cout << "The value of nVar is now " << nVar << "." << endl;
    IncrementVar( &nVar );
    cout << "The value of nVar is now " << nVar << "." << endl;
    return 0;
}

void IncrementVar( int* nVar )
{
    *nVar += 1;
}
```

Figure 9.3 shows how the address is used to change the value of a variable inside the IncrementVar function.

FIGURE 9.3.

Changing a variable's address inside a function.

```
int main()
{
    int nVar = 10;
    ChangeVar(&nVar);
    return 0;
}

void ChangeVar(int *pVar)
{
    *pVar = 42;
}
```

Address	Name	Initial Value
0000 0004	nVar	10

Address	Name	Initial Value
0000 0020	pVar	0000 0004

Another use for pointers is to keep a reference to memory that has been requested at run-time from the operating system. You will use pointers like this later, in the section called "Using new and delete to Create Dynamic Objects."

Using References

In addition to using pointers to refer to other variables, the C++ language also has a derived type known as a *reference*. A reference is declared using the reference operator &, which bears an uncanny resemblance to the address-of operator. Both operators use the same symbol; however, you use them in different contexts. The only time & is used for a reference is in a declaration, like this:

```
int myAge;
int& myRef = myAge;
```

This code defines a reference variable named myRef, which is a reference, or alias, for the myAge variable. The advantage of using a reference instead of a pointer variable is that no indirection operator is required. However, after it is defined the reference variable can't be bound to another variable. For example, code such as that in Listing 9.3 often is misunderstood.

LISTING 9.3. USING REFERENCES TO CHANGE THE VALUE OF A VARIABLE.

```
void refFunc()
{
    int nFoo = 5;
    int nBar = 10;
    // Define a reference to int that is an alias for nFoo.
    int& nRef = nFoo;

    // Change the value of nFoo.
    nRef = nBar;
```

```
        CString strMsg;
        strMsg.Format("nFoo = %d, nBar = %d", nFoo, nBar);

        AfxMessageBox(strMsg);
}
```

If you use the `refFunc` function in a Windows program, you will see that the line

```
nRef = nFoo;
```

does not change the binding of the `nRef` reference variable; instead, it assigns the value of `nBar` (10) to `nFoo`, with `nFoo` being the variable to which `nRef` is a reference.

References are most commonly used when passing parameters to functions. Passing a class object as a function parameter often is quite expensive in terms of computing resources. Using a pointer to pass a parameter is subject to errors and affects the function's readability. However, if you use references as function parameters you eliminate unnecessary copies, and you can use the parameter as if a copy were passed. To prevent the called function from changing the value of a reference variable, you can declare the parameter as `const`, like this:

```
void Print( const int& nFoo )
{
    nFoo = 12;  // error - not allowed to change const
    cout << "The value is " << nFoo << endl;
}
```

> You should use references to const objects when passing large objects to a function. It can be expensive, in terms of computing resources, to generate a copy of a large object that is used only during a function call.

Using new and delete to Create Dynamic Objects

So far, you've learned about variables allocated as local objects that are created when a function or block is entered and destroyed when the function or block is exited. Most programs that work in the real world use variables and objects that have a dynamic lifetime, meaning they are explicitly created and explicitly destroyed.

In a C++ program, you can use the `new` and `delete` operators to allocate and destroy variables dynamically, as shown in Listing 9.4.

LISTING 9.4. USING new AND delete FOR FUNDAMENTAL TYPES.

```
void ptrFunc()
{
    int *pFoo = new int;
    *pFoo = 42;

    CString strMsg;
    strMsg.Format("Foo = %d", *pFoo);
    AfxMessageBox(strMsg);

    delete pFoo;
}
```

Using new[] and delete[] to Create Arrays

You also can create arrays dynamically using new[], with the size of the array specified inside the square brackets. When you create an array using new[], you must use delete[] to release the memory allocated for the array. The size of the array is not specified when delete[] is used. Using delete[] is the only clue to the compiler indicating that the pointer is the beginning of an array of objects. Listing 9.5 is an example of a function showing how to allocate and free a dynamic array.

LISTING 9.5. USING new[] TO CREATE A DYNAMIC ARRAY.

```
void ptrArrayFunc()
{
    // Create array
    const int nMaxFoo = 5;
    int *arFoo = new int[nMaxFoo];
    // Fill array
    for(int n= 0; n < nMaxFoo; n++)
    {
        arFoo[n] = 42 + n;
    }
    // Read array
    for(n = 0; n < nMaxFoo; n++ )
    {
        CString strMsg;
        strMsg.Format("Index %d = %d", n, arFoo[n]);
        AfxMessageBox(strMsg);
    }
    // Free array
    delete[] arFoo;
}
```

Note that in Listing 9.5, it's possible to use a variable to specify the size of the array.

Using Pointers with Derived Classes

An instance of a class can be allocated and used dynamically, just as if it were one of the fundamental types, like this:

```
CRect* pRect = new CRect;
```

This example allocates space for a CRect object and calls the CRect constructor to perform any needed initializations. Of course, after the CRect object is no longer needed, you should make sure that the program calls delete to free the allocated memory and cause the class's destructor to be called.

```
delete pRect;
```

When using a pointer to a class or structure, you use the member selection operator, or ->, to access member data and functions:

```
pRect->left = 0;
int nHeight = pRect->Height();
```

Using a Pointer to a Base Class

Because a class derived from a base class actually contains the base, it's possible to use a pointer to a base class when you work with a derived object. For example, in the MFC library you can use a pointer to a CWnd object in place of a CDialog object. This makes a design much easier to implement because all the functions that work with any type of window can just use pointers to CWnd instead of trying to determine the type of each object. In other words, because CDialog is a CWnd, you should be able to do this:

```
CWnd* pWnd = new CDialog(/*Initialization info deleted*/);
pWnd->EnableWindow();
```

You might be wondering how this code works—after all, how does the compiler know to call the CWnd version of EnableWindow or the CDialog version of EnableWindow? In order to solve this problem, you must declare functions used through base-class pointers as virtual functions. When a function is declared with the virtual keyword, the compiler generates code that determines the actual type of the object at runtime and calls the correct function.

Using Virtual Functions

NEW TERM A *virtual function* is a function that is resolved at runtime. When a virtual function is used, the compiler constructs a special table, called a virtual function table. This table is used to keep track of the correct functions to be called for every object of that class. When a virtual function is called, the virtual function table is used to access the correct function indirectly, as shown in Figure 9.4.

FIGURE 9.4.

The virtual function table is used to determine the correct virtual function called at runtime.

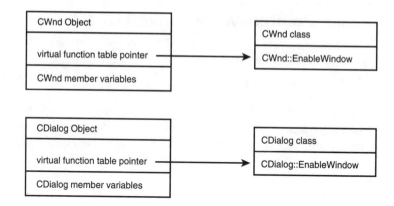

The added overhead of using the virtual function table is fairly small, but it could be significant if you have thousands of small objects or if execution speed is critical. For that reason, a function must be specified as virtual; it doesn't happen by default. Listing 9.6 is an example of a class declaration that uses a virtual function.

LISTING 9.6. AN EXAMPLE OF DECLARING A VIRTUAL FUNCTION.

```
class CUser
{
public:
    virtual void ClearInfo();
} ;
```

The virtual keyword is used only in the class declaration, not in the function definition.

Exploring Document/View Interfaces

The most commonly used interfaces in a Document/View program handle communication between the document and view objects, and between Windows and the document and view objects. Each of these interfaces has a particular purpose. Some are always overridden in the classes you include in your project; many are overridden only when needed. These are three of the major interfaces used in a Document/View program:

- GetDocument, a CView member function used to retrieve a pointer to its document
- UpdateAllViews, a CDocument member function used to update views associated with a document

- OnNewDocument, a CDocument member function used to initialize the document's member data

Remember, this list is just an overview of the major interfaces. The list does not cover all the interfaces required in an SDI or MDI program. Your mileage might vary; after using the Document/View architecture for a while, you might have another set of favorite interfaces.

The interfaces defined by the Document/View architecture represent guarantees about how each of the MFC classes that make up an application behave with regard to each other. For example, the MFC framework always calls the CDocument::OnNewDocument function when a new document is created. The MFC framework, and other classes that might be part of an MFC-based program, expect the new document to be initialized after this function has been called.

Using well-defined interfaces like CDocument::OnNewDocument to perform specific tasks enables you to modify only the functions where you must take special action; you can let the MFC framework handle most functions and interfaces if you want the default behavior.

The Document/View architecture also makes it easy to separate work. For example, data belongs only to the document; a view calls the GetDocument function to collect a document pointer and then uses member functions to collect or update data.

Creating a Data Model

Each of the interfaces discussed earlier has a specific role. For the remaining examples in this chapter, you will use the DVTest example created earlier in this hour.

Return to the DVTest example and add a CArray template object to the document class as a private data member. To do this, add the source code from Listing 9.7 to the CDVTestDoc class header, found in the DVTestDoc.h file. Add the source code to the attributes section of the class declaration, which begins with the // Attributes comment generated by AppWizard.

INPUT   **LISTING 9.7.** CHANGES TO THE CDVTestDoc CLASS DECLARATION.

```
// Attributes
public:
    CString GetName( int nIndex ) const;
    int     AddName( const CString& szName );
    int     GetCount() const;
private:
    CArray<CString, CString>    m_arNames;
```

Because the CDVTestDoc class contains a CArray member variable, the template collection declarations must be included in the project. Add an #include statement at the bottom of the StdAfx.h file.

#include "afxtempl.h"

The next step is to implement the functions described in the CDVTestDoc class interface. These functions provide access to the data stored in the document. Add the source code in Listing 9.8 to the end of the DVTestDoc.cpp file.

INPUT   **LISTING 9.8.** NEW FUNCTIONS ADDED TO THE CDVTestDoc CLASS.

```
CString CDVTestDoc::GetName( int nIndex ) const
{
    ASSERT( nIndex < m_arNames.GetSize() );
    return m_arNames[nIndex];
}

int CDVTestDoc::AddName( const CString& szName )
{
    return m_arNames.Add( szName );
}

int CDVTestDoc::GetCount() const
{
    return m_arNames.GetSize();
}
```

Every document class must specify some access functions to add and retrieve data. The three functions in Listing 9.8 are typical access functions in that they do not just expose the CArray template. The data could also be stored in another type of collection. Storing the data in a CArray object is an implementation detail that should not be of interest to users of the CDVTestDoc class. This enables the internal implementation of CDVTestDoc to be changed in the future, if necessary.

Initializing a Document's Contents

You create and initialize document objects in two different ways, depending on the type of application using the document:

- A new MDI document object is created for every new document opened by the program.
- SDI programs create a single document object that is reinitialized each time a new document is opened.

In most cases, the best place to perform any initialization is in the
`CDocument::OnNewDocument` member function. This function is provided
with some default code inserted by AppWizard. Edit the `OnNewDocument` function
so it looks like the code provided in Listing 9.9.

INPUT   **LISTING 9.9.** CHANGES TO THE `CDVTestDoc::OnNewDocument` MEMBER
FUNCTION.

```
BOOL CDVTestDoc::OnNewDocument()
{
    TRACE( "CDVTest::OnNewDocument" );
    if (!CDocument::OnNewDocument())
        return FALSE;

    m_arNames.RemoveAll();
    m_arNames.Add( "Curly" );
    m_arNames.Add( "Moe" );
    m_arNames.Add( "Shemp" );
    return TRUE;
}
```

The TRACE macro sends an output message to the compiler's debug window,
which displays useful information as the program executes.

In Listing 9.9, the TRACE macro displays a line of text when a new document
is created. It's a good idea to have your program provide tracing information whenever an interesting event occurs.

Listing 9.9 clears the contents of the `m_arNames` collection and adds three new names.

Getting the Document Pointer

Every view is associated with only one document. When a view must communicate with
its associated document, the `GetDocument` function is used. If the view is created by
AppWizard, as `CDVTestView` is, the `GetDocument` function returns a pointer to the proper
document type. Listing 9.10 is a version of `OnDraw` that uses `GetDocument` to retrieve a
pointer to the `CDVTestDoc` class; then it uses the pointer to collect the names contained in
the document.

LISTING 9.10. USING GetDocument TO FETCH A DOCUMENT POINTER.

```
void CDVTestView::OnDraw(CDC* pDC)
{
    CDVTestDoc* pDoc = GetDocument();
    ASSERT_VALID(pDoc);
    // Calculate the space required for a single
    // line of text, including the inter-line area.
    TEXTMETRIC  tm;
    pDC->GetTextMetrics( &tm );
    int nLineHeight = tm.tmHeight + tm.tmExternalLeading;
    CPoint  ptText( 0, 0 );
    for( int nIndex = 0; nIndex < pDoc->GetCount(); nIndex++ )
    {
        CString szName = pDoc->GetName( nIndex );
        pDC->TextOut( ptText.x, ptText.y, szName );
        ptText.y += nLineHeight;
    }
}
```

There are three main parts to Listing 9.10:

- In the first part, the document pointer is retrieved using GetDocument. The pointer value is validated using the ASSERT_VALID macro. You should always use this macro after an old-style cast to ensure that the pointer is accurate.

- In the second part, the size of a line of text is calculated using the CDC::GetTextMetrics function. This function fills the TEXTMETRICS structure with information about the current font used by the device context. The tmHeight member is the maximum height of a character, and the tmExternalLeading member is the spacing between character lines. Adding these two values together results in a good spacing value between displayed rows of text.

- Finally, the third part collects each name in turn from the document, using the functions added earlier to the document class. After each line of text is displayed, the ptText.y value is increased by the line spacing value calculated earlier.

Compile and run the DVTest project. DVTest displays the names stored in the document class, as shown in Figure 9.5.

In Hour 22, "Using MFC to Save Program Data," you'll learn how to save the document to a file.

FIGURE 9.5.

DVTest displays three names in its view window.

9

Summary

In this hour you've learned about pointers and references, as well as the basic Document/View architecture used in most MFC programs. You learned how to use AppWizard and ClassWizard in SDI and MDI applications, and created a sample program demonstrating the use of Document/View.

Q&A

Q **When I use pointers, sometimes I get an Unhandled Exception error from Windows and my program crashes. The code that causes the problem looks something like this:**

```
int *pBadInt;
*pBadInt = 42;   // Error here
```

A There are two problems. First, the pointer isn't initialized. You should always initialize a pointer to either NULL or to an area of memory that is dynamically allocated, like this:

```
int *pInt = NULL;
int *pInt = new int;
```

A pointer doesn't automatically set aside any storage area—in the preceding code, pBadInt is uninitialized and is pointing to a random area of memory. You must assign the pointer either an address of an existing variable or the address of a block of dynamically allocated memory:

```
int n;
int *pInt;
pInt = &n;
*pInt = 42;   // Okay
pInt = new int;
*pInt = 42;   // Okay
delete pInt;
```

Q I don't get all this Document/View stuff. Wouldn't it be easier to store all the data in the view class?

A It might seem easier at first. However, the MFC framework will provide a great deal of help for free if you follow the Document/View rules. For example, if you try to store your data in your view class, it will be very difficult to provide multiple views for the same document. As you will see in Hour 23, it's fairly straightforward if you follow the Document/View model. Also, as you will see in Hour 22, MFC gives you a great deal of support for loading and storing data stored in your document classes.

Workshop

The Workshop is designed to help you anticipate possible questions, review what you've learned, and begin thinking ahead to putting your knowledge into practice. The answers to the quiz are in Appendix A, "Quiz Answers."

Quiz

1. What are some of the differences between pointers and references?
2. What is more efficient to pass as a parameter: a pointer or an object? Why?
3. What keyword is used to dynamically allocate memory?
4. What keyword is used to release dynamically allocated memory?
5. In the Document/View architecture, which classes are responsible for maintaining the user interface?
6. What are the four main categories of classes in the Document/View architecture?
7. What part of the Document/View architecture is responsible for the application's data?
8. What CView member function is used to retrieve a pointer to the document associated with the view?
9. What CDocument member function is used to notify a document's views that their user interface might need to be updated?

Exercises

1. Use the TRACE macro to see when the view requests information from the document. Add a TRACE macro to the document's GetName function, and experiment with resizing and moving the view to see when the view requests the data.
2. Modify the DVTest project so that a line number is displayed for each item in the view.

HOUR 10

Menus

Menus are an essential part of most Windows programs. With the exception of some simple dialog box–based applications, all Windows programs offer some type of menu.

In this hour, you will learn

- How menus are used in Windows programs
- How the MFC CMenu class is used to support menus
- How to add accelerators to your menu items

In this hour you will also modify a menu created by AppWizard and create a floating context menu.

What Is a Menu?

NEW TERM A *menu* is a list of command messages that can be selected and sent to a window. To the user, a menu item is a text label that indicates a task that can be performed by the application. Each menu item also has an ID that is used to identify the item when routing window messages. This ID is also used when modifying attributes for the menu item.

Menus are usually attached to a window, although many applications support floating pop-up menus that can appear anywhere on the desktop. Later in this hour, in the section "Creating a Shortcut Menu," you create a floating pop-up menu that is displayed when the right mouse button is pressed. These menus are often used to provide context-sensitive help and offer different menu choices depending on the window that creates the menu.

In order to make Windows programs easier to use, most programs follow a common set of guidelines regarding the appearance of their menus. For example, menu items leading to dialog boxes that require additional user input are usually marked with an ellipsis (...).

Another user interface requirement is a mnemonic, or underlined letter for each menu item. When this letter is pressed, the appropriate menu item is selected. This letter is usually the first letter of the menu item; however, in some cases another letter is used. For example, the Exit menu item found on the File menu uses X as its mnemonic. You must be careful not to duplicate letters used for mnemonics; if you do, the menu might not work as expected—the first menu item will be highlighted using the mnemonic, but the menu item will not be selected until Enter is pressed. Continuing to press the mnemonic key will cause the next menu item with the mnemonic to be highlighted.

Menus are sometimes nested, which means that one menu item is actually a submenu with a series of additional menu items. A menu item that leads to a nested submenu has a right arrow to indicate that more selections are available. You can see an example of a nested menu structure in the File menu used by Visual C++, as shown in Figure 10.1.

FIGURE 10.1.

Displaying a list of recent workspaces in Visual C++.

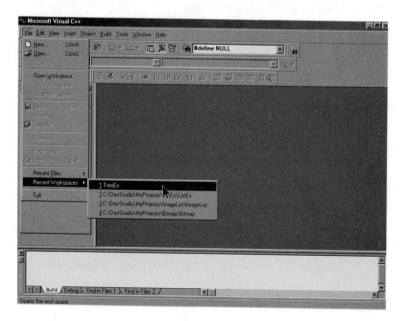

Command Message Routing

Before you learn about creating and modifying menus, look at how menu messages are handled by Windows programs in general and MFC programs in particular.

A menu is always associated with a particular window. In most MFC programs, it is associated with the main frame window, which also contains the application's toolbar and status bar. When a menu item is selected, a WM_COMMAND message is sent to the main frame window; this message includes the ID of the menu item. The MFC framework and your application convert this message into a function call, as described in Hour 8, "Messages and Event-Driven Programming."

Which Class Handles the Menu Selection Message?

In an MFC application, many classes can receive a menu selection message. In general, any class that is derived from the CCmdTarget class is plugged into the MFC framework's message loop. When a menu item is selected, the message is offered to all the command target objects in your application, in the following order:

1. The CMainFrame object
2. The main MDI frame window
3. The active child frame of an MDI frame window
4. The view that is associated with the MDI child frame
5. The document object associated with the active view
6. The document template associated with the document object
7. The CWinApp object

> This list might seem like a large number of steps to take, but it's actually not very complicated in practice. Usually, a menu item is handled by one type of object: a view or main frame. Menu messages are rarely handled directly by the document template or child frame objects.

Figure 10.2 shows a simplified map of how commands are routed in an MFC application.

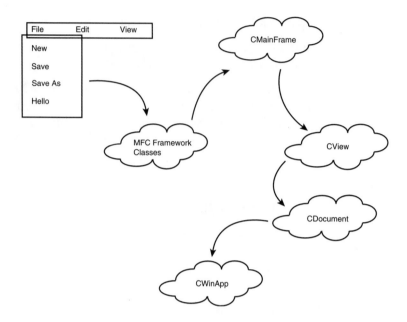

FIGURE 10.2.

Menu command routing in an MFC application.

In most cases, you can use ClassWizard to configure the message maps required to route menu selection messages to their proper destinations.

Creating a Menu

You can create menus dynamically or as static resources that are added to your program. The MFC class library provides a CMenu class that simplifies handling menus and is used for the examples in this hour.

AppWizard generates a menu resource for programs that it creates. You can edit this menu resource to add extra menu items for your application, or you can create new menu resources for your application.

For the examples used in this hour, create a sample SDI application called Menu. This program is used to demonstrate how menu resources are created and modified.

Adding New Menu Items

It is easy to add a new item to a menu. In order to use a new menu item, you must do two things:

- Modify the menu resource to include the new menu item.
- Add a message-handling function using ClassWizard.

These steps are explained in the next two sections.

Opening the Menu Resource

To display the current menu resources, select the ResourceView tab in the project workspace window. Expand the resource tree to show the different resource types defined for the current project; one of the folders is labeled Menu.

Open the Menu folder to display the resources defined for the project's menus. Every multiple-document application created by AppWizard has two menu resources. MDI applications use an IDR_MAINFRAME menu when no views are active. They also have an additional menu item used when a view is active. The name of this menu resource is based on the application name, such as IDR_xxxTYPE, where xxx is replaced by the program's name. For example, IDR_FOOTYPE is the second menu resource created for a program named Foo.

SDI applications, such as the Menu example, have a single menu created by AppWizard named IDR_MAINFRAME. This is the menu displayed by default for single-document applications. Every AppWizard program begins with the same menu; supplying any modifications that are required for your application is up to you.

Editing the Menu Resource

Open the menu resource by double-clicking the menu resource icon. The menu is displayed in the resource editor ready for editing. When the menu is initially loaded into the editor, only the top-level menu bar is displayed. Clicking any top-level menu item displays the pop-up menu associated with that item, as shown in Figure 10.3.

FIGURE 10.3.

*Using the Developer
Studio resource editor
to edit a menu
resource.*

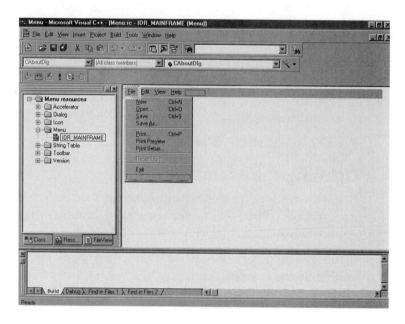

The last item of every menu is an empty box. You use this box to add new menu items to the menu resource. All menu items are initially added to the end of a menu resource and then moved to their proper position. To add a new menu item, follow these steps:

1. Double-click the empty box on the File menu to display the Menu Item Properties dialog box.

2. To add a menu item, provide a menu ID and caption for the new menu item. By convention, menu IDs begin with ID_, and then you include the name of the top-level menu. For this example, enter ID_FILE_HELLO as the menu ID and &Hello as the menu caption.

3. Optionally, you can provide a prompt that is displayed in the status bar when the new menu item is highlighted.

4. Click anywhere outside the Properties dialog box to return to the editor.

After you've added the new menu item you can move it to a new position by dragging it with the mouse. Changing the menu position does not change any of its attributes.

Menu Item Properties

Several optional properties can be applied to a menu item via the Properties dialog box:

- *ID* is used for the menu's resource ID. This ID is sent as part of the WM_COMMAND message to your application and is used by ClassWizard to identify the menu item.

- *Caption* is the name used to identify the menu item. The mnemonic letter is preceded by an ampersand (&) and is used to select the item without using the mouse.

- *Separator* is used to indicate that this menu item is a separator, or horizontal line that divides logical sections of a menu. This check box is usually cleared.

- *Checked* is used to indicate that the menu item should display a check mark to indicate the menu item is selected. This check box is usually cleared.

- *Pop-up* is used to indicate that this menu item is the top level of a pop-up or submenu. This option is usually cleared except on the top-level menu bar.

- *Grayed* indicates that this menu item is grayed. This check box is usually cleared.

- *Inactive* indicates that this menu item is inactive. This check box is usually cleared.

- *Help* places the menu item to the far right side of the menu bar. This option is rarely used, even for the Help menu.

- *Break* is used to split the menu at this menu item. The default choice is none and is used in almost all cases.

- *Prompt* is used to specify the text that will be displayed in the status bar when the menu item is highlighted.

10

Adding a Message-Handling Function

After adding a menu item to the application's menu, the next step is to add a message-handling function to handle the new menu item. As discussed in Hour 8, ClassWizard is used to create message-handling functions for MFC-based Windows programs. To add a message-handling function for the Hello menu item in the earlier example, follow these steps:

1. Open ClassWizard by pressing Ctrl+W or by right-clicking in a source code window and selecting ClassWizard from the menu.

2. Select the Message Maps tab and select the class that will handle the message from the Class Name combo box—in this case, CMainFrame.

3. Select the object that is generating the message from the Object ID list box—in this case, ID_FILE_HELLO. Remember that the ID is the value you entered earlier when you created the menu item. Two message-handling functions are displayed in the Messages list box.

4. Select the COMMAND message from the Messages list box and click the Add Function button. Accept the default name suggested by ClassWizard for the function name—OnFileHello.

5. Click OK to close ClassWizard.

Edit the `CMainFrame::OnFileHello` function so that it looks like the function provided in Listing 10.1.

LISTING 10.1. THE `CMainFrame::OnFileHello` MESSAGE-HANDLING FUNCTION.

```
void CMainFrame::OnFileHello()
{
    AfxMessageBox( "Hello from the File menu" );
}
```

These basic steps are used to add all the menu items used in examples for the remaining hours in this book. The Developer Studio tools are so easy to use that adding a new menu item will be second nature in no time.

Build the Menu project. If you select Hello from the File menu, a message box will be displayed.

Creating a Shortcut Menu

You display a shortcut menu, sometimes called a pop-up or context menu, by right-clicking on a window. Shortcut menus provide a list of commonly used actions.

Creating a shortcut menu is similar to modifying an existing menu except that a new menu resource must be created as the first step. Most shortcut menus are displayed in response to the `WM_CONTEXTMENU` message, which is sent when you press the right mouse button.

Creating the Resource for a Pop-Up Menu

Use the Developer Studio resource editor to create the context menu. To create the new menu resource, use one of the following techniques:

- Select Resource from the Insert menu and then select Menu from the Insert Resource dialog box.
- Right-click the Menu folder in the ResourceView and then select Insert Menu from the pop-up menu.

Both of these methods open a new menu resource for editing. Add a single space as a dummy caption for the first top-level item on the menu bar. This caption is not displayed by the menu; it is used only as a placeholder.

Open the Properties dialog box for the menu resource by right-clicking the edge of the menu resource, and change the resource ID to ID_POPUP. Using the values from Table 10.1, add three menu items under the dummy label.

TABLE 10.1. MENU ITEMS ADDED TO THE ID_POPUP MENU RESOURCE.

Menu ID	Caption
ID_LIONS	&Lions
ID_TIGERS	&Tigers
ID_BEARS	&Bears

Adding Message-Handling Functions

The new context menu will be displayed when a right mouse click is detected on the application's view. After a menu item has been selected, a message is displayed at the menu's location, similar to the message displayed in the MouseTst example from Hour 8.

You must add two new variables to the CMenuView class: a CString variable that stores the message and a CPoint variable that stores the location of the pop-up menu. Add the source code provided in Listing 10.2 to the CMenuView class after the //Implementation comment.

LISTING 10.2. NEW MEMBER VARIABLES FOR THE CMenuView CLASS.

```
// Implementation
protected:
    CPoint  m_ptMsg;
    CString m_szMsg;
```

The constructor for CMenuView must initialize the m_ptMsg variable. Edit the constructor for CMenuView, found in MenuView.cpp, so it looks like the source code in Listing 10.3.

LISTING 10.3. THE CONSTRUCTOR FOR CMenuView.

```
CMenuView::CMenuView()
{
    m_ptMsg = CPoint(0,0);
}
```

10

The `CMenuView::OnDraw` member function resembles the `OnDraw` member function from `CMouseTestView` in Hour 8. Both functions use the `TextOut` function to display a message at a certain point in the view. Edit the `CMenuView::OnDraw` function so that it looks like the function provided in Listing 10.4. You must remove a few lines of AppWizard-supplied code.

LISTING 10.4. THE `CMenuView::OnDraw` MEMBER FUNCTION.

```
void CMenuView::OnDraw(CDC* pDC)
{
    pDC->TextOut( m_ptMsg.x, m_ptMsg.y, m_szMsg );
}
```

Trapping Messages

As discussed earlier, menu selection messages are routed through your application when a menu item is selected. You must add a message-handling function for each menu item; this function will be executed whenever the menu item is selected. The easiest way to add a message-handling function is to use ClassWizard.

Use ClassWizard to add four new message-handling functions to the `CMenuView` class: three message-handling functions for the new menu items and one message-handling function to detect the right-click from the mouse button. The steps used to add the message-handling functions are similar to the ones used earlier when modifying an existing menu, except these messages are handled by the `CMenuView` class.

1. Open ClassWizard by pressing Ctrl+W or right-clicking in a source code window and selecting ClassWizard from the menu.
2. Select the Message Maps tab and select the class that will handle the message from the Class Name combo box—in this case, `CMenuView`.
3. Select the object in the Object ID list box that will generate the message—in this case, use one of the values from Table 10.2.
4. Select a message from the Messages list box and click the Add Function button. Accept the default name suggested by ClassWizard for the function name.
5. Repeat this process for all entries in Table 10.2.
6. Click OK to close ClassWizard.

TABLE 10.2. VALUES USED TO CREATE MESSAGE-HANDLING FUNCTIONS.

Object ID	Message	Function
CMenuView	WM_CONTEXTMENU	OnContextMenu
ID_LIONS	COMMAND	OnLions
ID_TIGERS	COMMAND	OnTigers
ID_BEARS	COMMAND	OnBears

The source code for the CMenuView::OnContextMenu message-handling function is provided in Listing 10.5.

LISTING 10.5. POPPING UP A MENU WHEN A RIGHT MOUSE BUTTON IS CLICKED.

```
void CMenuView::OnContextMenu(CWnd* pWnd, CPoint point)
{
    CMenu    zooMenu;
    // Store popup point, and convert to client coordinates.
    // for the drawing functions.
    m_ptMsg = point;
    ScreenToClient( &m_ptMsg );

    zooMenu.LoadMenu( ID_POPUP );
    CMenu* pPopup = zooMenu.GetSubMenu( 0 );
    pPopup->TrackPopupMenu( TPM_LEFTALIGN¦TPM_RIGHTBUTTON,
                            point.x,
                            point.y,
                            this );
}
```

10

When a right mouse click is detected, the WM_CONTEXTMENU message is sent to the application and the MFC framework calls the OnContextMenu message handler. The OnContextMenu function creates a CMenu object and loads the ID_POPUP menu resource. The floating menu is displayed by calling GetSubMenu and TrackPopupMenu.

The GetSubMenu function is used to skip past the dummy menu item at the top of the ID_POPUP menu resource. The GetSubMenu function returns a temporary pointer to the pop-up menu. Calling TrackPopupMenu causes the pop-up menu to be displayed and the menu item selection to automatically follow the mouse cursor.

The source code for handling menu selection messages sent to the CMenuView class is provided in Listing 10.6.

LISTING 10.6. MESSAGE-HANDLING FUNCTIONS FOR FLOATING MENU ITEMS.

```
void CMenuView::OnLions()
{
    m_szMsg = "Lions are out";
    InvalidateRect( NULL );
}
void CMenuView::OnTigers()
{
    m_szMsg = "Tigers are afoot";
    InvalidateRect( NULL );
}
void CMenuView::OnBears()
{
    m_szMsg = "Bears are hungry";
    InvalidateRect( NULL );
}
```

Each message-handling function in Listing 10.6 works in a similar way: A message is stored in the m_szMsg member variable, and the view rectangle is invalidated. This causes a WM_PAINT message to be sent to the MFC framework, which in turn calls the OnDraw function to display the message.

Build the Menu project. Experiment by right-clicking in the main view window. Selecting any menu item from the shortcut menu will cause a message to be displayed, as shown in Figure 10.4.

FIGURE 10.4.

Selecting an item from the context menu.

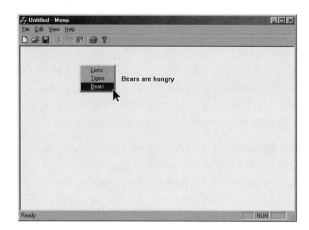

Using Keyboard Accelerators

NEW TERM *Keyboard accelerators* are keyboard shortcuts to message-handling functions. A keyboard accelerator provides easy access to commonly accessed program functions. Each keyboard accelerator is a sequence of keystrokes that are translated into a Windows WM_COMMAND message, just as if a menu item were selected. This message is routed to a specific command handler.

AppWizard creates several keyboard accelerators automatically for your SDI and MDI applications. The following are some of the more common accelerators:

- Ctrl+N is used to call the ID_FILE_NEW command handler.
- Ctrl+C is used to call the ID_EDIT_COPY command handler.
- Ctrl+V is used to call the ID_EDIT_PASTE command handler.

10

There is no requirement that a keyboard accelerator must be mapped to a menu item. However, finding an action that is useful as a keyboard accelerator but not useful as a menu item is extremely rare.

Displaying Keyboard Accelerator Resources

Keyboard accelerators are resources and are displayed and edited much like menu resources. To see the keyboard accelerators for the Menu sample project, open the IDR_MAINFRAME Accelerator resource folder in the project workspace. The keyboard accelerators used by the project will be displayed as shown in Figure 10.5.

An MDI program will have at least two accelerator resources. Only one resource identifier is in use at a time; the current accelerator resource has the same identifier as the current menu resource.

FIGURE 10.5.

Displaying the keyboard accelerators associated with the Menu sample project.

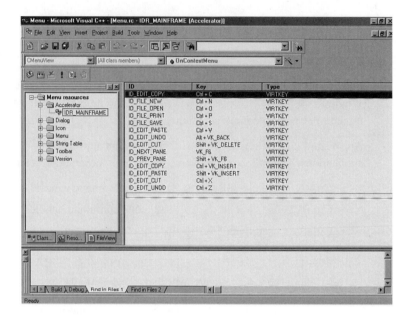

Adding Keyboard Accelerators

To create a new keyboard accelerator, bring up the Accel Properties dialog box by double-clicking the empty line at the bottom of the accelerator list. The Accel Properties dialog box is shown in Figure 10.6.

FIGURE 10.6.

The Accel Properties dialog box.

You can also bring up the Accel Properties dialog box by pressing the Insert key on your keyboard.

Each keyboard accelerator has several properties:

- *ID* is the WM_COMMAND message that will be sent when the accelerator is invoked. This value is usually a menu item identifier.
- *Key* is the keyboard key that is used to start the accelerator.

- *Modifiers* is used to indicate whether one or more of the Shift, Control, or Alt keys is pressed as part of the accelerator combination.
- *Type* is used to specify whether the Key value is a virtual key code or an ASCII value.

The simplest way to fill in the Accel Properties dialog box is to click the button labeled Next Key Typed. After clicking this button, the dialog box will use the next keystroke combination to fill in the properties for the accelerator.

> Avoid using the ASCII value type for your keyboard accelerators because they behave unpredictably in the presence of Shift and Caps Lock keys. The virtual keycode is much more reliable and is not affected by your keyboard's Shift and Caps Lock states.

A Keyboard Accelerator Example

To illustrate how accelerators are added to Windows applications, you can add a keyboard accelerator to the Menu sample project. The accelerator will perform the same action as selecting Bears from the pop-up shortcut menu.

Open the `IDR_MAINFRAME` accelerator resource folder, and add a new accelerator resource to the Menu project using the values from Table 10.3.

TABLE 10.3. THE NEW ACCELERATOR RESOURCE FOR THE MENU PROJECT.

ID	Key	Modifiers	Type
ID_BEARS	B	Ctrl	VirtKey

Build the Menu project. Instead of selecting an item from the shortcut menu, try pressing Ctrl+B on your keyboard; you will get the same message as when you select Bears from the shortcut menu.

Summary

In this hour, you learned about the use of menus in Windows applications. You learned about the routing of menu command messages, as well as methods for modifying and creating your own menus. Not only did you learn how to work with regular menus, but you also discovered how to create pop-up menus that appear when the right mouse button is clicked. You ended the hour by learning how to add accelerators to your menu items.

Q&A

Q Can a dialog box have a menu?

A According to the Windows User Interface guidelines, only top-level windows may have menus. Dialog boxes and MDI windows are considered child windows and cannot have menus.

Q I added a new item to my menu, but it's disabled. I've checked the menu attributes to make sure that the menu should be enabled; why is the menu item still disabled?

A Make sure that you have provided a message-handling function for the menu item. The MFC framework will not enable a menu item that doesn't have a message handler.

Q All the menu items with keyboard accelerators that are provided by MFC and AppWizard place the accelerator label to the far right of the menu window. How can I provide that effect for my controls?

A Use the \t tab escape sequence between your menu item and the accelerator text. For example, the caption for the Bears menu item would be

```
&Bears\tCtrl+B
```

Workshop

The Workshop is designed to help you anticipate possible questions, review what you've learned, and begin thinking ahead to putting your knowledge into practice. The answers to the quiz are found in Appendix A, "Quiz Answers."

Quiz

1. What MFC class is used to manage menus?
2. What message is handled when providing a shortcut menu?
3. What visual cue should be provided for a menu that leads to a dialog box that requires further input from the user?
4. What is a mnemonic?
5. What is a keyboard accelerator?
6. What visual cue is provided automatically to indicate a submenu?
7. What character is used in a menu caption to create a mnemonic?
8. What Windows message is sent to your application when a menu item is selected?
9. In an MDI application, which menu resource is used when no documents are open?

10. What menu item property is used to create a horizontal line that divides logical menu sections?

Exercises

1. Add accelerators for the Lions and Tigers shortcut menu items in the Menu project.

2. The File | Enable Hello and File | Check Hello menu items are not updated to reflect the current state of the application. Add update command UI handlers for these menu items so that their captions read File | Disable Hello and File | Uncheck Hello when appropriate.

10

PART IV
The Graphics Interface

Hour

HOUR 11

Device Contexts

All output in a program written for Windows must be done using a device context. A device context is an important part of the Windows Graphics Device Interface, or GDI. Device contexts are used by Windows and applications to provide device-independent output.

In this hour, you will learn

- The different type of device contexts used in Windows and the MFC classes that support them
- How to use device map modes
- How to use GDI objects in your Windows applications
- How to use the different options for text output in Windows

You also will build a sample program that demonstrates how a device context is used with text output.

What Are Device Contexts?

NEW TERM A *device context*, often abbreviated as *DC*, is a structure maintained by Windows that stores information needed when a program displays output to a device. The device context stores information about the drawing surface and its capabilities. Before using any of the GDI output functions, you must create a device context.

> Deep down inside Windows, device contexts are actually structures that the GDI uses to track the current output state for a window. However, you never have access to the individual members of a device context; instead, all access to device contexts occurs through function calls.

The simplest reason to use device contexts is because they are required; there's simply no other way to perform output in a Windows program without them. However, using a device context is the first step toward using many of the GDI features that are available under Windows. Understanding how device contexts work can also help make your Windows programs more efficient.

Types of GDI Objects

NEW TERM Associating a GDI object with a device context is commonly referred to as *selecting* a GDI object into the device context. A GDI object can be selected into a device context in order to provide specific drawing capabilities for the DC. Each GDI object can be used to create a different type of output. The GDI objects most commonly used with device contexts are listed in Table 11.1.

TABLE 11.1. COMMONLY USED GDI OBJECTS IN WINDOWS PROGRAMS.

Object	Purpose
Pen	Drawing lines
Brush	Filling regions
Bitmap	Displaying images
Font	Typeface characteristics

Types of Device Contexts

Windows and the MFC class library provide the following four different basic types of device contexts. Although you use these device contexts in different situations, the basic rules for their use are consistent.

- *Display DCs*, used to display information to a standard video terminal. These are the most commonly used device contexts in a Windows program.
- *Printer DCs*, used to display output on a printer or plotter.
- *Memory DCs*, sometimes called *compatible device contexts*, used to perform drawing operations on a bitmap.
- *Information DCs*, used to collect information on a device. These DCs are small and fast but cannot be used for actual output.

With the exception of the information device contexts, each of the different DC types is used to create a different type of output.

Hardware Independence

The goal behind using device contexts is to give programs written for Windows hardware independence. With a little care, your program can run on any display or printer that's supported by a Windows hardware driver. Most new output devices supply a driver if Windows doesn't currently provide automatic support. This means that programs you write today will work with display devices that have not yet been developed.

> Because of the way device contexts insulate a program written for Windows from the actual device hardware, output is often said to be "written to a device context."

In order to achieve true hardware independence, you must take a few precautions:

- Don't hard-code any dimensions into your program. Larger or smaller screens or printers will cause hard-coded dimensions to look skewed or distorted.
- Don't assume that Windows is running on a display with a particular resolution. Making assumptions about video monitors, in particular, is a bad idea. It's a sure bet that many people don't use your screen resolution or dimensions.
- Don't assume that a certain set of colors are available or are appropriate in all cases. For example, don't assume the workspace background is always white. A large number of Windows users have laptops that simulate VGA displays. Other users often change the available color scheme. The selection of colors used is strictly up to the user.

Device contexts can help by providing much of the information you need to stay hardware-independent.

How to Use Device Contexts

When using Visual C++, you almost always use an MFC class to gain access to a device context. The MFC class library offers not just one, but four different display device context classes that can help make your life easier, at least when displaying output in a Windows program:

- CDC: The base class for all the device context classes
- CPaintDC: Performs some useful housekeeping functions that are needed when a window responds to WM_PAINT
- CClientDC: Used when a device context will be used only for output to a window's client area
- CWindowDC: Used when the entire window can be drawn on

There are more MFC device context classes, but they are used for specialized purposes and are discussed elsewhere in this book. For example, the CPrinterDC class is discussed in Hour 21, "Printing."

Wizard Support for Device Contexts

When you create a class using ClassWizard or AppWizard, often code that uses or creates a device context is provided automatically. For example, the OnDraw function for a typical view class is provided in Listing 11.1.

LISTING 11.1. A TYPICAL OnDraw FUNCTION.

```
void CDisplayView::OnDraw(CDC* pDC)
{
    CDocument* pDoc = GetDocument();
    // TODO: add draw code here
}
```

The device context used for the OnDraw function is created by the MFC framework before the OnDraw function is called. Because every OnDraw function must display some output, the device context is provided for you automatically, without the need for you to write any code.

Most functions that need a device context have one provided as a parameter, just like OnDraw. This is one of the ways MFC helps make your code easier to write and more reliable at the same time.

Selecting a GDI Object

One of the most common mistakes made when using device contexts occurs when selecting a GDI object into a DC. When a device context is created, it contains a set of default GDI objects, as shown in Figure 11.1.

FIGURE 11.1.

A device context created with a collection of default GDI objects.

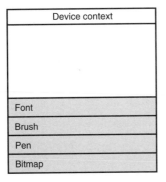

When a new GDI object—for example, a bitmap—is selected into a device context, the default GDI bitmap is passed as a return value to the caller. This return value must be saved so that it can be returned to the device context later. Listing 11.2 is an example of selecting a new bitmap into a DC and returning the previously selected GDI object at the end of the function.

LISTING 11.2. SELECTING AND RESTORING A GDI OBJECT.

```
CBitmap      bmpHello;
bmpHello.LoadBitmap( IDB_HELLO );
CBitmap* pbmpOld = dcMem.SelectObject( &bmpHello );
if( pbmpOld != NULL )
{
    //
    // Use the bitmap...
    //
    dcMem.SelectObject( pbmpOld );
}
```

Notice that the pbmpOld value is checked to make sure that it isn't NULL. If the call to SelectObject fails, the original bitmap is not returned. In that case, there's no need to return the original bitmap to the DC because a new one never was selected.

11

You must restore the device context to its original state when you are finished with it. If you don't, resources that you have selected into a device context might not be properly released, causing your program to consume more and more GDI resources. This type of problem is known as a *resource leak* and is very difficult to track down—getting into the habit of always restoring the original object back into the device context is much better.

Stock Objects

A group of commonly used GDI objects known as stock objects are maintained by Windows. These objects are much easier to use than objects that you create yourself. To select a stock object into a device context, use the SelectStockObject function:

```
HPEN hOldPen = pDC->SelectStockObject(BLACK_PEN);
```

Although stock objects do not need to be destroyed after they are used, attempting to destroy a stock object is not harmful. Windows will simply ignore any attempts to destroy one of the stock objects.

When a device context is created, it already has several stock objects selected. For example, the default pen is a stock object BLACK_PEN, and the default brush is the stock object NULL_BRUSH.

Setting the Device Context Map Mode

NEW TERM   The *map mode* is the current coordinate system used by a device context. In Windows, you use map modes to define the size and direction of units used in drawing functions. As a Windows programmer, several different coordinate systems are available to you. Map modes can use physical or logical dimensions, and they can start at the top, bottom, or at an arbitrary point on the screen.

A total of eight different map modes are available in Windows. You can retrieve the current map mode used by a device context using the GetMapMode function, and set a new map mode using SetMapMode. Here are the available map modes:

- MM_ANISOTROPIC: Uses a viewport to scale the logical units to an application-defined value. The SetWindowExt and SetViewportExt member functions are used to change the units, orientation, and scaling.

- MM_HIENGLISH: Each logical unit is converted to a physical value of 0.001 inch. Positive x is to the right; positive y is up.

- MM_HIMETRIC: Each logical unit is converted to a physical value of 0.01 millimeter. Positive x is to the right; positive y is up.

- MM_ISOTROPIC: Similar to MM_ANISOTROPIC, where logical units are converted to arbitrary units with equally scaled axes. This means that one unit on the x-axis is always equal to one unit on the y-axis. Use the SetWindowExt and SetViewportExt member functions to specify the units and orientation of the axes.

- MM_LOENGLISH: Each logical unit is converted to a physical value of 0.01 inch. Positive x is to the right; positive y is up.

- MM_LOMETRIC: Each logical unit is converted to a physical value of 0.1 millimeter. Positive x is to the right; positive y is up.

- MM_TEXT: Each logical unit is converted to one device pixel. Positive x is to the right; positive y is down.

- MM_TWIPS: Each logical unit is converted to 1/20 of a point. Because a point is 1/72 inch, a twip is 1/1440 inch. This map mode is useful when sending output to a printer. Positive x is to the right; positive y is up.

A Device Context Example

11

To demonstrate some basic ideas about how device contexts can be used, you will create a sample SDI program named DCTest. To help reduce the amount of typing required for GDI examples, the DCTest program will be used through Hour 14, "Icons and Cursors."

DCTest is an SDI program that displays some information about the current device context, its map mode, and information about the default font. It will be possible to change the view's map mode using a dialog box.

To begin building the DCTest example, create an SDI program named DCTest using MFC AppWizard. Feel free to experiment with options offered by AppWizard because none of the options will affect the sample project.

Creating the Map Mode Dialog Box

Using Figure 11.2 as a guide, create a dialog box that changes the map mode for the view display. Give the dialog box a resource ID of IDD_MAP_MODE, and set its caption property to Map Mode.

FIGURE 11.2.

The IDD_MAP_MODE
dialog box in the
resource editor.

The dialog box contains two controls:

- A drop-down combo box
- A static text control

Change the resource ID of the combo box to IDC_COMBO. Change the caption property of the static text control to Map Mode.

Using ClassWizard, add a class named CMapModeDlg to handle the IDD_MAP_MODE dialog box. Add a CString member variable to the class as shown in Table 11.2.

TABLE 11.2. NEW CString MEMBER VARIABLE FOR THE CMapModeDlg CLASS.

Resource ID	Name	Category	Variable Type
IDC_COMBO	m_szCombo	Value	CString

That's the beginning of the DCTest project. It doesn't do much now, but you will add source code to the example as new device context topics are discussed in the rest of this hour.

Modifying the Map Mode Dialog Box

Modify the combo box in the IDD_MAP_MODE dialog box so that it can be used to track the current map mode. You can set the contents of the combo box control by selecting the tab labeled Data in its properties dialog box. Because this combo box contains a fixed list of items, adding them in the resource editor is easier than adding the necessary code to OnInitDialog. Add the items from the following list to the combo box:

```
MM_ANISOTROPIC
MM_HIENGLISH
MM_HIMETRIC
MM_ISOTROPIC
MM_LOENGLISH
MM_LOMETRIC
MM_TEXT
MM_TWIPS
```

Adding a Menu Item

Use the values from Table 11.3 to add a menu item to the View menu and a message-handling function to the CDCTestView class. The CDCTestView class will handle this menu selection because the dialog box changes data that is interesting only for the view class.

TABLE 11.3. NEW MEMBER FUNCTIONS FOR THE CDCTestView CLASS.

Menu ID	Caption	Event	Function Name
ID_VIEW_MAP_MODE	&Map Mode...	COMMAND	OnViewMapMode

Listing 11.3 contains the source code for the OnViewMapMode function, which handles the message sent when the new menu item is selected. If the OK button is clicked, the new map mode is calculated based on the value contained in the combo box. The view rectangle is invalidated, which causes the view to be redrawn.

INPUT   **LISTING 11.3.** THE CDCTestView::OnViewMapMode FUNCTION.

```
void CDCTestView::OnViewMapMode()
{
    CMapModeDlg dlg;

    if( dlg.DoModal() == IDOK )
    {
        POSITION    pos;
        pos = m_map.GetStartPosition();
        while( pos != NULL )
        {
            CString szMapMode;
            int     nMapMode;
             m_map.GetNextAssoc(pos, nMapMode, szMapMode);
            if(szMapMode == dlg.m_szCombo)
            {
                m_nMapMode = nMapMode;
                break;
            }
        }
        InvalidateRect( NULL );
    }
}
```

11

Add an #include statement to the DCTestView.cpp file so the CDCTestView class can have access to the CMapModeDlg class declaration. Add the following line near the top of the DCTestView.cpp file, just after the other #include statements:

```
#include "MapModeDlg.h"
```

Collecting Information from a Device Context

The CDC class has two member functions that are commonly used to collect information:

- GetDeviceCaps, used to return information about the physical device that is associated with a device context
- GetTextMetrics, used to retrieve information about the currently selected font

Using the GetDeviceCaps Function

One common use for GetDeviceCaps is to determine the number of pixels per logical inch for the device associated with the DC. To retrieve the number of pixels per logical inch in the horizontal direction (also known as the x-axis), call GetDeviceCaps and pass an index value of LOGPIXELSX as a parameter:

```
int cxLog = pDC->GetDeviceCaps( LOGPIXELSX );
```

Later, in the section "Modifying the CDCTestView Class," you will use GetDeviceCaps to display this information in the DCTest example.

GetDeviceCaps is used primarily when printing; you can use this function to determine whether the printer supports specific GDI functions. In Hour 21 you will see how GetDeviceCaps is used to determine whether a printer can have bitmaps transferred to it.

Using the GetTextMetrics Function

GetTextMetrics is used to fill a TEXTMETRIC structure with a variety of information:

```
TEXTMETRIC tm;
pDC->GetTextMetrics(&tm);
```

The TEXTMETRIC structure has a large number of member variables that contain information about the currently selected font. The most commonly used members of the TEXTMETRIC structure are shown in Table 11.4.

TABLE **11.4.** COMMON MEMBER VARIABLES OF THE TEXTMETRIC STRUCTURE.

Member	Specifies
tmAscent	The number of units above the baseline used by characters in the current font.
tmDescent	The number of units below the baseline used by characters in the current font.
tmHeight	The total height for characters in the current font. This value is equal to adding the tmAscent and tmDescent values together.
tmInternalLeading	The area reserved for accent marks and similar marks associated with the font. This area is inside the tmAscent area.
tmExternalLeading	The area reserved for spacing between lines of text. This area is outside the tmAscent area.
tmAveCharWidth	The average width for non-bold, non-italic characters in the currently selected font.
tmMaxCharWidth	The width of the widest character in the currently selected font.

To get the height of the currently selected font, call the GetTextMetrics function and use the value stored in the tmHeight member variable:

```
TEXTMETRIC   tm;
pDC->GetTextMetrics(&tm);
nFontHeight = tm.tmHeight;
```

Modifying the CDCTestView Class

In order to display information about the current map mode, you must first create a collection based on CMap, one of the template collection classes. The CMap variable, m_map, associates an integer map mode value with a CString object that describes the map mode. As shown in Listing 11.4, add two new variables to the CDCTestView class declaration in the Attributes section.

NEW TERM

LISTING **11.4.** NEW MEMBER VARIABLES ADDED TO THE CDCTestView CLASS DECLARATION.

```
// Attributes
private:
    CMap< int, int, CString, CString > m_map;
    int     m_nMapMode;
```

When using one of the MFC collection classes in a project, you must always add an
#include "afxtempl.h" statement to the stdafx.h file in the project directory. This
include directive adds the MFC template declarations to the project's precompiled header, reducing project build time.

```
#include "afxtempl.h"
```

The source code for CDCTestView::OnDraw is provided in Listing 11.5. The current map
mode is displayed, along with text and device metrics. The text metrics vary depending
on the current logical map mode, while the device measurements remain constant. Some
of the map modes will display the information from top to bottom, whereas some of the
modes cause the information to be displayed from bottom to top.

INPUT   **LISTING 11.5.** THE CDCTestView::OnDraw FUNCTION.

```
void CDCTestView::OnDraw(CDC* pDC)
{
    // Set map mode
    pDC->SetMapMode( m_nMapMode );
    // Get client rect, and convert to logical coordinates
    CRect   rcClient;
    GetClientRect( rcClient );
    pDC->DPtoLP( rcClient );
    int x = 0;
    int y = rcClient.bottom/2;
    CString szOut;
    m_map.Lookup( m_nMapMode, szOut );
    pDC->TextOut( x, y, szOut );
    // Determine the inter-line vertical spacing
    TEXTMETRIC  tm;
    pDC->GetTextMetrics( &tm );
    int nCyInterval = tm.tmHeight + tm.tmExternalLeading;
    y += nCyInterval;
    szOut.Format( "Character height - %d units", tm.tmHeight );
    pDC->TextOut( x, y, szOut );

    y += nCyInterval;
    szOut.Format( "Average width - %d units", tm.tmAveCharWidth );
    pDC->TextOut( x, y, szOut );

    y += nCyInterval;
    szOut.Format( "Descent space - %d units", tm.tmDescent );
    pDC->TextOut( x, y, szOut );

    y += nCyInterval;
    szOut.Format( "Ascent space - %d units", tm.tmAscent );
    pDC->TextOut( x, y, szOut );
```

```
    int cxLog = pDC->GetDeviceCaps( LOGPIXELSX );
    y += nCyInterval;
    szOut.Format( "%d pixels per logical horiz. inch", cxLog );
    pDC->TextOut( x, y, szOut );

    int cyLog = pDC->GetDeviceCaps( LOGPIXELSY );
    y += nCyInterval;
    szOut.Format( "%d pixels per logical vert. inch", cyLog );
    pDC->TextOut( x, y, szOut );
}
```

Add the source code from Listing 11.6 to the CDCTestView constructor, which can be found in the DCTestView.cpp file.

INPUT

LISTING 11.6. INITIALIZING THE MAP COLLECTION IN THE CDCTestView CONSTRUCTOR.

```
CDCTestView::CDCTestView()
{
    m_nMapMode = MM_TEXT;
    m_map.SetAt( MM_ANISOTROPIC, "MM_ANISOTROPIC" );
    m_map.SetAt( MM_HIENGLISH, "MM_HIENGLISH" );
    m_map.SetAt( MM_HIMETRIC, "MM_HIMETRIC" );
    m_map.SetAt( MM_ISOTROPIC, "MM_ISOTROPIC" );
    m_map.SetAt( MM_LOENGLISH, "MM_LOENGLISH" );
    m_map.SetAt( MM_LOMETRIC, "MM_LOMETRIC" );
    m_map.SetAt( MM_TEXT, "MM_TEXT" );
    m_map.SetAt( MM_TWIPS, "MM_TWIPS" );
}
```

11

Compile and run the DCTest example. Figure 11.3 shows the DCTest main window, with device measurements and text metrics displayed.

FIGURE **11.3.**

Running the DCTest
example.

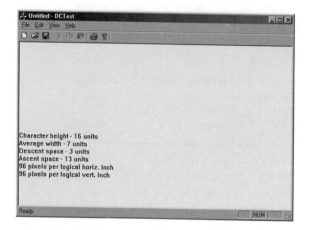

Using Color in Windows Applications

As a final topic in this hour, it's important to understand how colors are represented in Windows applications. Color values are stored in COLORREF variables, which are 32-bit variables defined as

```
typedef DWORD COLORREF;
```

Each COLORREF is a 32-bit variable, but only 24 bits are actually used, with 8 bits reserved. The 24 bits are divided into three 8-bit chunks that represent the red, green, and blue components of each color.

A COLORREF is created using the RGB macro, which stands for Red, Green, and Blue—the three colors used for color output in a Windows program. The RGB macro takes three parameters, each ranging from 0 to 255, with 255 signifying that the maximum amount of that color should be included in the COLORREF. For example, to create a COLORREF with a white value, the definition would look like this:

```
COLORREF clrWhite = RGB(255,255,255);
```

For black, the definition would look like this:

```
COLORREF clrBlack = RGB(0,0,0);
```

You can change the current text color used for a device context through the SetTextColor function. SetTextColor returns the previous text color used by the device context.

Listing 11.7 shows two different ways in which you can use the SetTextColor function. The first method uses the RGB macro inside the SetTextColor function call; the next method creates a COLORREF value that is passed as a parameter.

INPUT   **LISTING 11.7.** CHANGING THE TEXT COLOR USING THE SetTextColor FUNCTION.

```
// Change text color to pure green
COLORREF colorOld = pDC->SetTextColor(RGB(0,255,0));

// Change text color to pure blue
COLORREF colorBlue = RGB(0,0,255);
pDC->SetTextColor(colorBlue);

// Restore original text color
pDC->SetTextColor(colorOld);
```

Summary

In this hour you learned about the Graphics Device Interface, or GDI. You also learned the basics of the device context, as well as some of the MFC classes that are used to manage them. You built a sample program that enables you to change and display information about an output device and its map mode. You finished the hour by learning how to set colors in Windows programs.

Q&A

Q I'm having trouble drawing an ellipse that is exactly six inches across. I used GetDeviceCaps to retrieve the LOGPIXELSX and LOGPIXELSY values, but the image is drawn either too small or too large. How can I draw an image to an exact physical size?

A The LOGPIXELSX and LOGPIXELSY values are supplied by the video driver. These values are approximate, and are really just a wild guess. There's no way to determine the true number of pixels per inch on your display adapter.

Q Why is a CPaintDC class created and used for WM_PAINT messages instead of a normal CDC object?

A The CPaintDC class is exactly like the CDC class, except that its constructor and destructor do some extra work that is needed when handling a WM_PAINT message. This extra work tells Windows that the window has been repainted. If a CDC object is used, Windows will not be notified that the window has been repainted and will continue to send WM_PAINT messages.

11

Workshop

The Workshop is designed to help you anticipate possible questions, review what you've learned, and begin thinking ahead to putting your knowledge into practice. The answers to the quiz are in Appendix A, "Quiz Answers."

Quiz

1. What is the difference between a device context and an information device context?

2. What CDC member function is used to select a stock object?

3. How many twips are in an inch?

4. What type of GDI object is used to draw lines?

5. What type of GDI object is used to fill areas?

6. How do you determine the height and other characteristics of characters in the currently selected font?

7. What is the RGB macro used for?

8. What MFC class is used as a base class for all device contexts?

9. How can you tell that a call to SelectObject has failed?

10. What map mode maps one device pixel per measurement unit?

Exercises

1. Modify the DCTest program to change the color for each line of output.

2. Modify the DCTest program so that every line starts with its x and y coordinates.

HOUR 12

Using Pens and Brushes

In this hour you will look at pens and brushes. Specifically, you will learn

- How pens are used to draw lines and geometric shapes in Windows programs
- How brushes are used to fill areas with colors and patterns
- What MFC class library support is available to simplify the use of pens and brushes

You also modify the DCTest sample program from Hour 11, "Device Contexts," to draw a variety of figures using pens and brushes.

What Is a Pen?

NEW TERM A *pen* is a Windows GDI object used to draw lines and figures. Think of a Windows pen as being like an ink pen at your desk. A pen is perfect in situations in which you must draw a geometric shape or line. Although you can use a bitmap for complicated images, you easily can draw squares, rectangles, circles, and other basic shapes using a pen.

Pens are also useful for drawing three-dimensional highlighting or other effects. It's not uncommon for pens and other GDI objects to be used to simulate controls in Windows. For example, before Windows 95 was released, early versions of property pages used pens to draw simulated "tabs."

Like other GDI objects, you normally use a pen by creating an MFC object. Use the CPen class to create and manage both cosmetic and geometric pens. When creating a pen, you must specify at least three attributes:

- Width: Normally one pixel wide, although a pen can be as wide as you like
- Style: Can be any of the pen styles discussed in this chapter
- Color: Can be any Windows color packed into a COLORREF structure

Types of Pens

Programs written for Windows use two types of pens:

- *Cosmetic pens*, which are always drawn in device units, regardless of the current map mode.
- *Geometric pens*, which are drawn in logical units and are affected by the current map mode. Geometric pens have more style and drawing options than cosmetic pens.

Cosmetic pens are extremely quick and are mapped directly into device units. This makes them useful for drawing things like frames, borders, grid lines, and other screen objects that should not be affected by the current device context-map mode. Geometric pens require more CPU power but offer more styles. You can manipulate geometric pens using any of the available map modes. The next few sections discuss the various options available for cosmetic and geometric pens.

> You should use cosmetic pens whenever possible. Although the number of styles available for geometric pens is much larger than for cosmetic pens, cosmetic pens have much less overhead.

Using Cosmetic Pens

Cosmetic pens are not affected by the current map mode's scaling factor because they are always drawn in device units. Therefore, they are useful where a line must overlay another view that can be scaled. These basic styles (illustrated in Figure 12.1) are available for cosmetic pens:

- PS_SOLID: Creates a solid pen.
- PS_DOT: Creates a dotted pen. This style is also valid only for pens with a width of one. Wider pens are drawn as PS_SOLID.
- PS_DASH: Creates a dashed pen. If the pen width is greater than one, the pen is drawn as PS_SOLID.
- PS_DASHDOT: Creates a pen with alternating dashes and dots. If the pen width is greater than one, the pen is drawn as PS_SOLID.
- PS_DASHDOTDOT: Creates a pen with alternating dashes and double dots. If the pen width is greater than one, the pen is drawn as PS_SOLID.
- PS_NULL: Creates a null pen; this pen doesn't draw at all.
- PS_INSIDEFRAME: Creates a pen that draws a line inside the frame of closed shapes produced by GDI functions, such as the Ellipse and Rectangle functions.
- PS_ALTERNATE: Can be applied only to cosmetic pens and creates a pen that sets every other pixel.

FIGURE 12.1.

Examples of the styles available for pens.

PS_SOLID

PS_DOT

PS_DASH

PS_DASHDOT

PS_DASHDOTDOT

PS_NULL

PS_INSIDEFRAME

12

Using Geometric Pens

Geometric pens can use all the styles available for cosmetic pens except for the PS_ALTERNATE style, and they also have access to four additional attributes:

- A pattern used to draw the pen
- A hatch style used for some types of patterns
- The type of end cap used to terminate a line
- A joining style, used when two lines intersect

Using the CPen Class

The CPen class is simple to use because there really are only a few things that can be done to a pen object; most of the fun occurs when the pen object is selected into a device context. The CPen class provides three constructors: two simple constructors primarily for cosmetic pens and another extremely flexible constructor primarily for geometric pens.

The first constructor has no arguments:

```
CPen     aGreenPen;
aGreenPen.Create( PS_SOLID, 1, RGB(0,255,0);
```

As shown in the preceding, if you use this constructor you must use the Create member function to actually create the pen and make it ready for use.

The second constructor provided for CPen also is used for cosmetic pens:

```
CPen     penDottedAndRed( PS_DOT, 1, RGB(255,0,0) );
```

This version of the constructor accepts three parameters: the pen style, width, and color. In this case, the CPen instance is a dotted red pen.

The third constructor used for CPen objects enables any type of pen to be created. It also uses more parameters, as shown in Listing 12.1.

LISTING 12.1. CREATING A BRUSH USING A LOGBRUSH STRUCTURE.

```
LOGBRUSH     lbrGrnHatch;

lbrGrnHatch.lbStyle = BS_HATCHED;
lbrGrnHatch.lbColor = RGB(0,255,0);
lbrGrnHatch.lbHatch = HS_DIAGCROSS;

CPen     penGeometric( PS_DOT ¦ PS_GEOMETRIC ¦ PS_ENDCAPROUND,
                       50,
                       &lbrGrnHatch,
                       0,
                       NULL );
```

The constructor's first parameter is the pen's style, with the C++ OR operator, ¦, used to combine all styles that are applied to the pen. The second parameter for the constructor is the width; if the pen is cosmetic, it must be set to 1. The third parameter is a pointer to a LOGBRUSH structure. In Listing 12.1, lbrGrnHatch is defined as a diagonally cross-hatched green brush.

The last two parameters are rarely used; they define a user-supplied pattern for the pen. These two parameters are used only if the pen is created with the PS_USERSTYLE attribute. The fourth parameter is the number of elements in the style array, whereas the fifth parameter is an array of DWORD values, each used to define the length of a dash or space in the pen's pattern.

Using Stock Pens

The simplest pens to use are known as stock objects. Stock objects were introduced in Hour 11; they are GDI objects that belong to the operating system. Windows provides three stock pens:

- BLACK_PEN: Provides, oddly enough, a black pen
- WHITE_PEN: Provides a white pen
- NULL_PEN: Provides a null pen and is exactly the same as creating a pen with the PS_NULL style

Each of these pens is exactly one unit wide. If you need a wider pen, you must create one using the CPen class. These pens are used through a CDC object by calling the SelectStockObject function, passing the stock object as a parameter, as follows:

```
CPen* pOldPen = pDC->SelectStockObject( BLACK_PEN );
```

Drawing with Pens

After a pen has been selected into a device context, several different drawing functions can be performed with the device context. The CDC class used to represent device contexts, as you learned in Hour 11, includes these drawing functions often used with pens:

- Ellipse: Used to draw an ellipse. This function is also used to draw circles because a circle is just a special type of ellipse.
- Arc: Used to draw a portion of an ellipse.
- LineTo and MoveTo: Used to draw lines. Together they are often used to draw highlighting, squares, rectangles, and other types of figures.

As an example using pens, you can modify the DCTest program you created in Hour 11. The changes use three pens to draw three figures in the view window in a variety of styles and colors. Modifying the existing project also gives you a chance to see how different map modes affect the figures drawn using pens. Although some of the listings might look long, most of them require only a few changes in the source code that is already present.

12

Modifying the Map Mode Dialog Box

As the first step in the sample program, modify the Map Mode dialog box and the CMapModeDlg class to support extra options used when drawing with pens. The new version of the IDD_MAP_MODE dialog box is shown in Figure 12.2.

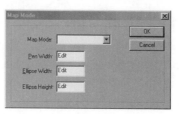

Use the values from Table 12.1 for the new controls you add to the Map Mode dialog box, using ClassWizard to add member variables to the CMapModeDlg class. All existing controls should remain as they are.

TABLE 12.1. VALUES FOR NEW EDIT CONTROLS YOU ADD TO THE MAP MODE DIALOG BOX.

Edit Control	Resource ID	Variable Name	Type
Pen Width	IDC_WIDTH	m_nPenWidth	int
Ellipse Width	IDC_CXELLIPSE	m_cxEllipse	int
Ellipse Height	IDC_CYELLIPSE	m_cyEllipse	int

Modifying the CDCTestView Class

You must modify the CDCTestView class slightly to add three new member variables that store the pen height and the ellipse variables you just added to the dialog box class. Add three new member variables to the attributes section of the CDCTestView class declaration, as shown in Listing 12.2.

INPUT   **LISTING 12.2.** NEW MEMBER VARIABLES ADDED TO THE CDCTestView CLASS.

```
// Attributes
private:
    // Variables added for Hour 11
    CMap< int, int, CString, CString > m_map;
    int     m_nMapMode;
    // Variables added for Hour 12 - pens
    int     m_cxEllipse;
    int     m_cyEllipse;
    int     m_nPenWidth;
```

Do not modify the declarations for existing member variables.

Modifying the `CDCTestView` Member Functions

You must modify three `CDCTestView` member functions:

- The `CDCTestView` constructor
- The `CDCTestView::OnViewMapMode` menu handler
- The `CDCTestView::OnDraw` member function

None of these member functions are new; all are used in the current DCTest project.

Add three new lines to the `CDCTestView` constructor to initialize the new variables added to the `CDCTestView` class. Listing 12.3 is the new version of the `CDCTestView` constructor. Most of the function should already be entered; you must add only the last three lines before the closing parenthesis.

INPUT   **LISTING 12.3.** THE NEW VERSION OF THE `CDCTestView` CONSTRUCTOR.

```
CDCTestView::CDCTestView()
{
    m_nMapMode = MM_TEXT;
    m_map.SetAt( MM_ANISOTROPIC, "MM_ANISOTROPIC" );
    m_map.SetAt( MM_HIENGLISH, "MM_HIENGLISH" );
    m_map.SetAt( MM_HIMETRIC, "MM_HIMETRIC" );
    m_map.SetAt( MM_ISOTROPIC, "MM_ISOTROPIC" );
    m_map.SetAt( MM_LOENGLISH, "MM_LOENGLISH" );
    m_map.SetAt( MM_LOMETRIC, "MM_LOMETRIC" );
    m_map.SetAt( MM_TEXT, "MM_TEXT" );
    m_map.SetAt( MM_TWIPS, "MM_TWIPS" );
    m_nPenWidth = 1;
    m_cxEllipse = 100;
    m_cyEllipse = 200;
}
```

12

Modify the `CDCTestView::OnViewMapMode` function to handle the changes in the Map Mode dialog box. Listing 12.4 provides the source code for the new version of `OnViewMapMode`. There are a total of six new source code lines, each marked with a comment. You should need to add only these six lines; the rest of the function should have been created already.

INPUT **LISTING 12.4.** THE NEW VERSION OF THE `CDCTestView::OnViewMapMode` FUNCTION.

```
void CDCTestView::OnViewMapMode()
{
    CMapModeDlg dlg;
    // The next three lines are added for Hour 12 - pens
    dlg.m_nPenWidth = m_nPenWidth;  // 1
    dlg.m_cxEllipse = m_cxEllipse;  // 2
    dlg.m_cyEllipse = m_cyEllipse;  // 3
    // Set the combo box to the current map mode.
    CString szMapMode;
    m_map.Lookup(m_nMapMode, szMapMode);
    dlg.m_szCombo = szMapMode;
    if( dlg.DoModal() == IDOK )
    {
        // The next three lines are added for Hour 12 - pens
        m_nPenWidth = dlg.m_nPenWidth;  // 4
        m_cxEllipse = dlg.m_cxEllipse;  // 5
        m_cyEllipse = dlg.m_cyEllipse;  // 6
        POSITION    pos;
        pos = m_map.GetStartPosition();
        while( pos != NULL )
        {
            CString szMapMode;
            int     nMapMode;
            m_map.GetNextAssoc( pos, nMapMode, szMapMode );
            if( szMapMode == dlg.m_szCombo )
            {
                m_nMapMode = nMapMode;
                break;
            }
        }
        InvalidateRect( NULL );
    }
}
```

Last but not least, you must create a new version of the OnDraw function. Most of this version of OnDraw is new because you are now drawing with pens instead of listing device attributes. Use the source code provided in Listing 12.5 for the new version of CDCTestView::OnDraw.

LISTING 12.5. THE NEW VERSION OF `CDCTestView::OnDraw`.

```
void CDCTestView::OnDraw(CDC* pDC)
{
    pDC->SetMapMode( m_nMapMode );
    // Draw an ellipse based on the current map mode and values
    // supplied by the user.
    CRect   rcClient;
    GetClientRect( rcClient );
    pDC->DPtoLP( rcClient );     // Convert device units to logical
    CPoint  ptCenter( rcClient.Width()/2, rcClient.Height()/2 );
    CRect   rcEllipse( ptCenter.x - ( m_cxEllipse/2 ),
    ptCenter.y - ( m_cyEllipse/2 ),
    ptCenter.x + ( m_cxEllipse/2 ),
    ptCenter.y + ( m_cyEllipse/2 ) );
    CPen    penRed( PS_SOLID, m_nPenWidth, RGB(255,0,0) );
    CPen*   pOldPen = pDC->SelectObject( &penRed );
    pDC->Ellipse( rcEllipse );
    // Draw a black box around the ellipse, using one of the stock
    // pens.
    pDC->SelectStockObject( BLACK_PEN );
    pDC->MoveTo( rcEllipse.TopLeft() );
    pDC->LineTo( rcEllipse.right, rcEllipse.top );
    pDC->LineTo( rcEllipse.BottomRight() );
    pDC->LineTo( rcEllipse.left, rcEllipse.bottom );
    pDC->LineTo( rcEllipse.left, rcEllipse.top );
    // Draw an arc using the client area as a bounding rectangle.
    // Clip the arc so that only the lower-left half is displayed.
    CPen    penDottedAndGreen( PS_DOT, 1, RGB(0,255,0) );
    pDC->SelectObject( &penDottedAndGreen );
    pDC->Arc(rcClient, rcClient.TopLeft(),rcClient.BottomRight());
    pDC->SelectObject( &pOldPen );
}
```

12

Compile and run the DCTest project, and experiment by changing the values in the Map Mode dialog box. Figure 12.3 shows the DCTest project running with the map mode set to MM_TEXT.

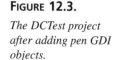

FIGURE 12.3.

The DCTest project after adding pen GDI objects.

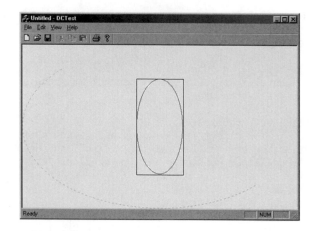

What Are Brushes?

NEW TERM   A *brush* is a GDI object used to fill a control, window, or other area when programming for Windows. A brush is much like a pen; both are selected the same way, some of the attributes are similar, and you can use a series of stock objects without much overhead. However, you use a brush to fill an area rather than draw a line or a figure. A common use for brushes is to color windows, controls, or dialog boxes.

Every brush has several attributes:

* Color: Specifies the brush color. You use a COLORREF value, just as when you specify a pen color.
* Pattern: Defines the pattern used by the brush.
* Hatching Style: Specifies a hatch pattern.

By choosing different values for attributes given to a brush, you can achieve a wide variety of effects.

MFC Support for Brushes

In a program you write with Visual C++, you normally create and use CBrush objects the way you create and use CPen objects. Every brush has a set of attributes that define how it appears and behaves.

Your Windows program can create four basic types of brushes:

* *Solid brushes*: Similar to solid pens, except they are used to fill areas instead of drawing lines. You normally give these brushes a color when you use a COLORREF to create them.

- *Stock brushes*: Predefined brushes stored and maintained by Windows.
- *Hatch brushes*: Fill an area with a predefined hatch pattern.
- *Pattern brushes*: Fill an area with a pattern supplied in an 8 × 8 bitmap.

You create each of these brush types using a different function call. For example, a solid brush is created using CreateSolidBrush, whereas a hatched brush is created using CreateHatchBrush. When using the CBrush class, it's also possible to call a specialized CBrush constructor to construct the CBrush object in the desired style. You will use the CBrush class later in this hour.

You can create solid and hatch brushes with a color attribute that specifies the color used when the brush fills an area. In the case of a hatched brush, the color specifies the color of the hatching lines.

Using the CBrush Class

To use a brush in an MFC program, you create a CBrush object and select it into a device context. You can create the brush using single-step construction, like this:

```
CBrush    brBlack( RGB(0,0,0) );
```

Alternatively, you use two-step construction, where the brush object is constructed and then explicitly created, like this:

```
CBrush    brBlack();
brBlack.CreateSolidBrush( RGB(0,0,0) );
```

The advantage of using two-step construction is that the function used to create a brush returns FALSE if the function fails.

Unlike pens, which use style bits to determine the type of pen to be created, separate functions are used for different brush types. In two-step construction, you use one of three functions to create a brush after you construct the CBrush object:

- CreateSolidBrush
- CreateHatchBrush
- CreatePatternBrush

Constructing a Brush

Four different constructors are provided for CBrush. In addition to the default constructor, you can use one of three constructors that each create a specific type of brush in one step. The second constructor is used to create a solid brush and takes one COLORREF parameter, indicating the color used for the brush.

```
CBrush    brGreen( RGB(0,0,255) );
```

12

Using this brush is equivalent to using the default constructor and then calling
CreateSolidBrush.

The third form of the CBrush constructor is used to create a hatched brush and takes the
hatching style and hatch color as parameters:

```
CBrush    brGray( HS_CROSS, RGB(192,192,192) );
```

This constructor is equivalent to using the default constructor and then calling
CreateHatchBrush.

Use the fourth and final constructor for CBrush to create brushes that have bitmap patterns. You will learn more about bitmaps in Hour 16, "Using Bitmaps and Image Lists";
for now, just remember that a bitmap can be used as a pattern for a brush. The constructor takes a pointer to a CBitmap object as a parameter:

```
CBrush    brArrow( &bmpArrow );
```

The CBitmap object can be up to 8 × 8 pixels. If the bitmap is larger, only the upper-left
eight pixel squares are used for the brush pattern.

Logical Brushes

Logical brushes are defined using the LOGBRUSH structure. A logical brush often is used
when specifying how a brush should be constructed. For example, earlier in this hour
you used a LOGBRUSH structure to specify the characteristics of a geometric pen. Think of
a LOGBRUSH as a recipe for a brush that might be created: It's not a brush yet, but it might
help build a brush in the future.

The LOGBRUSH structure has three data members:

- lbrStyle contains the brush style.
- lbrColor stores a COLORREF value for the brush.
- lbrHatch stores a hatch style if needed.

Each of the three LOGBRUSH data members corresponds to one of the style attributes available for brushes, discussed earlier in this hour. To create a logical brush, just assign values to the three data members, as with any structure. Listing 12.6 uses a logical brush to
create a red hatched brush.

LISTING 12.6. FILLING A LOGBRUSH STRUCTURE.

```
LOGBRUSH     lbrRed;
lbrRed.lbrStyle = BS_HATCH;
lbrRed.lbrColor = RGB(255,0,0);
lbrRed.lbrHatch = HS_CROSS;

CBrush       theRedBrush;
theRedBrush.CreateBrushIndirect( &lbrRed );
```

Using Stock Brushes

Just like stock pens discussed earlier in this hour, Windows maintains a set of stock brushes. Windows provides seven stock brushes:

- BLACK_BRUSH: Provides a black brush.
- DKGRAY_BRUSH: Provides a dark gray brush.
- GRAY_BRUSH: Provides a gray brush.
- HOLLOW_BRUSH: Equivalent to NULL_BRUSH.
- LTGRAY_BRUSH: Provides a light gray brush.
- NULL_BRUSH: Provides a null brush.
- WHITE_BRUSH: Provides a white brush.

As with other stock objects, you use these brushes through a CDC object by calling the SelectStockObject function, passing the stock object as a parameter, as follows:

```
CPen* pOldBrush = pDC->SelectStockObject( BLACK_BRUSH );
```

12

Using the Common Color Dialog Box

The Windows operating system includes a series of dialog boxes as part of the operating system known as the *common dialog boxes*. These dialog boxes are guaranteed to be present, and using them requires just a few lines of code. Use these dialog boxes for common operations where it's beneficial for all Windows programs to have a similar look and feel. The common dialog boxes shipped with Windows can help you do the following:

- Select a file to be opened
- Choose a font
- Choose a color
- Create a standard Find and Replace dialog box
- Choose options and print to a supported printer

As with pens, brushes can be created in a wide variety of colors. You can allow the user to select a brush color by using the Common Color dialog box. To use the Common Color dialog box, just create a CColorDialog object and call DoModal, just as with any other dialog box:

```
CColorDialog    dlgColor;
if( dlgColor.DoModal() )
{ //....
```

If IDOK is returned from the dialog box, the CColorDialog::GetColor function gets the selected color value. The example in the next section uses the Common Color dialog box to choose a brush color. You will use other common dialog boxes in later hours. (For example, the font-selection dialog box is used in Hour 13, "Fonts.")

Allowing the User to Control Colors

As an example of how to use brushes, continue to modify the DCTest project that you worked with earlier this hour. The new version of the project will display a colored ellipse on a gray view background. Both the ellipse and background color are filled using CBrush objects. You can change the color of the ellipse using the Common Color dialog box; as a bonus, the Map Mode dialog box color changes to match the ellipse.

Modify the Map Mode dialog box to allow the user to choose a color for the dialog box and a brush used for the view. The CMapModeDlg class needs two new variables: a COLORREF for the currently selected color and a CBrush object that has been created using the current color. Listing 12.7 contains the changes to the CMapModeDlg class declaration. Add the new code in the Dialog Data section, just after the AFX_DATA comments.

| INPUT | **LISTING 12.7.** CHANGES TO THE CMapModeDlg CLASS DECLARATION. |

```
// Dialog Data
    //{{AFX_DATA(CMapModeDlg)
    enum { IDD = IDD_MAP_MODE };
    CString    m_szCombo;
    int        m_cyEllipse;
    int        m_cxEllipse;
    int        m_nPenWidth;
    //}}AFX_DATA
    // Variable added in Hour 12
public:
    COLORREF m_clrChoice;
private:
    CBrush    m_brControl;
```

You must change the Map Mode dialog box slightly for this example. Remove the pen-width edit control and add a pushbutton control, as shown in Figure 12.4. Use ClassWizard to remove the m_nPenWidth member variable from the CMapModeDlg class.

FIGURE 12.4.

The new version of the Map Mode dialog box.

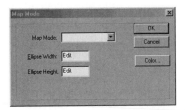

Use the values from Table 12.2 for the new button control.

TABLE 12.2. VALUES FOR THE NEW COLOR BUTTON.

Resource ID	Caption	Function
IDC_COLOR	&Color...	CMapModeDlg::OnColor

Using ClassWizard, add a new message-handling function to the CMapModeDlg class named CMapModeDlg::OnColor. The source code for OnColor is provided in Listing 12.8.

INPUT   **LISTING 12.8.** THE CMapModeDlg::OnColor MEMBER FUNCTION.

```
void CMapModeDlg::OnColor()
{
    CColorDialog    dlgColor;
    if( dlgColor.DoModal() == IDOK )
    {
        m_clrChoice = dlgColor.GetColor();
        // If the brush already exists, delete the current
        // GDI object before calling CreateSolidBrush
        if( m_brControl.Detach() )
            m_brControl.DeleteObject();
         m_brControl.CreateSolidBrush( m_clrChoice );
        InvalidateRect( NULL );
    }
}
```

The OnColor function creates a Common Color dialog box and displays it using DoModal. If the user selects a new color, the color is collected and the brush is updated. If the brush has previously been created, the Detach and DeleteObject functions must be called to destroy the current brush before creating a new brush.

12

Changing Dialog Box and Control Colors

Before displaying any control or dialog box, Windows asks for the control's color by sending a WM_CTLCOLOR message to the owner of the control. To specify a color to be used for the control or dialog box, return a solid brush containing the color in response to this message, as shown in Listing 12.9. The m_brControl brush is a class member variable because it must survive for the life of the control.

INPUT   **LISTING 12.9.** CHANGING THE COLOR OF A DIALOG BOX BY HANDLING WM_CTLCOLOR.

```
HBRUSH CMapModeDlg::OnCtlColor(CDC* pDC,CWnd* pWnd,UINT nCtlColor)
{
    if( nCtlColor == CTLCOLOR_DLG || nCtlColor == CTLCOLOR_STATIC )
    {
        pDC->SetBkMode( TRANSPARENT );
        return (HBRUSH)m_brControl.GetSafeHandle();
    }
    else
        return CDialog::OnCtlColor(pDC, pWnd, nCtlColor);
}
```

You should set the text drawing mode to transparent if you are drawing text on a colored background. In Listing 12.9, the text drawing mode is set to transparent by calling SetBkMode. If this line is commented out, you will see that the static text control has uncolored areas around the text. By setting the drawing mode to transparent, the text is drawn without including the text background color, allowing the dialog box color to show through.

The GetSafeHandle function is used with all GDI objects to return a handle to the underlying object. A CBrush object returns an HBRUSH handle; a CPen object returns an HPEN, and so on.

The WM_CTLCOLOR message is sent for every control type found in the dialog box. It's possible to set different colors for each control type by testing for the values found in Table 12.3. If a brush is not returned, determine the return value by calling CDialog::OnCtlColor.

TABLE 12.3. CONTROL-TYPE MESSAGE RETURN VALUE.

Control Message Value	Control Type
CTLCOLOR_BTN	Button control
CTLCOLOR_DLG ✓	Dialog box
CTLCOLOR_EDIT ✓	Edit control
CTLCOLOR_LISTBOX	List box control
CTLCOLOR_MSGBOX	Message box
CTLCOLOR_SCROLLBAR	Scrollbar control
CTLCOLOR_STATIC ✓	Static control

Updating the `CDCTestView` Class

The `CDCTestView` class must store the color and brush selected by the user to color the ellipse and Map Mode dialog box. One new variable is added to the attributes section of the `CDCTestView` class, as shown in Listing 12.10. The `m_clrChoice` variable stores the currently selected color for the ellipse.

INPUT   **LISTING 12.10.** CHANGES TO THE `CDCTestView` CLASS DECLARATION.

```
// Attributes
private:
    // Variables added for Hour 11
    CMap< int, int, CString, CString > m_map;
    int     m_nMapMode;
    // Variables added for Hour 12 - pens
    int     m_cxEllipse;
    int     m_cyEllipse;
    // Variable added for Hour 12 - brushes
    COLORREF m_clrChoice;
```

12

Using Brushes in `CDCTestView`

To update the DCTest project to use brushes instead of pens, you must make four basic changes to the `CDCTestView` member functions:

- All references to `m_nPenWidths` must be removed.
- The new variable, `m_clrChoice`, must be initialized in the constructor.
- The `OnViewMapMode` function must update the `m_clrChoice` variable if the user changes the color.
- The `OnDraw` function must be changed to use brushes instead of pens.

Edit the constructor for CDCTestView so it looks like the source code provided in
Listing 12.11. The m_nPenWidth variable has been removed, and one line has been added
to initialize the m_clrChoice variable.

LISTING 12.11. THE CDCTestView CONSTRUCTOR.

```
CDCTestView::CDCTestView()
{
    m_nMapMode = MM_TEXT;
    m_map.SetAt( MM_ANISOTROPIC, "MM_ANISOTROPIC" );
    m_map.SetAt( MM_HIENGLISH, "MM_HIENGLISH" );
    m_map.SetAt( MM_HIMETRIC, "MM_HIMETRIC" );
    m_map.SetAt( MM_ISOTROPIC, "MM_ISOTROPIC" );
    m_map.SetAt( MM_LOENGLISH, "MM_LOENGLISH" );
    m_map.SetAt( MM_LOMETRIC, "MM_LOMETRIC" );
    m_map.SetAt( MM_TEXT, "MM_TEXT" );
    m_map.SetAt( MM_TWIPS, "MM_TWIPS" );
    // The next two lines are added for Hour 12 - pens
    m_cxEllipse = 100;
    m_cyEllipse = 200;
    // The next line is added for Hour 12 - brushes
    m_clrChoice = RGB(0,0,0);
}
```

Modify the CDCTestView::OnViewMapMode function as shown in Listing 12.12. The code
in this listing removes all references to the m_nPenWidth variable, and the function now
tracks the color selected by the user. A total of two lines have been removed and one line
added to the existing function.

LISTING 12.12. THE OnViewMapMode FUNCTION.

```
void CDCTestView::OnViewMapMode()
{
    CMapModeDlg dlg;
    // The next two lines are added for Hour 12 - pens
    dlg.m_cxEllipse = m_cxEllipse;
    dlg.m_cyEllipse = m_cyEllipse;
    // The next line is added for Hour 12 - brushes
    dlg.m_clrChoice = m_clrChoice;
    CString szMapMode;
    m_map.Lookup(m_nMapMode, szMapMode);
    dlg.m_szCombo = szMapMode;    if( dlg.DoModal() == IDOK )
```

```
{
    // The next two lines are added for Hour 12 - pens
    m_cxEllipse = dlg.m_cxEllipse;
    m_cyEllipse = dlg.m_cyEllipse;
    // The next line is added for Hour 12 - brushes
    m_clrChoice = dlg.m_clrChoice;
    POSITION    pos;
    pos = m_map.GetStartPosition();
    while( pos != NULL )
    {
        CString szMapMode;
        int     nMapMode;
        m_map.GetNextAssoc( pos, nMapMode, szMapMode );
        if( szMapMode == dlg.m_szCombo )
        {
            m_nMapMode = nMapMode;
            break;
        }
    }
    InvalidateRect( NULL );
}
}
```

Modify the `CDCTestView::OnDraw` function as shown in Listing 12.13. The new version of OnDraw uses a CBrush object to fill the view window with a red brush. Another CBrush object is used to draw an ellipse in the center of the view using a user-defined color to fill the figure.

INPUT **LISTING 12.13.** THE OnDraw MEMBER FUNCTION MODIFIED TO USE BRUSHES.

12

```
void CDCTestView::OnDraw(CDC* pDC)
{
    CRect rcClient;
    GetClientRect( rcClient );
    pDC->DPtoLP( rcClient );
    CBrush  brBackground( RGB( 255, 255, 100 ) );
    pDC->FillRect( rcClient, &brBackground );
    CPoint  ptCenter( rcClient.Width()/2, rcClient.Height()/2 );
    CRect   rcEllipse( ptCenter.x - ( m_cxEllipse/2 ),
    ptCenter.y - ( m_cyEllipse/2 ),
    ptCenter.x + ( m_cxEllipse/2 ),
    ptCenter.y + ( m_cyEllipse/2 ) );
    CBrush  brEllipse( m_clrChoice );
    CBrush* pOldBrush = pDC->SelectObject( &brEllipse );
    pDC->Ellipse( rcEllipse );
    pDC->SelectObject( &pOldBrush );
}
```

Compile and run the DCTest project, and experiment by changing the values in the Map Mode dialog box. Also experiment with different colors for the dialog box and ellipse by clicking the Color button. Figure 12.5 shows an example of the DCTest project running.

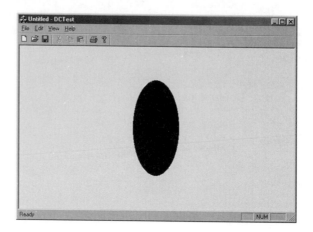

Summary

In this hour you learned about two GDI objects—pens and brushes—and how they are used to draw figures and fill shapes in Windows programs. You also learned about the MFC classes CPen and CBrush that are used to manage pen and brush objects. Finally, you modified the DCTest program to use the MFC CPen and CBrush classes.

Q&A

Q Can a pen and a brush be used at the same time?

A Yes; in fact, you are always drawing with both a pen and a brush. Earlier in this hour the ellipse and rectangle were drawn with specific pens; the shapes weren't filled in because the default brush for a device context is the hollow, or null brush. Because this brush has no effect no brush seems to be used.

Q Why aren't pushbuttons affected by handling WM_CTLCOLORBTN?

A The WM_CTLCOLORBTN message will affect radio buttons and check boxes, but not pushbuttons. To change the color of a pushbutton you must make it an owner-drawn pushbutton and take over responsibility for drawing every aspect of the button.

Workshop

The Workshop is designed to help you anticipate possible questions, review what you've learned, and begin thinking ahead to putting your knowledge into practice. The answers to the quiz are in Appendix A, "Quiz Answers."

Quiz

1. What are the three attributes of a pen?
2. What are the two types of pens?
3. What MFC class is used to manage pens?
4. What stock pens are maintained by Windows?
5. What styles are available for cosmetic pens?
6. What styles are available for geometric pens?
7. What are the four types of brushes?
8. What stock brushes are maintained by Windows?
9. What MFC class is used to manage brushes?
10. What function is used to draw a circle?

Exercises

1. Modify the DCTest example and change the edit control color to red.
2. Modify the DCTest example so that four objects are drawn in the view window:

    - A black rectangle
    - A red circle with a green border
    - A blue square with no border
    - A green circle with a blue border

12

HOUR 13

Fonts

Fonts define the symbols and characters used to display text in a Windows program. In this hour, you will learn

- The basic attributes that are available for fonts
- How to use the Common Font dialog box provided as part of Windows
- MFC class library support for creating and managing fonts

At the end of the hour is some sample code that extends the DCTest example to show how fonts are used in a Windows program.

What Are Fonts?

Fonts are GDI objects, much like the pens and brushes discussed in Hour 12, "Using Pens and Brushes," and are used to define the characters used for output in a Windows program. A collection of characters and other symbols that share the same attributes is a font.

Strictly speaking, it is not necessary to deal with fonts in most programs written for Windows. A default font is selected into every device context automatically, and it can work just fine for most applications. However, almost every program can benefit from using fonts that have been selected to suit its specific needs.

Fonts are maintained by Windows. Information about each currently installed font is stored in a system table known as the font table.

When you're working with text output, the MFC CFont class makes using a font easy. There are two basic ways to use a font in your program:

- You can specify exactly which font should be used.
- You can specify font-general attributes and let Windows select a font for you.

No matter which method you use, Windows will attempt to match your request with one of the fonts available on your system. If a reasonable match is available, the font will be created and returned to you.

After you have created a font you can't change any of its characteristics. If you want to provide text output using different character styles, you must create separate fonts for each character style.

Types of Fonts

There are three different types of fonts; each type has different characteristics:

- *Raster fonts* are created from bitmaps and are stored in resource files with an .FON extension. Each bitmap is created for a specific screen resolution and is used by Windows to map out exactly how the individual character will look when it is displayed.
- *Vector fonts* consist of a series of endpoints that are connected together to create each glyph and also are found in files with an .FON extension. Unlike raster fonts, vector fonts are device independent, but they are the slowest of the three font types.
- *TrueType fonts* are the most flexible of all Windows fonts. First introduced in Windows 3.1, TrueType fonts consist of line and curve information, as well as hints about each individual character. Each TrueType font is stored in two files: one with an .FOT extension, the other with a .TTF extension.

Scaleable fonts that can display italic, bold, or underlined text give a program an extra amount of usability. Most printers supported by Windows
allow TrueType fonts to be printed exactly as they appear on a video screen;
this is an extra advantage because it greatly simplifies the work required for
printing.

Font Families

Fonts are also arranged into six families that define the general attributes of the font.
Fonts in the same family share similar strokes, serifs, and pitch.

New Term The *font pitch* refers to the width of individual characters. Fixed pitch means that
each character has the same width, whereas variable pitch means that some characters will be wider than others.

New Term A *serif* is the small cross at the ends of some characters. A font with a serif has
short crosses at the ends of lines making up the font; Times New Roman is such
a serif font. A font without serifs is often called a sans-serif font. Figure 13.1 shows
examples of a serif and a sans-serif font.

Figure 13.1.

*Examples of serif and
sans serif fonts.*

The following are the six font families:

- *Decorative* specifies novelty fonts such as Old English.
- *Dontcare* specifies a generic group of fonts; either the font family information
  doesn't exist or the font family is unimportant.
- *Modern* specifies fonts that have fixed pitch and might or might not have serifs.
  Courier New is an example of a Modern font.
- *Roman* specifies fonts that have both variable pitch and serifs, such as Times New
  Roman.
- *Script* specifies fonts that are similar to handwriting.
- *Swiss* specifies a font that is fixed pitch and doesn't have serifs, such as Arial.

13

Specifying Font Attributes

In addition to the font families discussed earlier in this hour, you can use other general attributes to specify a font. Many font attributes exist, mainly because there are so many different ways to display characters. After you've used fonts a few times, you'll be able to create fonts with no trouble at all.

There are two ways to create a font using MFC:

- By calling the CFont::CreateFont function, passing the font's attributes as parameters

- By describing the font using a LOGFONT structure and passing the structure to the CFont::CreateFontIndirect function

> As discussed earlier, after a font is created its characteristics cannot be changed. If you need a font with a different attribute, you must create a new font.

The CreateFont member function is called for a CFont object, with several attributes passed as parameters:

```
CFont fnt;
fnt.CreateFont(100,              // Height
               0,                // Width
               0,                // Escapement
               0,                // Orientation
               FW_BOLD,          // Weight
               TRUE,             // Italic
               FALSE,            // Underline
               FALSE,            // Strikeout
               ANSI_CHARSET,     // Character set
               OUT_DEFAULT_PRECIS,   // Output precision
               CLIP_DEFAULT_PRECIS,  // Clipping precision
               DEFAULT_QUALITY,  // Quality
               DEFAULT_PITCH,    // Pitch and family
               "Arial");         // Typeface name
```

The LOGFONT structure is often used to describe a font. Just as the LOGBRUSH structure discussed in Hour 12, "Using Pens and Brushes," was used to describe a particular brush, the LOGFONT structure is used to describe a particular font. A LOGFONT isn't a font; it's just a description, so it contains members for all the attributes available for a font.

The LOGFONT structure has members that are identical to the parameters passed to CreateFont. The address of a LOGFONT structure is filled and passed to the CreateFontIndirect function:

```
LOGFONT lf;
ZeroMemory(&lf, sizeof(lf));
lf.lfWeight = FW_DEMIBOLD;
lf.lfHeight = 300;
lf.lfWidth = 50;
fnt.CreateFontIndirect(&lf);
```

As shown in the preceding code fragment, you don't need to provide a value for every member of the LOGFONT structure. If you clear the contents of the structure using the ZeroMemory function, default values will be assigned to any font attributes that you don't specify.

The next few sections describe each of the attributes that are used to describe fonts.

Font Height and Width Attributes

You can specify the height of the font using one of the following methods:

- If a height greater than zero is specified, Windows tries to match the requested height with one of the available fonts, and the font is mapped using logical units.
- If a font height of zero is specified, a reasonable default font is used. In this case, "reasonable" is defined by Windows.
- If the specified height is a negative number, the font is mapped using hardware units. Windows searches for a font that matches the absolute value of the size provided.

Logical units normally are used for screen display, and physical units are normally used for printing. In Hour 21, "Printing," you use MM_TWIPS to create fonts based on device units.

13

The width of a font normally is set to zero, which tells Windows to select an appropriate default width. However, in some cases you might want to specify your own font width to display compressed or elongated text.

The Font Character Set

One of the attributes that can be specified for a font is the character set. These three character sets are available:

- ANSI_CHARSET: Used for most output when programming in Windows. This is the character set you're most likely to use. The symbol ANSI_CHARSET is defined as equal to zero, which makes it easy to use as a default parameter.
- OEM_CHARSET: Used mainly for console-mode programs; it is almost identical to the ANSI character set. This character set is system dependent and can't be used reliably for every machine capable of running Windows. Some of the low- and high-numbered characters are different, but these are rarely used in Windows.
- SYMBOL_CHARSET: Used to display symbols such as the ones used in math formulas.

Attributes that Affect Font Output

Three parameters specify output attributes of the selected font: *output precision*, *clipping precision*, and *output quality*.

Output Precision of a Font

Output precision is used to specify how closely the font returned by Windows must match the requested font. A range of options is available, from allowing Windows to select a reasonable match to requiring an exact match.

- OUT_DEFAULT_PRECIS: Used when Windows can choose a "reasonable" font. This is the option selected most often and is equivalent to using zero as a parameter.
- OUT_STRING_PRECIS: Used to specify that the font chosen by Windows must match the requested font's size.
- OUT_CHARACTER_PRECIS: Used to specify that the font must match all requested attributes except orientation and escapement, which are defined later in the section "Other Font Attributes."
- OUT_STROKE_PRECIS: Used to specify that the font chosen must exactly match the requested font.

Clipping Precision of a Font

Clipping precision is used to specify how characters are treated when part of a character will be hidden or *clipped*. Clipping occurs when a font is used in an area that is too small to contain the text. There are three options:

- CLIP_DEFAULT_PRECIS: Allows Windows to select a "reasonable" font. This is the option selected most often and is equal to zero.

- `CLIP_CHARACTER_PRECIS`: Requires Windows to select a font that allows individual characters to be clipped if any part of the character lies outside the clipping region.

- `CLIP_STROKE_PRECIS`: Requires Windows to choose a font that allows portions of an individual character to be clipped if a character falls on the clipping boundary.

The Output Quality of a Font

The *output quality* of the font refers to the degree to which GDI routines must match logical font attributes to the physical representation of the font. Here, again, there are three options:

- `DEFAULT_QUALITY`: Appearance doesn't matter; Windows is free to provide a "reasonable" font. This is a commonly selected option and is equivalent to using zero as a parameter.

- `DRAFT_QUALITY`: Fast output is given higher priority than print quality. Some effects, such as strikethrough, bold, italic, and underlined characters, are synthesized by GDI routines if necessary.

- `PROOF_QUALITY`: The output quality is given higher priority than output speed. The quality of the font is more important than exact matching of the logical-font attributes. Some effects, such as strikethrough, bold, italics, and underlined characters, are synthesized by GDI routines if necessary.

Font Pitch and Family Attributes

All fonts have a certain pitch. When requesting a font from Windows, you have three different choices for the pitch:

- `DEFAULT_PITCH`: Windows selects a reasonable font, based on other specified attributes.

- `FIXED_PITCH`: The font created by Windows must have a fixed pitch.

- `VARIABLE_PITCH`: The font is specified to have a variable pitch.

As discussed earlier, the font family describes general characteristics for a type of font and can be used when a specific font might not be available on all machines. Here are the values for font families:

- `FF_DECORATIVE`

- `FF_DONTCARE`

- `FF_MODERN`

- `FF_ROMAN`

- `FF_SCRIPT`

- `FF_SWISS`

13

The pitch attribute can be combined with a font family attribute using the bitwise OR operator. For example, if you're using a LOGFONT, you can combine DEFAULT_PITCH and FF_SWISS like this:

```
lfHeading.lfPitchAndFamily = DEFAULT_PITCH | FF_SWISS;
```

> Combining the pitch and family attributes isn't necessary; often, the family name implies a pitch. In the preceding example, it's possible to specify just FF_SWISS.
>
> FF_ROMAN and FF_SWISS always imply a variable pitch. FF_MODERN always implies a fixed pitch. Other family types contain fonts that have both fixed and variable pitch.

Font Weight Attributes

You can specify the relative weight of a font based on a scale from 0 to 1,000. A weight of 400 describes a normal font, whereas 700 is used for a bold font. If you use 0, Windows uses a reasonable default weight for the font. Each of the weight options between 0 and 900 has a symbolic name, as shown in Table 13.1.

TABLE 13.1. SYMBOLIC NAMES FOR FONT WEIGHTS.

Symbol	Weight
FW_DONTCARE	0
FW_THIN	100
FW_EXTRALIGHT	200
FW_ULTRALIGHT	200
FW_LIGHT	300
FW_NORMAL	400
FW_REGULAR	400
FW_MEDIUM	500
FW_SEMIBOLD	600
FW_DEMIBOLD	600
FW_BOLD	700
FW_EXTRABOLD	800
FW_ULTRABOLD	800
FW_BLACK	900
FW_HEAVY	900

Although not every weight is available for every font, Windows tries to select a font weight close to the requested value.

Other Font Attributes

It's possible to define the escapement and orientation of a font. The *escapement* is the angle, in tenths of a degree, formed by a line of text in relation to the bottom of the page. Each degree in escapement adds 10 to the parameter value. For example, an escapement parameter value of 900 (90° × 10) describes a font where each line of text is rotated 90 degrees counterclockwise. The *orientation* of a font is similar to the escapement, but applies to each character rather than to an entire line of text.

Italic, underline, and strikethrough effects are assigned by specifying TRUE or FALSE for each of these attributes.

Finally, you can specify the typeface name. This is the name of a font that should be a good match for the parameters specified in other parts of the font description. If this parameter is set to NULL, Windows uses the other parameters when searching for a font. If you specify a name, that name is used to search for a font. If a font with that name is found, it is used.

Examples of Creating Fonts Using MFC

As discussed earlier, you can create a font by passing parameters to CFont member functions or by passing a LOGFONT structure to a CFont member function. If you are creating a small number of fonts, you can use the CFont class and its CreateFont member function. If you're creating several similar fonts or a large number of fonts, you can use the LOGFONT structure.

Creating a Font Using CFont

The first time you consider creating a CFont object, you might be intimidated by the large number of parameters it takes. Most of the parameters can actually be set to default values or zero, and the Windows font mapper selects a font for you.

Listing 13.1 shows how you can easily create an Arial font using CFont and CreateFont. All parameters are set to zero except for the font name, which is set to Arial. This code asks the font mapper to select a reasonable font, and specifies only that the font should have the name Arial.

13

LISTING 13.1. AN EASY WAY TO CREATE AND USE A CFont OBJECT.

```
void CMyView::OnDraw(CDC* pDC)
{
    CFont    fntArial;
    fntArial.CreateFont( 0, 0, 0, 0, 0, 0, 0, 0,
                         0, 0, 0, 0, 0, "Arial");
    CString szMsg = "Hello! I'm an Arial Font");
    CFont* pOldFont = pDC->SelectObject( &fntArial );
    pDC->TextOut( 0, 50, szMsg );

    // Restore the old GDI objects
    pDC->SelectObject( pOldFont );
}
```

As with all GDI objects, you must save the original font that is returned when a new font is selected into a device context. If you fail to select the original font into the device context when you're finished with the DC, you will create a resource leak.

Creating a Font Using a LOGFONT Structure

As discussed earlier, a LOGFONT structure simplifies creating multiple fonts because many of the attributes for a series of fonts can be shared. Listing 13.2 is a version of CDCTestView::OnDraw that uses a LOGFONT structure to create several different fonts. The CDCTestView class is part of the DCTest project that was originally created in Hour 11, "Device Contexts."

LISTING 13.2. USING A LOGFONT STRUCTURE TO CREATE FONTS.

```
void CDCTestView::OnDraw(CDC* pDC)
{
    CRect rcClient;
    GetClientRect( rcClient );
    pDC->DPtoLP( rcClient );
    COLORREF clrOld = pDC->SetTextColor( m_clrChoice );
    int nOldMode = pDC->SetBkMode( TRANSPARENT );
    CString szMsg = "Hello! I'm an Arial font";
    CFont    fntArial;
    LOGFONT lf;
    ZeroMemory( &lf, sizeof(LOGFONT) );
    lstrcpy( lf.lfFaceName, "Arial" );
    fntArial.CreateFontIndirect( &lf );
```

```
    CFont* pOldFont = pDC->SelectObject( &fntArial );
    pDC->TextOut( rcClient.Width()/2, rcClient.Height()/2, szMsg );
    pDC->SelectObject( pOldFont );
    pDC->SetTextColor( clrOld );
    pDC->SetBkMode( nOldMode );
}
```

Selecting and Configuring the Right Fonts

In the rest of this hour you learn two ways to simplify and improve your font-handling code:

- By using stock fonts provided by Windows
- By using the Font Selection common dialog box

You will also make some changes to the DCTest example so that the user can select a font for the application.

Using Stock Font Objects

Just as with stock pens and brushes, discussed in Hour 12, "Using Pens and Brushes," Windows maintains a set of stock fonts. Windows provides six stock fonts:

- ANSI_FIXED_FONT: A fixed-pitch system font.
- ANSI_VAR_FONT: A variable-pitch system font.
- DEVICE_DEFAULT_FONT: A device-dependent font. This stock object is available only on Windows NT.
- DEFAULT_GUI_FONT: The default font for user interface objects such as menus and dialog boxes.
- OEM_FIXED_FONT: The OEM-dependent fixed-pitch font.
- SYSTEM_FONT: The system font.

As with other stock objects, these fonts are used through a CDC object by calling the SelectStockObject function, passing the stock object as a parameter, as follows:

```
CPen* pOldFont = pDC->SelectStockObject(SYSTEM_FONT);
```

Setting the Font for a Window

You can change the font used by a control or any other window by calling the CWnd::SetFont function. The SetFont function takes a pointer to a CFont object as a parameter:

```
pCtrl->SetFont(fntWingDings);
```

13

If you change the font for a window, you must be careful to keep the font that is passed as a parameter valid for as long as the window exists.

Using the Common Font Dialog Box

Like the other common dialog boxes, the Common Font dialog box enables you, as a programmer, to easily use a commonly used dialog box in your Windows programs. The Common Font dialog box is extremely flexible from a user's point of view; the user can change the color, style, typeface, and size of the font in a single dialog box.

You use the Common Font dialog box to select a font to be used in the view window. This is illustrated in the following example.

Programming Fonts

As an example that demonstrates how the MFC CFont class can be used in your applications, you can modify the DCTest project that was used in Hours 11 and 12.

Adding Support For a Common Font Dialog Box

In this hour, you will modify the DCTest project so that the user can control the font used to display text output. The user can select the font using the Common Font dialog box, and the DCTest program will use that font when displaying text. The font is represented by a LOGFONT variable that is a member of the CDCTestView class. After selecting a new font with the Common Font dialog box, the LOGFONT variable is updated and the view redrawn.

Five steps are involved in adding support for the Common Font dialog box:

1. Add a new LOGFONT variable to the CDCTestView class.
2. Modify the CDCTestView constructor.
3. Create a new menu item for changing the font.
4. Create a function in the CDCTestView class to handle the new menu item.
5. Modify the CDCTestView::OnDraw member function so that the new LOGFONT variable is used when creating a font.

Just to make things interesting, you modify the OnDraw function to display the text rotated around the center of the view.

Adding a LOGFONT Variable to the CDCTestView Class

The first step is to add a LOGFONT variable to the CDCTestView class. Although the font is created and destroyed every time the OnDraw member function is called, the LOGFONT variable stores the current attributes for the font selected for the view. Add this line to the attributes section of the CDCTestView class declaration, just below the variables added in Hour 12:

```
LOGFONT     m_logFont;
```

The CDCTestView class constructor must initialize this variable to a known value. Listing 13.3 contains the source code for the new version of the CDCTestView constructor. Only the last two lines of the source code have been added since the previous version.

LISTING 13.3. SOURCE CODE TO INITIALIZE THE m_logFont VARIABLE.

```
CDCTestView::CDCTestView()
{
    m_nMapMode = MM_TEXT;
    m_map.SetAt( MM_ANISOTROPIC, "MM_ANISOTROPIC" );
    m_map.SetAt( MM_HIENGLISH, "MM_HIENGLISH" );
    m_map.SetAt( MM_HIMETRIC, "MM_HIMETRIC" );
    m_map.SetAt( MM_ISOTROPIC, "MM_ISOTROPIC" );
    m_map.SetAt( MM_LOENGLISH, "MM_LOENGLISH" );
    m_map.SetAt( MM_LOMETRIC, "MM_LOMETRIC" );
    m_map.SetAt( MM_TEXT, "MM_TEXT" );
    m_map.SetAt( MM_TWIPS, "MM_TWIPS" );
    m_cxEllipse = 100;
    m_cyEllipse = 200;
    m_clrChoice = RGB(0,0,0);
    ZeroMemory( &m_logFont, sizeof(LOGFONT) );
    lstrcpy( m_logFont.lfFaceName, "Arial" );
}
```

Add a New Menu Item

Using the Developer Studio resource editor, add a new menu item to the View menu, using the values from Table 13.2.

TABLE 13.2. VALUES USED FOR THE FONT MENU ITEM.

Resource ID	Caption	Member Function
ID_VIEW_FONT	&Font...	CDCTestView::OnViewFont

Use ClassWizard to add a message-handling function to the CDCTestView class for the new menu item, using the default name of OnViewFont. The source code for OnViewFont is shown in Listing 13.4.

13

LISTING 13.4. THE CDCTestView::OnViewFont MEMBER FUNCTION.

```
void CDCTestView::OnViewFont()
{
    CFontDialog dlgFont( &m_logFont );
    dlgFont.DoModal();
    m_clrChoice = dlgFont.GetColor();
    InvalidateRect( NULL );
}
```

[handwritten annotations:]
OPENFILENAME m-openfile;
CString m-pathname;
CFileDialog dlgFile (&m-openfile);
dlgFile. DoModal();
m-pathname = dlgFile. GetPathName
AfxMessageBox(m-pathname, MB_ICON
                                        INFo...

The source code in Listing 13.4 is the heart of this example. The current LOGFONT is passed during construction to the Common Font dialog box, which uses it as a starting point when the dialog box is initially displayed. After the user dismisses the dialog box, the LOGFONT will contain any modifications made by the user. Because the LOGFONT structure doesn't store the text color, the GetColor function is called to update any color selections made in the Common Font dialog box.

Modify the OnDraw Member Function

The final step in this example is to use the selected font to draw a rotating text message in the view. The lfEscapement field from the LOGFONT structure is used to specify the angle of the text line. The source code in Listing 13.5 updates the font's escapement in a for loop, causing the text to rotate.

LISTING 13.5. DISPLAYING A ROTATING TEXT MESSAGE USING A LOGFONT.

```
void CDCTestView::OnDraw(CDC* pDC)
{
    CRect rcClient;
    GetClientRect( rcClient );
    pDC->DPtoLP( rcClient );
    COLORREF clrOld = pDC->SetTextColor( m_clrChoice );
    int nOldMode = pDC->SetBkMode( TRANSPARENT );
    CString szMsg = "  ...Help! I'm Spinning and I can't get up!";
    CFont   fntRotate;
    for( int nDegrees = 0; nDegrees < 3600; nDegrees += 200 )
    {
        m_logFont.lfEscapement = nDegrees;
        fntRotate.CreateFontIndirect( &m_logFont );
        CFont* pOldFont = pDC->SelectObject( &fntRotate );
        pDC->TextOut( rcClient.Width()/2,
                      rcClient.Height()/2,
                      szMsg );
        pDC->SelectObject( pOldFont );
        fntRotate.DeleteObject();
    }
```

```
        pDC->SetTextColor( clrOld );
        pDC->SetBkMode( nOldMode );
}
```

The text will rotate around the center of the view, as shown in Figure 13.2. The font and color are updated when a new selection is made in the Common Font dialog box.

FIGURE 13.2.

The DCTest application with new fonts.

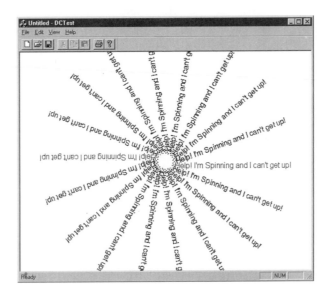

Summary

In this hour you learned about using fonts in Windows programs, as well as how to use the CFont and CFontDialog classes. Sample programs illustrated the use of the LOGFONT structure, the use of the Common Font dialog box, and rotating fonts.

Q&A

Q I have problems determining the correct text metrics for my device context. I call GetTextMetrics and then select my font into the device context. What am I doing wrong?

A The GetTextMetrics function returns information about the currently selected font—you must select the font into the device context before calling GetTextMetrics.

13

Q **If a family attribute has a default pitch can you override it? For example, what happens if you set the `lfPitchAndFamily` value to `FF_SWISS` and `FIXED_PITCH`?**

A When font parameters conflict with each other, a part of the Windows operating system known as the font mapper will try to match your request with a font based on other parameters. If it can't find a font that matches your requested font, it chooses a reasonable font. For example, if you specify a type face name, that name has precedence.

Q **When I change the font for a pushbutton control nothing happens—the original font is still used to display the caption for the button. What am I doing wrong?**

A This problem usually occurs when the `CFont` object is destroyed before the control is destroyed. The control doesn't copy the font passed to it during the `SetFont` function call—it must be available as long as the control exists. If you change the font for a control, you should make the `CFont` object a member of the `CDialog`-derived class that contains the control.

Workshop

The Workshop is designed to help you review what you've learned and begin thinking ahead to putting your knowledge into practice. The answers to the quiz and exercises are in Appendix A, "Quiz Answers."

Quiz

1. Give some examples of serif and sans-serif fonts.
2. What are the stock font objects maintained by Windows?
3. What is the font escapement attribute used for?
4. What MFC class is used to manage fonts?
5. What are the six font families?
6. What are the three pitch choices for a font?
7. What function is used to change the font used by a window?

Exercises

1. Modify the DCTest project so that a different font is used for the Color pushbutton.
2. Modify the DCTest project to display text metric information for the currently selected font.

HOUR 14

Icons and Cursors

Icons and cursors are two commonly used GDI objects. In this hour, you will learn how to

- Use icons in your MFC program
- Add icons to button controls
- Manage cursors in your MFC program

There are several examples in this hour; you will add icons to pushbutton controls, clip cursors to a specific rectangle, and change the cursor to an hourglass to indicate that a long process is in progress.

What Is an Icon?

NEW TERM An *icon* is a small bitmap that represents another object in a Windows program. Icons are used to represent minimized child windows in an MDI application. Icons also are widely used by Windows itself. When a program is minimized, its icon is displayed in the Windows taskbar. When you're using the Explorer, the icon representing an application associated with each file is displayed next to the file's name. Windows displays the program's icon in the upper-left corner of the main window title bar.

The Windows Explorer uses the icon resources associated with your program when determining which icons to display. If large and small icons are available, the Explorer uses the icon resources from your application's EXE file. However, if you provide only a large icon, the Explorer synthesizes a small icon, which can result in a small, distorted icon.

> Icons also are used in dialog boxes. For example, the message dialog boxes discussed in Hour 4, "Using Dialog Boxes," use icons to indicate the type of message conveyed. It's also common practice to include an application's icon in the About dialog box.

Types of Icons

There are several different types of icon resources. Four different types of icons are available:

- Large icons: Used for most programs written for Windows before the release of Windows 95, these icons are 32×32 pixels in size and support 16 colors.
- Small icons: First introduced with Windows 95, these icons are usually a smaller (16×16 pixels) version of a program's large icon.
- 256-color icons: These icons support more than the standard 16 colors available to other types of icons. These icons are 48×48 pixels in size and are never displayed as a program's icon when the window is minimized.
- Monochrome icons: These icons support only two colors and are 32×32 pixels.

Icons are similar to bitmaps, which are covered in Hour 16, "Using Bitmaps and Image Lists." However, the code required to use an icon is so simple that there's not even an icon MFC class. Instead, you manipulate an HICON, or handle to an icon, directly.

Creating Icons Using the Image Editor

Because icons are resources, you add them to a program's resource file just as you do bitmaps, menus, and dialog boxes. You create new icons using the resource editor.

When creating a new project, AppWizard creates a set of default icons for your project automatically. You can use the Developer Studio image editor to edit or create new icons for your project.

To open the image editor, open the ResourceView in the project workspace and then open the Icon folder. Double-click any icon resource contained in the folder to open the editor. In an MDI application created by AppWizard, two icon resources will be defined for a new project:

- IDR_MAINFRAME: An icon that is associated with the application; this is the MFC cube icon by default.
- IDR_MYAPPTYPE: Where MyApp is the name of the project. This icon is used to represent the MDI child window. By default, this icon is the standard MFC Doc icon.

The color palette is displayed whenever you are editing an image resource. The color palette consists of several colored boxes. To change the color of the current drawing tool, click the color you want. There are two special color icons in the color palette:

- The transparent color: The background shows through the icon
- The reverse video color: The background shows through after reversing the video

You can find the transparent and reverse video colors on the color palette. Switch to the transparent color by clicking the small video display icon with a green screen, and switch to the reverse video color by clicking the small video display with the red screen.

Inserting a New Icon Resource

To insert a new icon resource into an existing project, right-click the Icon folder in the resource view, and select Insert Icon from the pop-up menu; this opens the image editor with a blank icon, ready for editing. You can change attributes for icon resources, as with all resources, by double-clicking the edge of the icon resource or by pressing Alt+Enter on the keyboard.

Changing a Program's Icon

The icon used for a program is created by AppWizard when you initially create the project. To change this icon, open the image editor by double-clicking the application's icon in the resource view Icon folder.

Remember, every application written for Windows can have its icon displayed in large and small formats. If you edit one of the icon formats, make sure you make corresponding changes in all formats supported by the icon. To display and edit all the available formats, click the drop-down combo box above the image editor, which displays all the supported formats for the icon. Selecting a new format loads that version of the icon into the image editor.

Every child window type also has a unique icon. You can edit a child window's icon just as you do the program's main icon.

14

Loading an Icon in Your Programs

After you have added an icon to a project, loading and displaying it requires three lines of code. Depending on your application, your code may be in one of several places, but the basic steps are the same for all applications. For example, to display an icon in a view, you would add code to the view's OnDraw function.

To load an icon and prepare it for display, use the LoadIcon function to return a handle to the icon:

```
HICON hIcon = AfxGetApp()->LoadIcon( IDI_LOGO );
```

Because LoadIcon is a CWinApp member function, a pointer to the application's CWinApp object must be fetched using the AfxGetApp function.

After the icon has been loaded, display it by calling DrawIcon:

```
pDC->DrawIcon( 0,0, hIcon );
```

The DrawIcon function is a member of the CDC class. The coordinates and icon handle must be passed as parameters.

After using LoadIcon, release the icon resource by calling the DestroyIcon function:

```
DestroyIcon( hIcon );
```

> If you forget to call DestroyIcon, the memory allocated for the icon isn't released.

Displaying an Icon on a Button

Another useful way to use an icon is to display it in a button. Beginning with Windows 95, it's possible to display an icon in a button almost as easily as displaying a text string. Use the CButton member function SetIcon to set a button's icon. The icon must be loaded before it is used, and it must be destroyed after the button is destroyed.

Adding New Icon Resources to the Sample Program

As an example, add two buttons to the About dialog box from the DCTest project used in the previous hour. These two "stop-light" buttons work just like the traditional OK and Cancel buttons. Figure 14.1 shows the IDI_RED and IDI_GREEN icons. Although you can't tell from the figure, the icons consist of colored circles (one red and one green) surrounded by the transparent color. You will use these icons to label buttons in the DCTest About dialog box.

FIGURE 14.1.

The new icons used in the DCTest example.

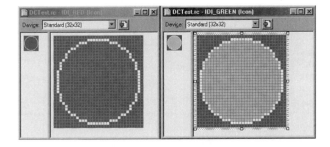

Modify the IDD_ABOUTBOX dialog box by adding an extra button to it, as shown in Figure 14.2.

FIGURE 14.2.

The About dialog box used in the Icon example.

Use the values from Table 14.1 to set the attributes for the two buttons in the About dialog box. Use ClassWizard to add the two buttons to the CAboutDlg class as CButton variables.

TABLE 14.1. VALUES USED FOR BUTTON CONTROLS IN THE DCTEST ABOUT DIALOG BOX.

ID	Variable Name	Control Type	Attributes
IDOK	m_btnOkay	CButton	Visible, Tabstop, Icon, Default
IDCANCEL	m_btnCancel	CButton	Visible, Tabstop, Icon

Buttons that have icon labels instead of text must have the Icon attribute set. Review each button's Properties dialog box under the Styles tab and make sure the Icon option is checked.

Working with Icon Handles

You must set up variables to store the handles of the icons displayed on the dialog box buttons. Add two new variables to the CAboutDlg class. Add the source code from Listing 14.1 to the Implementation section of the CAboutDlg project. Also, add a declaration for a destructor for the CAboutDlg class, just after the constructor declaration.

14

INPUT   **LISTING 14.1.** ADDITIONS TO THE CAboutDlg CLASS DECLARATION.

```
// Implementation
public:
    ~CAboutDlg();
protected:
    HICON    m_hIconOkay;
    HICON    m_hIconCancel;
```

The icons are added to the dialog box's buttons when the dialog box receives the
WM_INITDIALOG message. Using ClassWizard, add a message-handling function for
WM_INITDIALOG to the CAboutDlg class. Use the default name provided by ClassWizard,
OnInitDialog. Edit the OnInitDialog member function so it looks like the code provided
in Listing 14.2.

INPUT   **LISTING 14.2.** THE AboutDlg::OnInitDialog MEMBER FUNCTION.

```
BOOL CAboutDlg::OnInitDialog()
{
    CDialog::OnInitDialog();
    CWinApp* pApp = AfxGetApp();
    if( pApp != 0 )
    {
        m_hIconOkay = pApp->LoadIcon( IDI_GREEN );
        m_hIconCancel = pApp->LoadIcon( IDI_RED );
        ASSERT(m_hIconOkay);
        ASSERT(m_hIconCancel);
        m_btnOkay.SetIcon( m_hIconOkay );
        m_btnCancel.SetIcon( m_hIconCancel );
    }
    return TRUE;
}
```

ANALYSIS   The source code in Listing 14.2 loads the two stop-light icons created earlier.
After the icons are loaded, the icon handles are passed to the SetIcon function
for each of the buttons contained in the dialog box.

> When an icon is drawn on a button, the icon is clipped if necessary. The icon
> isn't scaled to fit inside the button; it is displayed "actual size." This might
> mean that you must experiment with the relative sizes of the icon and the
> button.

As the dialog box is destroyed, the icons previously loaded using LoadIcon must be destroyed. Use the source code from Listing 14.3 to create the CAboutDlg class destructor, and add it to the DCTest.cpp source file.

INPUT

LISTING 14.3. USING THE CAboutDlg CLASS DESTRUCTOR TO DESTROY THE PREVIOUSLY LOADED ICONS.

```
CAboutDlg::~CAboutDlg()
{
    DestroyIcon( m_hIconOkay );
    DestroyIcon( m_hIconCancel );
}
```

Compile and run the DCTest example. Figure 14.3 shows the DCTest About box with icons placed in the pushbutton controls.

FIGURE 14.3.

The DCTest dialog box after adding icons to the pushbutton controls.

What Is a Cursor?

NEW TERM

A *cursor* is the little bitmap that moves around the screen providing feedback about the current mouse position. The cursor also provides other types of feedback:

- If the application is busy and won't accept input, most applications change the regular cursor to the hourglass cursor.
- If the cursor is over a window or control that accepts text input, most applications change the regular cursor to the I-beam cursor.

The most commonly used cursors are supplied by Windows. The hourglass, I-beam, and arrow cursors are three of the more popular standard cursors. In addition, each program can have application-specific cursor resources.

The cursor is an important part of the feedback supplied to a user of a Windows program. Changing the style of cursor is an easy way to alert the user that a change of some type has occurred. Many times, changing the cursor is the only type of feedback required.

14

Using Cursors in Windows Programs

Most window classes have a cursor assigned to the class—in almost all cases it's the standard arrow cursor. This means that for most default behavior, you don't have to do anything to use a cursor; Windows provides it free of charge. However, there are some situations in which you must take control over the cursor yourself. For the examples in this hour, create an SDI project named Cursor that will demonstrate how cursors are used in a Visual C++ project.

Creating a Cursor Resource

You create a cursor image using the Developer Studio image editor, much like icons were created earlier this hour. Figure 14.4 shows the cursor used in later examples ready for editing in the image editor.

FIGURE 14.4.

The IDC_BANG *cursor inside the Developer Studio image editor.*

Create the cursor shown in Figure 14.4 and name it IDC_BANG. To create a cursor resource, right-click in the resource view window and choose Insert from the pop-up menu; then select Cursor from the Resource Type dialog box. The editing tools you use to create a cursor are the same ones you used to create icons earlier in this hour. The standard Windows naming convention is for cursors to have names beginning with IDC_.

Adding a Hotspot to a Cursor

NEW TERM   A *hotspot* is the actual point that determines the current cursor position. Every cursor has a hotspot. The hotspot for the arrow cursor is located at the very tip of the arrow. The default hotspot for a cursor is the upper-left corner of the cursor. The cursor-image editor enables you to move the hotspot to a position that is reasonable for the cursor image.

For example, the IDC_BANG cursor you created in the previous section will not work properly if a new hotspot isn't defined. Because the current hotspot is part of the background, this cursor won't work as well for operations in which the mouse clicks must be accurate. One solution, as shown in Figure 14.5, is to modify the cursor to add a well-defined hotspot to the cursor—in this case a bull's-eye, or target, in the upper-left corner of the cursor bitmap.

FIGURE 14.5.

The new version of IDC_BANG, with a hotspot and a bulls-eye.

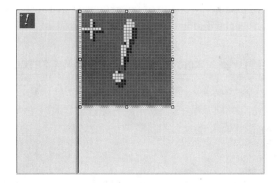

The hotspot control is a button located above the edited image. Click the hotspot button and then click the new hotspot pixel. For IDC_BANG, create a new hotspot in the center of the bull's-eye.

Changing a Cursor

Changing the current mouse cursor is probably the most common cursor-related activity in Windows programming. The operating system sends a WM_SETCURSOR message to a window as the mouse cursor passes over it. You can use this message to change the cursor, or you can let Windows choose the cursor that was defined for the window when it was registered.

To change the current cursor for a window, you handle the WM_SETCURSOR message. Using ClassWizard, add a message-handling function for WM_SETCURSOR to the CAboutDlg class. Listing 14.4 contains source code for OnSetCursor that changes the cursor to IDC_BANG.

14

LISTING 14.4. CHANGING THE CURSOR DURING WM_SETCURSOR.

```
BOOL CAboutDlg::OnSetCursor(CWnd* pWnd, UINT nHitTest,
                                        UINT message)
{
    // Load and set the new cursor. Return TRUE to stop
    // further processing of this message.
    CWinApp* pApp = AfxGetApp();
    HICON hIconBang = pApp->LoadCursor( IDC_BANG );
    SetCursor( hIconBang );
    return TRUE;
}
```

Conditionally Changing a Cursor

It's often convenient to change a cursor conditionally; for example, based on the cursor's location. Listing 14.5 is a new version of OnSetCursor that restores the arrow cursor when the cursor is over the dialog box's OK button.

LISTING 14.5. CONDITIONALLY CHANGING THE CURSOR DURING WM_SETCURSOR.

```
BOOL CAboutDlg::OnSetCursor(CWnd* pWnd, UINT nHitTest,
                                        UINT message)
{
    BOOL    bReturn;
    CRect   rcBtn;
    CPoint  ptCursor;
    //
    // Calculate the current cursor position, and change the
    // cursor if we're not over the OK button.
    //
    CWnd*   pBtn = GetDlgItem( IDOK );
    pBtn->GetWindowRect( rcBtn );
    GetCursorPos( &ptCursor );
    if( rcBtn.PtInRect( ptCursor ) == FALSE )
    {
        // Load and set the new cursor. Return TRUE to stop
        // further processing of this message.
        CWinApp* pApp = AfxGetApp();
        HICON hIconBang = pApp->LoadCursor( IDC_BANG );
        SetCursor( hIconBang );
        bReturn = TRUE;
    }
```

```
    else
    {
        // We're over the OK button, use the default cursor.
        bReturn = CDialog::OnSetCursor(pWnd, nHitTest, message);
    }
    return bReturn;
}
```

ANALYSIS The two key lines in Listing 14.5 retrieve the current mouse cursor position as a
CPoint object. The CPoint object is tested to see whether it is inside the boundary of the OK pushbutton:

```
GetCursorPos( &ptCursor );
if( rcBtn.PtInRect( ptCursor ) == FALSE )
{
    // cursor not over rectangle
}
```

Using the Standard Cursors

Windows provides 19 standard cursors for use in your programs. These cursors often are
used by Windows. For example, the IDC_APPSTARTING cursor is displayed when an application is launched by Windows. Table 14.2 lists the names and descriptions of the 19
standard cursors.

TABLE 14.2. THE STANDARD CURSORS PROVIDED BY WINDOWS.

Cursor Name	Description
IDC_ARROW	Arrow cursor
IDC_IBEAM	I-beam cursor
IDC_WAIT	Hourglass cursor
IDC_CROSS	Crosshair cursor
IDC_UPARROW	Up-arrow cursor
IDC_SIZENWSE	Sizing cursor, points northwest and southeast
IDC_SIZENESW	Sizing cursor, points northeast and southwest
IDC_SIZEWE	Sizing cursor, points west and east
IDC_SIZENS	Sizing cursor, points north and south
IDC_SIZEALL	Sizing cursor, points north, south, east, and west
IDC_NO	"No" cursor (circle with a slash through it)
IDC_APPSTARTING	Application-starting cursor

14

continues

TABLE 14.2. CONTINUED

Cursor Name	Description
IDC_HELP	Help cursor
IDI_APPLICATION	Application icon
IDI_HAND	Stop sign icon
IDI_QUESTION	Question mark icon
IDI_EXCLAMATION	Exclamation point icon
IDI_ASTERISK	Asterisk or information icon
IDI_WINLOGO	Windows logo icon

Using these cursors is similar to using stock objects. Listing 14.6 uses the IDC_UPARROW cursor in response to WM_SETCURSOR.

LISTING 14.6. USING A STANDARD WINDOWS CURSOR.

```
BOOL CAboutDlg::OnSetCursor(CWnd* pWnd, UINT nHitTest,
                           UINT message)
{
    // Load and set the new cursor. Return TRUE to stop
    // further processing of this message.
    CWinApp* pApp = AfxGetApp();
    HICON hIcon = pApp->LoadStandardCursor( IDC_UPARROW );
    SetCursor( hIcon );
    return TRUE;
}
```

A cursor set in response to the WM_SETCURSOR message will interfere with the remaining examples in the hour. After you are finished with this example, remove the OnSetCursor function using ClassWizard.

Changing the Cursor to the Hourglass

User input is often ignored during long initialization routines. Often a user interface is displayed, but user input is discarded until the initialization is complete. The initialization period can cause a noticeable delay before an application is ready for input, particularly in applications that work with large amounts of data. In these cases, you should use the BeginWaitCursor and EndWaitCursor functions.

When a large amount of processing is performed, it's common to ignore input from the user. It's considered good manners for a Windows program to change the cursor to an hourglass when user input won't be acknowledged.

To demonstrate how these functions are used, add two message-handling functions to the CAboutDlg class using ClassWizard. Add message-handling functions for WM_TIMER and WM_INITDIALOG and accept the default function names provided by ClassWizard. Listing 14.7 contains the source code for the OnInitDialog and OnTimer functions.

LISTING 14.7. MODIFYING OnInitDialog AND OnTimer TO USE THE HOURGLASS CURSOR.

```
BOOL CAboutDlg::OnInitDialog()
{
    CDialog::OnInitDialog();
    SetCapture();
    BeginWaitCursor();
    SetTimer( 1, 15000, NULL );
    return TRUE;
}

void CAboutDlg::OnTimer(UINT nIDEvent)
{
    ReleaseCapture();
    EndWaitCursor();
    KillTimer( 1 );
}
```

ANALYSIS In Listing 14.7, the OnInitDialog function simulates the beginning of a long processing period. The SetCapture and BeginWaitCursor functions are called to change the cursor to an hourglass. While changed, the cursor cannot be used to interact with any controls. A five-second timer is started, which calls the OnTimer function when the timer expires. The OnTimer function restores the cursor and kills the timer.

The order of the statements in OnInitDialog is important. Before calling BeginWaitCursor, the mouse must be captured using SetCapture; otherwise, the hourglass cursor immediately reverts to the arrow cursor.

14

Summary

In this hour you learned how to use icons in Windows programs. You learned how to change the main program icon, as well as child icons. You used a sample program to learn the functions used to load, draw, and destroy icon resources. You also learned how to use cursors to provide feedback when programming Windows applications.

Q&A

Q **What are the advantages of providing an icon for a button versus using the MFC `CBitmapButton` class?**

A Assigning an icon to a button is much simpler than using the `CBitmapButton` class. It is also more efficient because Windows will handle drawing the image instead of the MFC class library.

Q **The `CDC::DrawIcon` function will only draw an icon the size of its original image. How can I draw an icon larger than its original size?**

A You can use the `DrawIconEx` function to draw an icon to an arbitrary size. Unlike `DrawIcon`, the `DrawIconEx` function isn't a member of the `CDC` class. You must pass the internal handle used by the `CDC` object as the first parameter in the call to `DrawIconEx`, as shown in the `OnDraw` function:

```
void CMyTestView::OnDraw(CDC* pDC)
{
    CRect rc;
    GetClientRect(&rc);
    HICON hIcon = AfxGetApp()->LoadIcon(IDI_TEST);
    DrawIconEx(pDC->m_hDC,
               0,
               0,
               hIcon,
               rc.Width(),
               rc.Height(),
               0,
               NULL,
               DI_NORMAL);
    DestroyIcon(hIcon);
}
```

The really interesting parameters passed to `DrawIconEx` are parameters five and six; these are the width and height of the final image.

Workshop

The Workshop is designed to help you anticipate possible questions, review what you've learned, and begin thinking ahead to putting your knowledge into practice. The answers to the quiz are in Appendix A, "Quiz Answers."

Quiz

1. What function is used to associate an icon with a pushbutton?
2. What is the name of the area on the cursor that is used as the current mouse location?
3. What function is used to trap all mouse messages?
4. What function is used to change the current cursor?
5. What message must be handled in order to change the current cursor?
6. What is the size of an application's small icon?
7. What function is used to change to the hourglass cursor?

Exercise

1. Modify Listing 14.5 so that the hourglass cursor is shown unless the mouse is over the OK or Cancel button.

14

PART V
Common Controls

Hour

Hour **15**

Spin, Progress, and Slider Controls

In this hour, you will learn about controls that were first offered in Windows 95:

- The spin control, also known as the up-down control
- The slider control, also known as the trackbar control
- The progress control

The Common Controls

When Windows 95 was released, it included several brand-new controls. These controls, known collectively as the common controls, added exciting features to the Windows user interface. The controls covered in this book, along with their associated MFC classes, are shown in Table 15.1.

TABLE 15.1. SOME COMMON CONTROLS AND THEIR MFC CLASSES.

Control	Class
Spin (Up-down)	CSpinButtonCtrl
Progress	CProgressCtrl
Slider (Trackbar)	CSliderCtrl
Image List	CImageList
List	CListCtrl
Tree	CTreeCtrl

The Spin Control

The spin control, often called the up-down control, is a pair of small arrows that resemble the ends of a scrollbar but are smaller. Spin controls are often used to adjust the value of another control that is associated with the spin control.

 The control that is paired with the spin control is known as the *buddy control*. The buddy control is normally an edit control.

A spin control can also be aligned horizontally. A horizontal spin control is not called a left-right control; it keeps its original name.

By default, clicking the up arrow decreases the value of the buddy control, and clicking the down arrow increases the value contained in the buddy control. The up and down arrows work a lot like a scrollbar in a word-processing document—clicking the up arrow moves you to a lower-numbered page, clicking the down arrow moves you to a higher-numbered page. This behavior is confusing to most people; fortunately, it's easy to change, as you see in the section "Changing the Behavior of the Spin Control."

Spin controls are ideal for situations in which a set of values can be scrolled by a user. If the user must adjust the values by only a few units, a spin control is perfect because it enables the user to select a new value with only a few mouse clicks.

A spin control is very easy to use. To use the default functionality of the spin control, you must write exactly zero lines of source code! Even the most advanced uses for spin controls require just a few lines of source code; ClassWizard writes most of the code.

Using the Spin Control

For the examples in this hour, you use a dialog box-based project named Controls. This project starts with a spin control; later in the chapter, you add a slider and a progress control. To create the Controls project, use AppWizard to create a new project workspace. Select a dialog box-based project and click the Finish button.

Adding a Spin Control to a Dialog Box

Adding a spin control to the Controls dialog box is just like adding other controls. Open the main dialog box in the dialog box editor by selecting the ResourceView tab in the project workspace and opening the Dialog folder. Open the IDD_CONTROLS_DIALOG by double-clicking the dialog box icon or by right-clicking the icon and selecting Open from the pop-up menu. To place the spin control, you can either drag and drop the control from the control palette to the main dialog box, or you can select the spin control on the tool palette using the mouse and then click the desired position in the main dialog box.

Spin Control Properties

As with other controls, spin controls have properties that you can change using the Developer Studio resource editor. You can get to the properties by right-clicking the control and selecting Properties from the pop-up menu. The properties available for a spin control include the following:

- *ID* is used for the spin control's resource ID. A default resource ID, such as IDC_SPIN1, is supplied by Developer Studio.

- *Visible* is used to indicate that the control is initially visible. This check box is usually checked.

- *Disabled* is used to indicate the control should be initially disabled. This check box is usually cleared.

- *Group* is used to mark the first control in a group. This check box is usually cleared.

- *Tab Stop* indicates that this control can be reached by pressing Tab on the keyboard. This check box is usually left unchecked; this is different from most controls because the spin control is typically used to change the value of the buddy control. Normally the buddy control has the tabstop property enabled.

- *Help ID* indicates that a context-sensitive help ID should be generated for this control.

- *Orientation* indicates whether the spin control should be vertical or horizontal. The default selection is vertical.

- *Alignment* specifies how the buddy control and spin control are associated with each other. Possible values are Right, Left, and Unattached. The default value is Unattached, but in most cases you should select Left or Right.

- *Auto Buddy* indicates whether the spin control should use the previous control in the tab order as its buddy control. This check box is cleared by default but should be checked in most cases. If this box is not checked, the spin control will not be associated with a buddy control. You can still form this association by command, which is discussed in the next section.

- *Set Buddy Integer* indicates that the spin control should set the value of the attached buddy control. This check box is cleared by default but should be checked in most cases.

- *No Thousands* indicates that no separator should be provided for a value greater than 1,000 in the spin control. This check box is usually cleared.

- *Wrap* indicates that the spin control should "wrap around" after reaching its minimum or maximum value. If this option is not selected, the spin control stops after reaching its minimum or maximum limit. This check box is usually cleared.

- *Arrow Keys* indicates that the keyboard's arrow keys can be used to change the value of the spin control. This check box is usually cleared.

- *Hot Track* indicates that hot tracking should be enabled for this control.

In your sample program, change the control's resource ID to IDC_SPIN. All other properties should be set to their default values.

Adding a Buddy Control

The easiest way to add a buddy control to a spin control requires no source code; instead, you use the dialog box editor. Follow these steps to associate an edit control with a spin control:

1. Add an edit control to the dialog box. Most users expect the spin control to be placed against the buddy control; it helps emphasize the connection between the two controls.

2. Give the buddy control an ID. For your example, open the properties dialog box for the edit control and change the resource ID to IDC_EDIT. All other properties should be set to their default values.

3. Set the tab order for the edit control so that it is the control immediately before the spin control.

You can select the tab order by choosing Tab Order from the Layout menu (or press Ctrl+D). Each control is displayed with a small label that represents the control tab order. To change the tab order, use the mouse to click each control in the new tab order sequence.

4. Set an alignment property for the spin control. For the Controls project, the spin control is placed on the right side of the buddy control. Open the properties dialog box for the spin control and set the alignment value to Right.

5. Keep the Properties dialog box open and check the Auto Buddy and Set Buddy Integer check boxes.

The IDD_CONTROLS_DIALOG with a spin control and the buddy edit control is shown in Figure 15.1.

FIGURE 15.1.

The main dialog box used in the Controls sample program, including the spin control and buddy control.

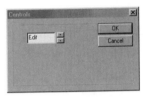

Believe it or not, that's all there is to using a spin control. If you compile and execute the Controls project, you can use the spin control to change the value contained in the edit control.

Assigning a tab stop to a spin control tends to confuse the user. The focus feedback given to the user is very subtle and easily overlooked. Also, the buddy control and spin button are normally paired into a single logical control. For these reasons, you should not set the tab stop property for the spin control in most cases.

To set, validate, or retrieve the value of the edit control, use ClassWizard to associate a CEdit object with the edit control or use one of the other techniques discussed in Chapter 6, "Using Edit Controls."

Using the CSpinButtonCtrl Class

The MFC class CSpinButtonCtrl can be used to manage a spin control. Use ClassWizard to associate the IDC_SPIN control in your sample program with a CSpinButtonCtrl object, using the values from Table 15.2.

TABLE 15.2. VALUES USED TO ADD A `CSpinButtonCtrl` MEMBER VARIABLE FOR `CControlsDlg`.

Control ID	Variable Name	Category	Type
IDC_SPIN	m_spin	Control	CSpinButtonCtrl

Changing the Behavior of the Spin Control

As discussed earlier, the default behavior for a spin control is to increment the control if the down arrow is clicked and decrement the control if the up arrow is clicked. You can change this behavior by reversing the range of the spin control.

To change the range of a spin control, use the `CSpinButtonCtrl`'s `SetRange` function. `SetRange` has two parameters: the first parameter is the lower-limit value for the control, the second parameter is the upper limit:

```
m_spin.SetRange( 0, 100 );
```

To set a new range for the spin control, add the source code from Listing 15.1 to the `CControlsDlg::OnInitDialog` member function. This source code should be added just after the `// TODO` comment.

INPUT   **LISTING 15.1.** SETTING THE RANGE FOR A SPIN CONTROL.

```
// TODO: Add extra initialization here
    m_spin.SetRange( 0, 100 );
```

Other `CSpinButtonCtrl` member functions are listed in Table 15.3.

TABLE 15.3. MEMBER FUNCTIONS FOR THE `CSpinButtonCtrl` CLASS.

Function	Description
SetAccel	Adjusts change rate for the spin position
GetAccel	Returns change rate for the spin position
SetBase	Sets the base for the spin position (10 or 16)
GetBase	Returns the base for the position (10 or 16)
SetPos	Sets the current spin position
GetPos	Returns the current spin position

15

Compile and execute the Controls project. The spin control now increments the edit control when its up arrow is clicked and decrements the edit control when the down arrow is clicked. This gives the spin control the behavior that most users expect.

Using the Slider Control

NEW TERM   A *slider control*, also known as a trackbar control, is a control that contains a slide bar that you can move between two points. A slider is used in the Display applet that is part of the Windows Control Panel. The Settings property page uses a slider to set the screen resolution.

The user moves the slide bar by dragging it with the mouse or by setting the keyboard focus to the slider and using the arrow keys on the keyboard. You can create sliders with optional tick marks that help the user to judge the position of the slide bar.

Deciding When to Use a Slider Control

Sliders are useful when a user is asked to select a value within a certain range. A slider gives the user immediate feedback about the control's current value, as well as the value's relationship to the high and low ranges.

Sliders are added to dialog boxes just like other controls; just drag and drop the control from the Controls palette to the dialog box. Although you can create a slider from scratch, adding one in the Developer Studio dialog box editor is much easier.

Open the IDD_CONTROLS_DIALOG resource and add a slider control by dragging a slider control from the control palette and dropping it on the dialog box. Figure 15.2 shows the Controls dialog box after you add the slider control.

FIGURE 15.2.

The main dialog box from the Controls project after you add a slider control.

Slider Control Properties

The Properties dialog box for a slider control contains many of the same options offered for spin controls, as well as a few that are exclusive to slider controls. The available options include the following:

- *ID* is used for the slider's resource ID. A default resource ID, such as IDC_SLIDER1, is supplied by Developer Studio.

- *Visible* is used to indicate that the control is initially visible. This check box is usually checked.
- *Disabled* is used to indicate the control should be initially disabled. This check box is usually cleared.
- *Group* is used to mark the first control in a group. This check box is usually cleared.
- *Tab Stop* indicates that this control can be reached by pressing Tab on the keyboard. This check box is usually checked.
- *Help ID* indicates that a context-sensitive help ID should be generated for this control.
- *Orientation* is used to specify whether the slider is vertical or horizontal. The default value is vertical.
- *Point* is used to indicate the position of optional tick marks. There are three options: Top/Left, Bottom/Right, or Both. The default value is Bottom/Right.
- *Tick Marks* indicates that tick marks should be drawn for the slider. This check box is usually cleared.
- *Auto Ticks* indicates that tick marks should be drawn at intervals along the slider control. This check box is usually cleared.
- *Enable Selection* enables the slider to be used to select a range of values. This check box is usually cleared.
- *Border* is used to specify that a border should be drawn around the control. This check box is usually checked.

In the next section, you use a slider to control a progress control. To prepare for that example, open the properties dialog box for your slider control and make sure the following slider properties are set:

- Set the ID to IDC_SLIDER
- Enable Tick Marks
- Enable Auto Ticks
- Enable Selection

Using the Progress Control

NEW TERM   A *progress control*, also known as a progress bar, is commonly used to indicate the progress of an operation and is usually filled from left to right as the operation is completed. You can also use progress controls to indicate temperature, water level, or similar measurements. In fact, an early term for this type of control was "Gas Gauge," back in the old days when programmers had mules and most Windows programs were written in C.

Progress controls are used in Developer Studio to indicate the progress of saving or loading a project workspace. Progress controls are also used by the Windows Explorer when copying or moving files.

> Progress controls are an easy way to give feedback to the user about the status of a task. Instead of waiting an unknown length of time, the user can see what portion of a job has yet to be completed.

CProgressCtrl member functions are listed in Table 15.4.

TABLE 15.4. MEMBER FUNCTIONS FOR THE CProgressCtrl CLASS.

Function	Description
SetRange	Sets the allowed range for the control
SetRange32	Same as SetRange, but also repaints the control
GetRange	Returns the allowed range for the control
SetPos	Sets the current progress bar position
GetPos	Returns the current progress bar position
OffsetPos	Increments the current progress bar position
SetStep	Sets the step amount for the progress bar
StepIt	Increments the position by the step amount

A progress control is added to a dialog box in the same way as the spin and slider controls discussed earlier. Using the Developer Studio dialog box editor, add a progress control to the Controls project main dialog box. Figure 15.3 shows the main dialog box from the Controls project after the progress control has been added.

FIGURE 15.3.

The Controls dialog box after adding the progress control.

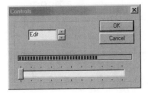

The available property options include the following:

- *ID* is used for the progress control's resource ID. A default resource ID, such as IDC_PROGRESS1, is supplied by Developer Studio.
- *Visible* is used to indicate that the control is initially visible. This check box is usually checked.
- *Disabled* is used to indicate the control should be initially disabled. This check box is usually cleared.
- *Group* is used to mark the first control in a group. This check box is usually cleared.
- *Tab Stop* indicates that this control can be reached by pressing Tab on the keyboard. This check box is usually checked.
- *Help ID* indicates that a context-sensitive help ID should be generated for this control.
- *Border* is used to specify that a border should be drawn around the control. This check box is usually checked.
- *Vertical* is used to indicate that the progress control should be aligned vertically rather than horizontally.
- *Smooth* is used to specify that the progress color should be drawn as one solid bar.

After you add the control to your sample program, open the properties dialog box and change the resource ID to IDC_PROGRESS. The rest of the properties can be left with their default values.

Using a Slider to Update a Progress Control

In this section, you use the IDC_SLIDER slider control to change the value displayed by the progress control. Using ClassWizard, add two new member variables associated with the slider and progress controls to the CControlsDlg class. Use the values from Table 15.5 for the new controls.

TABLE 15.5. VALUES FOR SLIDER AND PROGRESS CONTROL MEMBER VARIABLES.

Control ID	Variable Name	Category	Type
IDC_SLIDER	m_slider	Control	CSliderCtrl
IDC_PROGRESS	m_progress	Control	CProgressCtrl

15

Initializing the Slider and Progress Controls

The slider and progress controls must be initialized before you can use them. The CProgressCtrl and CSliderCtrl classes each provide a SetRange function that is used to set minimum and maximum values for their respective controls.

```
m_slider.SetRange( 0, 100 );
```

The slider also enables tick marks to be placed along the slider control if the Autoticks check box has been selected. Use the SetTicFreq function to specify the distance between each tick mark. To add tick marks every 10 positions, pass a value of 10 to SetTicFreq.

```
m_slider.SetTicFreq( 10 );
```

Listing 15.2 contains new source code for the initialization section of OnInitDialog. Add this source code just after the // TODO comment.

INPUT   **LISTING 15.2.** INITIALIZING THE CONTROLS IN CControlsDlg::OnInitDialog.

```
// TODO: Add extra initialization here
m_spin.SetRange( 0, 100 );
m_slider.SetRange( 0, 100 );
m_slider.SetTicFreq( 10 );
m_progress.SetRange( 0, 100 );
```

Handling Messages from the Slider to the Progress Control

When a slider is moved, it notifies its parent using WM_SCROLL and WM_HSCROLL messages. Because the slider in this example is a horizontal slider, it sends WM_HSCROLL messages to the main dialog box. Using ClassWizard, add a message-handling function to the CControlsDlg class for the WM_HSCROLL message. The source code for the OnHScroll function is provided in Listing 15.3.

INPUT   **LISTING 15.3.** USING SLIDER SCROLL MESSAGES TO UPDATE THE PROGRESS CONTROL.

```
void CControlsDlg::OnHScroll(UINT nSBCode, UINT nPos,
                             CScrollBar* pScrollBar )
{
    int nSliderPos = m_slider.GetPos();
    m_progress.SetPos( nSliderPos );
}
```

The code in Listing 15.3 is called whenever the trackbar position is changed. The CSliderCtrl::GetPos function is used to collect the current slider position, which is then used to update the progress control using the CProgressCtrl::SetPos function.

> There are many ways to use the progress control. Many times, you will update the progress control after receiving events that you don't have direct control over. For example, when copying a large number of files, your program might update a progress control after copying each file. During an installation, you might want to update a progress control after each phase of the installation is complete.

You can apply a large number of functions to a slider control. Other CSliderCtrl member functions are listed in Table 15.6.

TABLE 15.6. MEMBER FUNCTIONS FOR THE CSliderCtrl CLASS.

Function	Description
SetLineSize	Sets the amount the slider is changed with an arrow key
GetLineSize	Returns the amount the slider is changed with an arrow key
SetPageSize	Sets the amount the slider is changed with a page-up or page-down key
GetPageSize	Returns the amount the slider is changed with a page-up or page-down key
SetRange	Sets the allowed range for the control
SetRangeMin	Sets the minimum allowed value for the control
SetRangeMax	Sets the maximum allowed value for the control
GetRange	Returns the allowed range for the control
GetRangeMin	Returns the minimum allowed value for the control
GetRangeMax	Returns the maximum allowed value for the control
SetTic	Sets the position of a tick mark
GetTic	Returns the position of a tick mark
GetNumTics	Returns the number of ticks in a slider control
GetTicArray	Returns an array filled with tick mark positions
ClearTics	Removes the tick marks from a slider control
ClearSel	Clears the current selection in the control
VerifyPos	Tests to see whether the current position is inside a given range

Compile and run the Controls project. You can adjust the value displayed in the progress control by moving the slider control.

Summary

In this hour, you looked at spin, slider, and progress controls, three of the simpler controls offered by Windows. You examined the uses for each control and the MFC classes used to interact with them and created a small dialog box-based project that used all three controls.

Q&A

Q The spin control is paired with the wrong control when I run my program—what's wrong?

A The spin control must immediately follow the buddy control in the tab order. If the tab order isn't set correctly, the spin control will latch on to whatever control precedes it. When you are working with your dialog box in Developer Studio, press Ctrl+D to see the tab order.

Q Is there an easy way to increase the value displayed in the progress control by a specific amount, rather than setting a new value?

A Use `CProgressCtrl`'s `OffsetPos` function:

```
void CMyDlg::OnBump()
{
    m_progress.OffsetPos(5);
}
```

Workshop

The Workshop is designed to help you anticipate possible questions, review what you've learned, and begin thinking ahead to putting your knowledge into practice. The answers to the quiz are in Appendix A, "Quiz Answers."

Quiz

1. What property is used to change the spin control arrows to left/right instead of spin?

2. What property is used to indicate that the spin control is associated with a buddy control?

3. What function is used to set the limits of the spin control?

4. How do you specify which control is the buddy control?

5. What property is used to add division lines on the slider control?

6. What function is used to set the limits of the slider control?

7. What function is used to set the limits of the progress control?

Exercises

1. Change the Controls project so that the value of the spin control controls the progress control.

2. Experiment with changing the spin control's alignment and orientation from right to left, and from vertical to horizontal.

HOUR 16

Using Bitmaps and Image Lists

Bitmaps are one of the most important GDI objects offered by Windows. Image lists can be used to store collections of bitmaps, making them useful when several bitmaps are needed, such as in tree view and list view controls. In this hour, you learn

- How to use the MFC CBitmap class to simplify bitmap handling
- How to create an image list
- The properties and methods that can be applied to an image list
- How to use an image list as a bitmap container
- The advanced drawing features offered by image lists

Also, in this hour you will build a sample program that creates an image list and uses it as a storage location for bitmap images. This hour will build a foundation that you will use later in Hour 17, "List View Controls," and Hour 18, "Tree Views."

What Is a Bitmap?

NEW TERM   A *bitmap* is a graphical object that can be used to represent an image in programs written for Windows. As a bitmap, an image can be easily stored, loaded, and displayed.

Bitmaps provide a flexible way to store image data in a Windows program. The data structure used for a bitmap is straightforward and allows a wide variety of bitmap types that can be stored. Although image lists (described later in this hour) provide extra features, many times using a simple bitmap is the easiest way to display an image onscreen.

Creating a Bitmap Using Visual C++

The easiest way to create a bitmap is to use an image editor like the one that is integrated into Visual C++. You will use the Visual C++ image editor in this hour to create a bitmap that is displayed in a dialog box-based program's main dialog box.

After you've created the bitmap using the image editor, you can manipulate it by using the MFC CBitmap class. You can load the bitmap into your program by calling the LoadBitmap member function:

```
bmpHello.LoadBitmap( IDB_HELLO );
```

After the bitmap has been loaded, you can display it to any output device by using a device context.

Adding a Bitmap to a Project

A bitmap can be displayed in any project that handles the WM_PAINT message. As an example, create an SDI program named Bitmap. After you have created the project, open the resource file by clicking the ResourceView tab in the project workspace window.

Insert a new bitmap resource into the project by right-clicking the resource tree and selecting Insert from the shortcut menu. An Insert Resource dialog box is displayed; select Bitmap and click the New button. A new bitmap will be inserted into the project and loaded for editing.

The image editor displays a large grid that represents the bitmap surface, as well as two dockable toolbars:

- The Graphics toolbar consists of tools you can use to draw different shapes and text.
- The Colors palette contains the colors that are available for drawing the bitmap.

You can change the properties for a bitmap resource by right-clicking the bitmap's edge and selecting Properties from the pop-up menu. Change the name of the bitmap resource to IDB_HELLO.

> Using names that begin with IDB_ for bitmaps is a standard naming convention in Windows programming.

16

Select the text tool from the Graphics toolbar, and choose your favorite color from the Colors palette. Type a hello message as shown in Figure 16.1.

FIGURE 16.1.

The IDB_HELLO bitmap used in the Bitmap sample program.

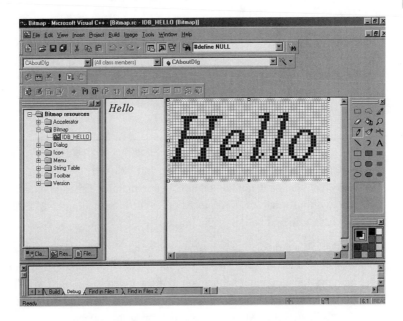

As with most resources, you can adjust the size of the bitmap by dragging the edges of the grid in any direction. Change the size of the bitmap so that the text fits inside the bitmap without any clipping. You can select a different font by pressing the Font button on the text tool. Feel free to add other effects by selecting other tools from the Graphics toolbar.

Loading and Displaying a Bitmap

Open the BitmapView.cpp source file and locate the member function CBitmapView::OnDraw. The function should already contain several lines of source code, which you can replace with the function provided in Listing 16.1.

LISTING 16.1. THE CBitmapView::OnDraw FUNCTION, USED TO DISPLAY A
BITMAP.

```
void CBitmapView::OnDraw(CDC* pDC)
{
    CBitmap     bmpHello;
    bmpHello.LoadBitmap( IDB_HELLO );

    // Calculate bitmap size using a BITMAP structure.
    BITMAP      bm;
    bmpHello.GetObject( sizeof(BITMAP), &bm );

    // Create a memory DC, select the bitmap into the
    // memory DC, and BitBlt it into the view.
    CDC         dcMem;
    dcMem.CreateCompatibleDC( pDC );

    CBitmap* pbmpOld = dcMem.SelectObject( &bmpHello );
    pDC->BitBlt( 10,10, bm.bmWidth, bm.bmHeight,
                &dcMem, 0,0, SRCCOPY );

    // Reselect the original bitmap into the memory DC.
    dcMem.SelectObject( pbmpOld );
}
```

Before the bitmap is displayed in Listing 16.1, information about the bitmap is collected using the SelectObject member function, which fills a BITMAP structure with information. Two pieces of useful information the BITMAP structure can provide are the width and height of the bitmap.

When displaying a bitmap, the bitmap is first selected into a special device context known as a *memory device context*, or *memory DC*. A memory DC is just a memory location that enables you to draw images offscreen, which improves performance. The BitBlt function is used to transfer the image from the memory DC to the view's device context, passed as a parameter to OnDraw.

BitBlt is an abbreviation for Bit-Block Transfer, which is the process used to move the image from the memory DC to the actual device context.

When you compile and run the Bitmap project, the IDB_HELLO bitmap is displayed in the view window. Experiment by changing the size and color of the bitmap or by combining the source code provided in Listing 16.1 with the DrawText function discussed in Hour 11.

If you play with the Bitmap program long enough, you might discover a problem that occurs when you use bitmaps. Although the background of the IDB_HELLO bitmap is white, it is not transparent. If the color of the view background were gray or another color, the bitmap would look like a white square containing text. It is possible to display a bitmap with a transparent background, although doing so takes a great deal of advanced graphics work. Fortunately, the image list, first introduced for Windows 95, is capable of drawing a transparent bitmap.

What Is an Image List?

An image list is similar to an array of bitmaps, just like a roll of film is an array of images, as shown in Figure 16.2. Unlike rolls of film, an image list can grow, if needed, as extra images are added to the list. Each bitmap stored in an image list is associated with an index, which can be used to retrieve a particular image.

16

FIGURE 16.2.

An image list is like a roll of bitmap images.

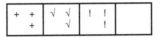

Image lists can also be used outside these new controls, and they provide an easy way to store a series of bitmaps because you must handle only a single image-list object instead of separate objects for each bitmap.

If your program must manage several different bitmapped images, a single image list is easier to use than a series of bitmaps. Accessing and displaying multiple images from an image list is much easier than handling multiple CBitmap objects. Windows Explorer has a much richer user interface than the older File Manager used in Windows 3.1. Much of this richness is achieved through the use of image lists, which offer an easy way to store and manage bitmaps.

In addition, image lists offer two features that are difficult to duplicate with regular bitmaps:

- Transparent images
- Overlaid images

Transparent Images

NEW TERM A *transparent image* is an image that enables the background to be seen through part of the image, as if part of the bitmap were transparent. A transparent image is difficult to achieve using a normal bitmap. In the simplest cases, about twice as many lines of code are required to draw a bitmap transparently as are required to draw it as an opaque image against a drawing surface. Using an image list, drawing a transparent bitmap is almost effortless, requiring little more than parameters that are set correctly.

Overlaid Images

NEW TERM   You create an *overlaid image* by combining two images to form a single, combined image. An overlaid image is useful to show special attributes for items represented by images stored in an image list. For example, when a shared directory is shown in the Explorer, a server "hand" is superimposed over the directory's folder. This is an overlaid image.

Using an Image List

As for almost everything else in Windows, there is an MFC class for image lists. You use the CImageList class to create, display, and otherwise manage image lists in an MFC-based Windows program.

Image lists often are used to provide item images for the list view control and the CListCtrl class covered in Hour 17, and for the tree control and the CTreeCtrl class covered in Hour 18. However, you can also use an image list as a collection of bitmaps, which you will do in this chapter. Using image lists in this way helps show off the different things you can do with image lists before they are used with the common controls.

As an example of using image lists, create an SDI project named ImageList. This project uses an image list to display a series of bitmaps in the program's client area.

Creating an Image List

The first step in creating an image list is to create a series of bitmaps, each of which is the same size. Although the images can be any size, the sample code in this section assumes the bitmaps are 32 pixels on each side. The bitmaps used in the example are shown in Figure 16.3.

Create the three bitmaps and name them as shown in Table 16.1.

TABLE 16.1. BITMAPS USED IN THE IMAGELIST PROJECT.

ID	Description
IDB_CROSS	Cross mark
IDB_CHECK	Check mark
IDB_BANG	Exclamation point

Storing a bitmap image in an image list consists of three steps:

1. Load the bitmap.
2. Create a new image index in the image list that contains a copy of the bitmap.
3. Delete the bitmap object.

FIGURE 16.3.

The bitmaps used in the ImageList example are all the same size.

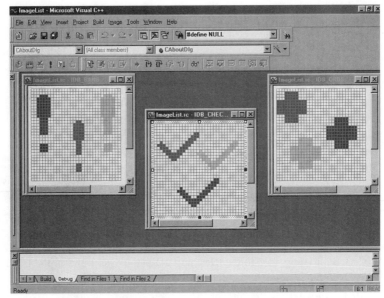

16

The bitmap object is deleted because the image list makes a copy of the bitmap and stores the image internally. As a rule of thumb, any time a Windows GDI object is loaded, it should be deleted to prevent memory leaks. The preceding steps are handled by AddBitmapToImageList, a new function added to the CImageListView class. Add the function provided in Listing 16.2 to the ImageListView.cpp source file.

INPUT **LISTING 16.2.** THE CImageListView::AddBitmapToImageList FUNCTION.

```
BOOL CImageListView::AddBitmapToImageList( UINT nResourceID )
{
    BOOL bReturn;
    CBitmap bmp;

    bReturn = bmp.LoadBitmap( nResourceID );
    if( bReturn != FALSE )
    {
        int nReturn = m_imageList.Add( &bmp, RGB(255,255,255) );
        bmp.DeleteObject();
    }
    return bReturn;
}
```

ANALYSIS The AddBitmapToImageList function is used because three bitmap resources are added to the image list. Adding the bitmaps using a new member function reduces the amount of code you must write and helps reduce the chance of errors because every bitmap is loaded using the same function.

The `CImageList::Add` member function is used to add an image to the image list. The version of `Add` used in Listing 16.2 takes two parameters:

- The address of the `CBitmap` image to be copied into the image list
- A `COLORREF` value that represents the background color of the bitmap

> The background color is used when drawing transparent images using masked bitmaps. If you aren't using a masked image list, the `COLORREF` value is ignored.

After adding the member function to the `ImageListView.cpp` file, add the source code from Listing 16.3 to the `CImageListView` class, found in the file `ImageListView.h`. Add the source code in the class implementation section, which is marked by the `//` `Implementation` comment. After the comment, there is a `protected:` label inserted by AppWizard for user-supplied variables and functions.

INPUT   **LISTING 16.3.** SOURCE CODE TO BE ADDED TO THE `CImageListView` CLASS.

```
protected:
    BOOL        AddBitmapToImageList( UINT nResourceID );
    CImageList  m_imageList;
```

The actual work of creating the image list is done when the view is constructed. The image list can be built at any time; however, creating an image list is costly in terms of computing power. Creating the image list in the constructor lets you build it once rather than each time it is used. Add the source code from Listing 16.4 to the constructor for `CImageViewList`.

INPUT   **LISTING 16.4.** THE `CImageListView` CONSTRUCTOR.

```
CImageListView::CImageListView()
{
    m_imageList.Create( 32, 32, TRUE, 3, 1 );

    AddBitmapToImageList( IDB_CROSS );
    AddBitmapToImageList( IDB_CHECK );
    AddBitmapToImageList( IDB_BANG );
}
```

ANALYSIS The image list is created using one of the `CImageList::Create` functions. This version of `Create` is useful when an image list is used as a bitmap collection. This version of `Create` has five parameters:

- The height of each bitmap; in this case, 32 pixels
- The width of each bitmap; in this case, 32 pixels
- Whether the image list is masked for transparency; in this case, TRUE
- The number of bitmaps stored initially in the image list; in this case, three
- The "grow-by," or the number of bitmaps added when the image list is expanded; in this case, one

NEW TERM A *masked image list* is an image list that contains two bitmaps for each image— the second bitmap is a mask that is used when drawing transparent images. Parts of the image that are visible are colored black in the mask, parts that are transparent are colored white in the mask.

Displaying an Image List Using the `CImageListDraw` Function

Individual items stored in an image list can be drawn using the `CImageList::Draw` member function, as shown in Listing 16.5.

LISTING **16.5.** USING `CImageList::Draw` TO DISPLAY A BITMAP FROM AN IMAGE LIST.

```
void CImageListView::OnDraw(CDC* pDC)
{
    CPoint ptImage( 0, 0 );
    for( int nImage = 0; nImage < 3; nImage++ )
    {
        m_imageList.Draw( pDC, nImage, ptImage, ILD_NORMAL );
        ptImage.x += 50;
    }
}
```

The Draw member function has four parameters:

- The device context that represents the drawing surface
- The image list index of the image to be drawn
- The location of the image, represented by a CPoint object
- The type of drawing operation to be performed

Compile and run the ImageList project. Figure 16.4 shows the current version of the ImageList application running.

There are eight different types of drawing operations:

- ILD_NORMAL draws the image directly onto the drawing surface. If the image is masked, the image will be drawn transparently if the background color for the image list is the default value of CLR_NONE.

- ILD_TRANSPARENT draws the image transparently. If the image is not masked, the image is drawn normally.

- ILD_MASK draws the image mask. If the image list doesn't have a mask, the image is drawn normally.

- ILD_BLEND25 draws the image and blends it 25 percent with the system highlight color. If the image list doesn't have a mask, the image is drawn normally.

- ILD_FOCUS is identical to ILD_BLEND25.

- ILD_BLEND50 draws the image and blends it 50 percent with the system highlight color. If the image list doesn't have a mask, the image is drawn normally.

- ILD_BLEND is identical to ILD_BLEND50.

- ILD_SELECTED is identical to ILD_BLEND50.

The individual image bitmaps stored in an image list can also be extracted as icons using the ExtractIcon member function:

```
HICON hicon = m_imageList.ExtractIcon( nImage );
```

The only parameter needed for ExtractIcon is the image index. You can then use the icon extracted just like any icon handle. Icons are discussed in Hour 14, "Icons and Cursors."

Displaying a Transparent Image

There are two methods you can use to display an image transparently:

- Define a background color for the images stored in the image list.
- Use the ILD_TRANSPARENT flag for the draw operation.

Using a Background Color

A simple method for drawing a transparent image is to define the background color that is used on the image background. The background color of the image list will then be adjusted to match the surface background color, allowing the drawing surface to "shine through," giving the image a transparent effect. Replace the CImageList::OnDraw function with the code provided in Listing 16.6, and then recompile and run the ImageList program.

16

INPUT

LISTING 16.6. USING THE CImageList::Draw FUNCTION TO DISPLAY A BITMAP TRANSPARENTLY.

```
void CImageListView::OnDraw(CDC* pDC)
{
    m_imageList.SetBkColor( RGB(0,255,0) );
    CPoint ptImage( 0, 0 );
    for( int nImage = 0; nImage < 3; nImage++ )
    {
        m_imageList.Draw( pDC, nImage, ptImage, ILD_NORMAL);
        ptImage.x += 50;
    }
}
```

ANALYSIS If you compile and run the ImageList project the background of the images will be set to green. By changing the RGB COLORREF value passed to the CImageList::SetBkColor function, you can match any background color.

Using the ILD_TRANSPARENT Flag

Another transparent drawing method is to use the ILD_TRANSPARENT flag when CImageList::Draw is called. This tells the image list to combine the image mask with the bitmap, if a mask exists. If the image list is not masked, the image is drawn as though ILD_NORMAL was used.

Displaying an Overlapped Image

An overlapped image is two images from the same bitmap, with one image superimposed on the other. Before you use an image as an overlay it must be defined as an overlay image. You can define up to four bitmaps per image list as overlays using the `CImageList::SetOverlayImage` function:

```
m_imageList.SetOverlayImage( 0, 1 );
```

The `SetOverlayImage` function takes two parameters: the image index used as the overlay and the overlay index used to identify the overlay.

> Just to make things more interesting, unlike almost every other index used in Windows, the overlay index starts at one instead of zero.

To use an overlaid image, the `CImageList::Draw` function is used as in previous examples, except that the `ILD_OVERLAYMASK` flag is used. The `INDEXTOOVERLAYMASK` macro is combined with the `ILD_OVERLAYMASK` flag to specify the overlay image index to be combined with the base image. Listing 16.7 is a new version of `OnDraw` that displays an overlaid image using an image list.

LISTING 16.7. USING THE `CImageList::Draw` FUNCTION TO DISPLAY AN OVERLAPPED IMAGE.

INPUT

```
void CImageListView::OnDraw(CDC* pDC)
{
    m_imageList.SetBkColor( CLR_NONE );
    CPoint ptOverlay( 50, 80 );
    m_imageList.SetOverlayImage( 0, 1 );
    m_imageList.Draw( pDC,
                      2,
                      ptOverlay,
                      INDEXTOOVERLAYMASK(1) );
}
```

Summary

In this hour you learned about image lists, a convenient way to display images in a Windows program. You used image lists to draw a series of bitmaps that were opaque, transparent, or overlaid with a second image.

Q&A

Q **I have a bitmap that has a white background color, and also uses white in the bitmap. How can I draw the background transparently and still draw the white parts of the bitmap?**

A Use the bitmap image mask instead of the color mask. One version of the `CImageList::Add` member function enables you to add two bitmaps to the image list:

```
nReturn = m_imageList.Add( &bmpImage, &bmpMask );
```

The second bitmap is a mask bitmap. The parts of the image bitmap that correspond to black pixels on the mask bitmap will be drawn. The parts of the image bitmap that correspond to white pixels will be transparent in the final image.

Q **How can I store an icon image in an image list?**

A A version of the `CImageList::Add` member function accepts an icon handle:

```
nReturn = m_imageList.Add( hIcon );
```

Workshop

The Workshop is designed to help you anticipate possible questions, review what you've learned, and begin thinking ahead to putting your knowledge into practice. The answers to the quiz are in Appendix A, "Quiz Answers."

Quiz

1. What are the two basic types of image lists?
2. Why would you want to have a "grow-by" parameter greater than one when creating an image list?
3. What is a transparent image?
4. The color mask is passed as a parameter when adding a bitmap image to the image list. What is the color mask used for?
5. What drawing style is used to draw the mask for a transparent image?
6. What are the drawing styles that begin with `ILD_BLEND` used for?
7. After a bitmap has been added to the image list, are you required to destroy the bitmap object or will the image list destroy it for you?
8. What is an overlapped image?
9. Which MFC class provides support for bitmaps?
10. What function is used to transfer a bitmap to an output device?

Exercises

1. Use an overlay image to combine two images.

2. Experiment by using the Draw function with the ILD_BLENDxx values to see how the system highlight color is combined with different types of images.

HOUR 17

List View Controls

List views are extremely flexible controls that allow information to be displayed in a variety of ways. In this hour, you will learn

- How to use image lists with the list view control
- How to switch between different display styles in a list view control
- How to allow the user to edit individual list items

What Is a List View Control?

List view controls, sometimes called list controls, are some of the common controls first released with Windows 95. A list view control is used to display information and an associated icon in one of four different formats:

- Icon view displays rows of 32×32 pixel icons.
- Small Icon view displays rows of smaller 16×16 pixel icons.
- List view displays small icons and list items arranged in a column.
- Report view displays items and their associated icons, along with subitems that are arranged in columns.

When you use a list view control, you can provide a menu or other method to enable the user to switch between the different viewing modes.

The Windows Explorer uses a list view control and offers all four viewing styles. The Explorer is shown in Figure 17.1 with the contents of the C:\ directory contained in a Large Icon view.

FIGURE 17.1.

The Windows Explorer uses a list view control.

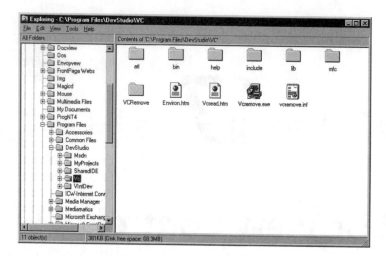

List views are very popular with users because they offer several different ways to display information. When you let the user switch between view styles, the list view control puts the user in charge of how information is displayed.

List view controls can be used to associate different icons with items stored in the list view control, as the Explorer does for filenames. The user is free to select between different sized icons or even the Report view, which can display extra information about each item. List view controls also support drag-and-drop operations, which enable the user to easily move items to or from a list view control.

List View Control Properties

The list view control's properties are set using the Properties dialog box in the same way other controls are. Some of the properties available for list view controls are also available for list boxes. The list view control property options include the following:

- *ID* is used for the list view control resource ID. A default resource ID, such as IDC_LIST1, is supplied by Developer Studio.

- *Visible* is used to indicate that the control is initially visible. This check box is usually checked.

- *Disabled* is used to indicate that the list should be initially disabled. This check box is usually cleared.

- *Group* is used to mark the first control in a group. This check box is usually cleared.

- *Tab Stop* indicates that this control can be reached by pressing Tab on the keyboard. This check box is usually checked.

- *Help ID* indicates that a context-sensitive help ID should be created for this control. This check box is normally cleared.

- *View* specifies the initial view used by the list view control. Possible values are Icon, Small Icon, List, or Report.

- *Align* specifies whether the items are aligned to the top or left sides of the control. This property applies only in the Icon or Small Icon views.

- *Sort* enables items to be sorted based on their labels as they are entered into the list view control.

- *Auto Arrange* specifies that items should be kept arranged when viewed in the Icon or Small Icon views.

- *Single Selection* enables a single list view item to be selected.

- *No Label Wrap* specifies that each item label must be displayed on a single line rather than wrapped, as is the standard behavior.

- *Edit Labels* enables the user to edit labels. If this property is enabled you must handle edit notification messages sent by the control.

- *No Scroll* disables scrolling.

- *No Column Header* removes the header control that is usually included in the report view.

- *No Sort Header* disables the sorting function that is available through the header control.

- *Share Image List* indicates that the image list used by the list view control is shared with other image lists. You must destroy the image list manually after the last list view control has been destroyed.

- *Show Selection Always* indicates that a selected item is always highlighted, even if the list view control doesn't have the focus.

- *Owner Draw Fixed* indicates that the owner of the control, instead of Windows, is responsible for drawing the control.

17

- *Owner Data* is used to create a virtual list view control that can hold millions of items. The control owner is responsible for storing all the data presented by the control.

- *Border* indicates that a border should be drawn around the control.

Using a List View Control

As an example of how the basic properties of list view controls are used, create a dialog box–based application. This program displays a list view control containing three items. You can use radio buttons to switch between the different view styles.

Use AppWizard to create a dialog box–based application named ListEx. Feel free to accept any of the options offered by AppWizard; this example works with any AppWizard parameters.

You must add a total of five controls to the ListEx main dialog box: four radio buttons and one list view control. Add the controls to the dialog box as shown in Figure 17.2.

FIGURE 17.2.

The ListEx main dialog box.

Properties for the list view and radio button controls are listed in Table 17.1. All properties that aren't listed should be set to the default values.

TABLE 17.1. PROPERTY VALUES FOR CONTROLS IN THE LISTEX MAIN DIALOG BOX.

Control	Resource ID	Caption
Icon view radio	IDC_RADIO_ICON	&Icon
Small radio	IDC_RADIO_SMALL	&Small
List radio	IDC_RADIO_LIST	&List
Report radio	IDC_RADIO_REPORT	&Report
List view control	IDC_LIST	None

Use ClassWizard to associate a CListCtrl member variable with IDC_LIST, using the values from Table 17.2.

TABLE 17.2. VALUES FOR A NEW CListCtrl MEMBER VARIABLE IN CListExDlg.

Control ID	Variable Name	Category	Type
IDC_LIST	m_listCtrl	Control	CListCtrl

Next, use ClassWizard to create message-handling functions that are called when the radio buttons are selected. Add four member functions to the CListExDlg class, using the values from Table 17.3.

TABLE 17.3. VALUES FOR NEW CListCtrl MEMBER FUNCTIONS IN CListExDlg.

Object ID	Class Name	Message	Function
IDC_RADIO_ICON	CListExDlg	BN_CLICKED	OnRadioIcon
IDC_RADIO_SMALL	CListExDlg	BN_CLICKED	OnRadioSmall
IDC_RADIO_LIST	CListExDlg	BN_CLICKED	OnRadioList
IDC_RADIO_REPORT	CListExDlg	BN_CLICKED	OnRadioReport

Associating Image Lists with a List Control

The images displayed in the list view next to each item are stored in image lists that are associated with the list view control. Constructing and managing image lists was discussed in Hour 16, "Using Bitmaps and Image Lists." An image list is added to a list view control with the SetImageList function:

```
m_listCtrl.SetImageList( &m_imageSmall, LVSIL_SMALL );
```

Two parameters are passed to the list view control: the address of the image list and a style parameter that indicates the type of images stored in the image list. There are three image list types.

- LVSIL_NORMAL is used for the image list used in the Icon view.
- LVSIL_SMALL is used for the image list used in the Small Icon view.
- LVSIL_STATE is used for optional state images, such as check marks.

 After the image list control has been added to the list view control, the list view control takes responsibility for destroying the image list.

> If the Share image list property has been selected, the list view control will not destroy the image list. You must destroy it yourself after the list view has been destroyed.
>
> If you don't destroy the image list you will create a memory leak. If you destroy the image list too early the list view control will behave unpredictably.

Creating the Image Lists

You must create two bitmaps for the ListEx application. One bitmap is used for the large icon bitmap and one for the small icon bitmap. The two bitmaps are shown in Figure 17.3. Each of the bitmaps contains two balls of the same size, and each ball is a different color.

FIGURE 17.3.

Bitmaps used for the ListEx image lists.

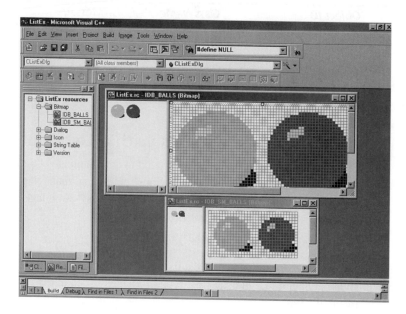

The properties for the two bitmaps are provided in Table 17.4.

TABLE 17.4. PROPERTIES FOR THE LISTEX IMAGE LIST BITMAPS.

Resource ID	Width	Height	Background
IDB_BALLS	64	32	White
IDB_SM_BALLS	32	16	White

Adding Items to a List View Control

The LV_ITEM structure is used to represent an item in a list view control. This structure is used when adding, modifying, or fetching list view items. The data members for the LV_ITEM structure include the following:

- mask is used to indicate which members are being used for the current function call. Possible values for this member are given later in this section.
- item contains the List View index of the item referred to by this structure. The first item contained in the list view control has an index of zero, the next has an index of one, and so on.
- iSubItem contains the index of the current subitem. A subitem is a string that is displayed in a column to the right of an item's icon and label in the report view. The first subitem has an index of one. The zero index is used by the actual list view item.
- state and stateMask contain the current state of the item and the valid states of the item.
- pszText contains the address of a string that is used as the item's label.
- cchTextMax specifies the size of the buffer provided in the pszText member if the structure is receiving item attributes. Otherwise, this member is not used.
- iImage contains the image list index for this item.

The LV_ITEM structure's mask member is used to indicate which parts of the structure are valid or should be filled in. It can be one or more of the following values:

- LVIF_TEXT indicates that the pszText member is valid.
- LVIF_IMAGE indicates that the iImage member is valid.
- LVIF_PARAM indicates that the lParam member is valid.
- LVIF_STATE indicates that the state member is valid.

> When more than one value is needed, combine them using the C++ OR ¦ operator:
>
> ```
> listItem.mask = LVIF_TEXT ¦ LVIF_IMAGE;
> ```

Inserting a List View Item

The InsertItem function is used to add an item to a list view control:

```
m_listItem.InsertItem( &listItem );
```

17

A pointer to an `LV_ITEM` structure is passed as the parameter to `InsertItem`. `LV_ITEM` data members are filled with data for the new item before it is inserted as shown in the following:

```
listItem.mask = LVIF_TEXT;
listItem.iItem = 0;
listItem.pszText = szText;
m_listCtrl.InsertItem( &listItem );
```

Adding Column Information for the Report View

Unlike the other three list view styles, the report view displays additional information for each item contained in the list. The extra items are subitems that are arranged in columns. Each list view item must have the same number of subitems. For example, in the Windows Explorer, the subitems are used for file information such as file size, file type, and modified date.

Columns for subitems are added to a list view control in two steps: first, the `LV_COLUMN` data structure is initialized and then the columns are added. List view columns are inserted using `LV_COLUMN` structures and the `InsertColumn` function. The `LV_COLUMN` structure has the following members:

- `mask` indicates the member variables that are used for the current function call. Values for the mask member variable are discussed at the end of this section.
- `fmt` specifies the alignment used for the column. There are three possible values: `LVCFMT_LEFT`, `LVCFMT_RIGHT`, and `LVCFMT_CENTER`. The first column must use the `LVCFMT_LEFT` value.
- `cx` specifies the width of the column in pixels.
- `pszText` points to a string containing the column text. If the structure is used to fetch information, this member holds the address of the buffer that contains the column heading text.
- `cchTextMax` stores the size of the buffer that is pointed to by `pszText`. This member is used only when receiving data.
- `iSubItem` specifies the column number.

The mask member variable is used to specify which member values are valid. Possible values include the following:

- `LVCF_FMT` indicates that the `fmt` member is valid.
- `LVCF_SUBITEM` indicates that the `iSubItem` member is valid.
- `LVCF_TEXT` indicates that the `pszText` member is valid.
- `LVCF_WIDTH` indicates that the `cx` member is valid.

After you fill in the values for an LV_COLUMN structure, the column is added to the list view control using the InsertColumn function:

```
m_listCtrl.InsertColumn( nColumn, &listColumn );
```

Determining Which Items Are Selected

Unlike a list box control, no single message or function exists to determine which items are selected in a list view control. Instead, you must use the CListCtrl::GetNextItem function, as in this example:

```
int nSel = m_listCtrl.GetNextItem( -1, LVNI_SELECTED );
```

This code returns the index of the first selected item in the list view control. GetNextItem has two parameters: the start item and a search flag. If the start item is -1, the search starts with the first item. The flag variable can include one geometric value and one state value. The following are the geometric values:

- LVNI_ABOVE: Searches for an item above the start item.
- LVNI_ALL: Searches for the next indexed item. This is the default value.
- LVNI_BELOW: Searches for an item below the start item.
- LVNI_TOLEFT: Searches for an item to the left of the start item.
- LVNI_TORIGHT: Searches for an item to the right of the start item.

The following are the possible state values:

- LVNI_DROPHILITED: Searches for an item that has the LVIS_DROPHILITED state flag set.
- LVNI_FOCUSED: Searches for an item that has the LVIS_FOCUSED state flag set.
- LVNI_HIDDEN: Searches for an item that has the LVIS_HIDDEN state flag set.
- LVNI_MARKED: Searches for an item that has the LVIS_MARKED state flag set.
- LVNI_SELECTED: Searches for an item that has the LVIS_SELECTED state flag set.

If no item can be found that matches the search parameters, –1 is returned. Otherwise, the index of the first list item that satisfies the criteria is returned.

Modifications to the CListExDlg Class

Returning to this hour's sample program, the ListEx program uses image lists to display icons, and also allows you to switch between different types of views offered by the list view control. The CListExDlg class must have two small modifications made to its class declaration:

- You must add two `CImageList` member variables for the list view control.
- You must add a `SetListView` member function. This function handles switching between different list view styles.

Add the source code provided in Listing 17.1 to the implementation section of the `CListExDlg` class declaration.

INPUT   **LISTING 17.1.** CHANGES TO THE `CListExDlg` CLASS DECLARATION.

```
// Implementation
protected:
    void SetListView( DWORD dwView );
    CImageList  m_imageLarge;
    CImageList  m_imageSmall;
```

The `CListExDlg::OnInitDialog` member function is called when the main dialog box is initialized. Add the source code in Listing 17.2 to the `OnInitDialog` function, just after the `// TODO` comment provided by AppWizard.

INPUT   **LISTING 17.2.** CHANGES TO THE `CListExDlg::OnInitDialog` FUNCTION.

```
// TODO: Add extra initialization here
// Create and set image lists
m_imageLarge.Create( IDB_BALLS, 32, 1, RGB(255,255,255) );
m_imageSmall.Create( IDB_SM_BALLS, 16, 1, RGB(255,255,255) );
m_listCtrl.SetImageList( &m_imageLarge, LVSIL_NORMAL );
m_listCtrl.SetImageList( &m_imageSmall, LVSIL_SMALL );
// Create list view columns
LV_COLUMN   listColumn;
LV_ITEM     listItem;
char*       arColumns[3] = { "City", "Football", "Baseball" };
listColumn.mask = LVCF_FMT|LVCF_WIDTH|LVCF_TEXT|LVCF_SUBITEM;
listColumn.fmt = LVCFMT_LEFT;
listColumn.cx = 60;
for( int nColumn = 0; nColumn < 3; nColumn++ )
{
    listColumn.iSubItem = nColumn;
    listColumn.pszText = arColumns[nColumn];
    m_listCtrl.InsertColumn( nColumn, &listColumn );
}
// Add list items
listItem.mask = LVIF_TEXT | LVIF_IMAGE;
listItem.iSubItem = 0;
char* arCity[3]     = { "Oakland", "San Diego", "Seattle" };
char* arFootball[3] = { "Raiders", "Chargers", "Seahawks" };
char* arBaseball[3] = { "Athletics", "Padres", "Mariners" };
```

```
for( int nItem = 0; nItem < 3; nItem++ )
{
    listItem.iItem = nItem;
    listItem.pszText = arCity[nItem];
    listItem.iImage = nItem % 2;
    m_listCtrl.InsertItem( &listItem );
    m_listCtrl.SetItemText( nItem, 1, arFootball[nItem] );
    m_listCtrl.SetItemText( nItem, 2, arBaseball[nItem] );
}
```

ANALYSIS The source code provided in Listing 17.2 creates two image lists for the list view control and then creates the list view's column headers. After the columns are created, the three list items are inserted into the list view. The SetItemText function is used to add subitem text strings to each list item—in this case, the name of the professional football and baseball teams for each city.

Changing the Current View for a List View Control

Switching views in a list view control requires just a few lines of code. The current view style is stored in a structure maintained by Windows. This information can be retrieved using the GetWindowLong function:

```
DWORD dwOldStyle = GetWindowLong( hWndList, GWL_STYLE );
```

The GetWindowLong function has two parameters:

- A window handle to the list view control
- A GWL constant that specifies the type of information requested—in this case, GWL_STYLE

The return value from GetWindowLong contains all the Windows style information for the list view control. If you are interested in the current view, the unnecessary information should be masked off using LVS_TYPEMASK.

```
dwOldStyle &= ~LVS_TYPEMASK; // Mask off extra style info
```

After the mask has been applied, the style information is one of the following values:

- LVS_ICON
- LVS_SMALLICON
- LVS_LIST
- LVS_REPORT

To change to another view you use the SetWindowLong function. When applying a new list view style, you must make sure that the style bits which are not associated with the list view style are left undisturbed. This is usually done in the following four steps:

17

1. Get the existing window style bit information using `GetWindowLong`.

2. Strip off the list view style information, leaving the other style information intact.

3. Combine a new list view style with the old style information.

4. Apply the new style information using `SetWindowLong`.

These steps are often combined into a few lines of code in the following way:

```
DWORD dwNewStyle = LVS_ICON;        // Changing to icon view
DWORD dwOldStyle = GetWindowLong( hWndList, GWL_STYLE );
dwNewStyle ¦= ( dwOldStyle &= ~LVS_TYPEMASK );
SetWindowLong( hWndList, GWL_STYLE, dwNewStyle );
```

Switching Between View Styles

The source code provided in Listing 17.3 is used to switch between list view styles.
When a radio button is selected, its message-handling function is called. Each message-handling function passes a different list view style parameter to the `SetListView` member function. The `SetListView` function uses the `SetWindowLong` function to change the list view to the selected style.

LISTING 17.3. FUNCTIONS USED TO CHANGE THE CONTROL'S VIEW STYLE.

```
void CListExDlg::OnRadioIcon()
{
    SetListView( LVS_ICON );
}
void CListExDlg::OnRadioList()
{
    SetListView( LVS_LIST );
}
void CListExDlg::OnRadioReport()
{
    SetListView( LVS_REPORT );
}
void CListExDlg::OnRadioSmall()
{
    SetListView( LVS_SMALLICON );
}
void CListExDlg::SetListView( DWORD dwNewStyle )
{
    DWORD    dwOldStyle;
    HWND     hWndList = m_listCtrl.GetSafeHwnd();

    dwOldStyle = GetWindowLong( hWndList, GWL_STYLE );

    if( (dwOldStyle & LVS_TYPEMASK) != dwNewStyle )
    {
```

```
        // Don't forget the tilde before LVS_TYPEMASK !
        dwOldStyle &= ~LVS_TYPEMASK;
        dwNewStyle |= dwOldStyle;
        SetWindowLong( hWndList, GWL_STYLE, dwNewStyle );
    }
}
```

Compile and run the ListEx sample program. The list view initially displays its contents in the Icon view. Try using the radio buttons to switch between views. When the report view is displayed, use the header control to change the spacing between columns. Figure 17.4 shows the ListEx program running.

FIGURE 17.4.

The ListEx sample program shows subitems and small icons in report view.

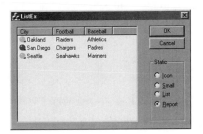

17

Congratulations! You now have an example of a basic list view control.

Summary

In this hour, you learned about the list view control and how it is used in an MFC-based program. You have also learned how this control interacts with image lists and header controls, and you built a sample application to demonstrate how a list view control is used.

Q&A

Q In a multiple selection list view, how can I determine which items have been selected?

A As discussed earlier this hour, you can use CListCtrl's GetNextItem member function to determine the first selected item in a list view control. To determine all selected items, you must use a while loop to continue to search for selected items until you reach the end of the list, like this:

```
void CListExDlg::OnTest()
{
    int nTotalSelected = 0;
```

```
int nSel = m_listCtrl.GetNextItem(-1, LVNI_SELECTED);
while(nSel != -1)
{
    nTotalSelected++;
    nSel = m_listCtrl.GetNextItem(nSel, LVNI_SELECTED);
}
TRACE("Total selected = %d\n", nTotalSelected);
}
```

Workshop

The Workshop is designed to help you anticipate possible questions, review what you've learned, and begin thinking ahead to put your knowledge into practice. The answers to the quiz are in Appendix A, "Quiz Answers."

Quiz

1. What styles are available for the list view?
2. What are the sizes of the icons used by the list view control?
3. What Windows function is used to change list view styles?
4. What steps are required to add a column to a list view?
5. How do you add text for a list view subitem?
6. What is the return value when the `InsertItem` function fails?
7. What MFC class is used to manage the list view control?
8. Can items stored in a list control have different numbers of subitems?
9. Which list view control style has columns that contain details about items stored in the control?
10. What structure is used to store information about a list view control item?

Exercises

1. Make it possible for a user to add new items to the list view control in the ListEx project.
2. Add a pop-up menu to the ListEx project that enables the user to select which list view style should be used. Display the pop-up menu when the user right-clicks the list view control.

HOUR 18

Tree Views

One of the most popular common controls first released with Windows 95 is the tree view control. In this hour, you will learn

- How to use the tree view control in a dialog box
- How to use the tree view control as a view in an SDI application
- How to use the MFC classes that support the tree view control

What Is a Tree View Control?

Tree view controls are similar to the list box controls discussed in Hour 7, "Using List Box and Combo Box Controls," except that they display information in a tree, or hierarchy. Tree view controls are often used to display disk directories or the contents of books or other documents.

NEW TERM A tree view control is composed of parent and child items. *Parent items* are located at the root, or top level, of the tree. In a tree view control, *child items* are located under parent items.

Items in a tree view control are arranged into groups, with child items located under parent items. Child items are also indented, or nested, under a parent.

A child item at one level can be the parent of child items at lower levels. The Windows Explorer is one of the applications that uses the new tree view control, shown in Figure 18.1.

FIGURE 18.1.

The Windows Explorer is one of the many applications that uses tree view controls.

The tree view control is a popular control because it enables you to display a great deal of information in a hierarchy. Unlike a list box, a small amount of high-level information can be presented initially, enabling the user to decide which parts of the tree should be expanded. The tree view control also enables information to be displayed so that relationships between different items in the control can be seen. For example, in the Explorer, subdirectories are nested in order to show their positions in the directory.

Tree view controls are also popular because they offer a wide range of options. As with list view controls, which were discussed in Hour 17, "List View Controls," tree view controls put the user in charge. As you see in an example later in this hour, letting a user edit the labels for individual tree view items is very easy.

You can create tree view controls with several different styles. For example, many tree view controls display a bitmap next to each item. Many also display a control button next to each item. This button contains a plus sign if an item can be expanded. If the button is clicked, the tree expands to display the item's children. When it is expanded, the item displays a button with a minus sign.

Tree view controls often contain a large amount of information. The user can control the amount of information displayed by expanding or collapsing tree items. When more horizontal or vertical room is needed, the tree view control automatically displays scrollbars.

MFC Support for Tree View Controls

There are two ways to use tree view controls in your MFC-based programs. When a tree view control is used in a dialog box, the control is added just as buttons, list boxes, and other controls have been added. The MFC class `CTreeCtrl` is used to interact with tree view controls and is associated with a tree view control using ClassWizard.

Tree view controls can also be used in a view. The `CTreeView` class is a specialized view that consists of a single tree view control. The `CTreeView` class is derived from `CCtrlView`, which is itself derived from `CView`.

Because `CTreeView` is derived from `CView`, it can be used just like `CView`. For the first example in this hour, you use `CTreeView` as the main view in an MFC-based application.

Using a Tree View Control as a View

The best way to understand a tree view control is to look at an example. For this example, create an SDI project named TreeEx using AppWizard. In AppWizard step 6 a checkered flag is displayed along with a list box containing classes that are generated for the application. Follow these steps to use a tree view as the application's main view:

1. Select the view class in the class list box, in this case `CTreeExView`.
2. Select `CTreeView` from the Base Class combo box.
3. Click the Finish button to end the AppWizard process and display the New Project Information dialog box.
4. Click OK to generate the code for the TreeEx project.

You can compile and run the TreeEx application; however, no items have been added to the tree view control yet. In the next section, you see how items are added to a tree view.

Adding Items to a Tree View

As discussed earlier, the `CTreeView` class is derived from `CView` and contains a tree view control that covers the entire view surface. To get access to the tree view control, you use the `GetTreeControl` function:

```
CTreeCtrl& tree = GetTreeCtrl();
```

Note that the return value from `GetTreeCtrl` is a reference to a `CTreeCtrl` object. This means that the return value must be assigned, or bound, to a `CTreeCtrl` reference variable.

After you have access to the tree view control, you can add items to the control in several different ways. The simplest methods are used when adding simple text items

18

without bitmap images to the tree view control. When adding simple items to a tree view control, only the label for the item must be provided:

```
HTREEITEM hItem = tree.InsertItem( "Foo" );
```

This line adds an item to the tree view control at the first, or root, level. The return value from InsertItem is a handle to the new item if it was inserted successfully or NULL if the item could not be inserted.

To add an item as a child, pass the parent's handle as a parameter when inserting the item.

```
tree.InsertItem( "Bar", hItem );
```

The source code provided in Listing 18.1 uses the functions discussed previously to add eight items in the CTreeExView::OnInitialUpdate function.

INPUT **LISTING 18.1.** ADDING ITEMS TO A CTreeView.

```
void CTreeExView::OnInitialUpdate()
{
    CTreeView::OnInitialUpdate();
    CTreeCtrl& tree = GetTreeCtrl();

    HTREEITEM hChapter = tree.InsertItem( "Chapter 1" );
    tree.InsertItem( "What", hChapter);
    tree.InsertItem( "Why", hChapter );
    tree.InsertItem( "How", hChapter );
    hChapter = tree.InsertItem( "Chapter 2" );
    tree.InsertItem( "What", hChapter );
    tree.InsertItem( "Why", hChapter );
    tree.InsertItem( "How", hChapter );
}
```

After you add the source code from Listing 18.1, compile and run the TreeEx project. This version of the tree view control is a minimal tree view control, as shown in Figure 18.2. There are no connecting lines, no bitmaps, and no pushbuttons; in short, it's fairly simple.

FIGURE 18.2.

The main view of the TreeEx example.

Applying Styles to a Tree View Control

In addition to other available view and window styles, you can apply four style options specifically to a tree view control:

- TVS_HASLINES adds connecting lines between parent and child items.
- TVS_LINESATROOT adds lines for the root items in the tree view control. This attribute is ignored if TVS_HASLINES is not selected.
- TVS_HASBUTTONS adds the plus and minus buttons for items that can be expanded.
- TVS_EDITLABELS enables the user to edit a tree view item label.

You usually don't need to get involved with defining the styles for a normal view; the default settings are good enough 99 percent of the time. For a tree view, however, you might want to select one or more of the optional styles by modifying the CTreeExView::PreCreateWindow function. The source code in Listing 18.2 applies all the optional attributes except for TVS_EDITLABELS.

INPUT   **LISTING 18.2.** MODIFYING THE TREE VIEW STYLE IN PreCreateWindow.

```
BOOL CTreeExView::PreCreateWindow(CREATESTRUCT& cs)
{
    cs.style |= ( TVS_HASLINES¦TVS_LINESATROOT¦TVS_HASBUTTONS );
    return CTreeView::PreCreateWindow(cs);
}
```

Compile and run the TreeEx example and you'll see that the example now has lines and buttons, as shown in Figure 18.3. It might sound like a small addition, but it makes the control much easier to use, especially if the tree must be expanded and collapsed frequently.

18

FIGURE 18.3.

The TreeEx example
after modifying the
tree view styles.

At first glance, you might think that the list view and tree view controls are almost identical as far as the API goes. The key word, unfortunately, is *almost*.

The biggest difference between the list view and tree view controls is in how individual items are referenced. In the list view control, an item index is used when communicating with the control. Because tree view controls allow items to be expanded and collapsed, however, the idea of an absolute index doesn't work. An item handle, or HTREEITEM, is used when referring to a tree view item.

In addition, several smaller differences can tend to be a bit aggravating. For example, CListCtrl::CreateDragImage takes two parameters, whereas the equivalent CTreeCtrl function takes only one parameter.

Adding Tree View Controls to Dialog Boxes

You can also add a tree view control to a dialog box. As an example you will add one to the TreeEx About dialog box. The tree view control used in the TreeEx About dialog box supports label editing and also displays bitmaps for each item.

Adding a tree view control to a dialog box is similar to adding any other control to a dialog box. Select the ResourceView tab in the project workspace window and open the Dialog folder. Open the IDD_ABOUTBOX dialog box resource by double-clicking the IDD_ABOUTBOX icon or by right-clicking the icon and selecting Open from the pop-up menu.

Remove the current controls except for the OK button from IDD_ABOUTBOX. Add a tree view control to the dialog box by dragging the tree view icon onto the dialog box or by selecting a tree view control and clicking on the dialog box. The modified dialog box is shown in Figure 18.4.

FIGURE 18.4.

Adding a tree view
control to a dialog
box.

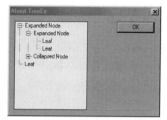

As shown in Figure 18.4, the tree view control displays a simulated tree to assist in sizing the control.

> A tree view control is often larger than a list box due to the space required for indenting the nested child items.

Setting Tree View Control Properties

The tree view control's properties are set using the Properties dialog box. Some of the properties available for tree view controls are also available for list boxes. The tree view control property options include the following:

- *ID* is used for the tree view control resource ID. A default resource ID, such as IDC_TREE1, is supplied by Visual C++.

- *Visible* is used to indicate that the control is initially visible. This check box is usually checked.

- *Disabled* is used to indicate the list should be initially disabled. This check box is usually cleared.

- *Group* is used to mark the first control in a group. This check box is usually cleared.

- *Tab Stop* indicates that this control can be reached by pressing Tab on the keyboard. This check box is usually checked.

- *Help ID* indicates that a context-sensitive help ID should be generated for this control.

- *Has Buttons* indicates that the control should be drawn with buttons. Each tree view control item that can be expanded has a button drawn to the left of the item. This check box is usually cleared.

- *Has Lines* is used to indicate that lines should be drawn connecting items in the control. This check box is usually cleared.

18

- *Border* is used to indicate that a border should be drawn around the tree view control. This check box is usually checked.
- *Lines at Root* indicates that lines should be drawn at the first, or "root," level of the control. This option is ignored if the Has Lines check box is not selected.
- *Edit Labels* enables a user to change the values of labels in the control. This check box is usually cleared.
- *Disable Drag Drop* prevents drag and drop for items contained in the tree view control. This item is usually cleared.
- *Show Selection Always* uses the system highlight colors for selected items. This item is usually cleared.
- *Check Boxes* creates a check box next to each item in the tree view control. This item is usually cleared.
- *Full Row Select* causes the entire row to be highlighted when an item is selected. This item is usually cleared.
- *Info Tip* indicates that info-tips should be displayed in this control. This item is usually cleared.
- *Scroll* enables scrolling for this control. This item is usually checked.
- *Tool Tips* indicates that tooltips should be displayed for items in this control. This item is normally checked.
- *Non Even Height* specifies that an item's height can be set to an odd value instead of even values. This item is normally cleared.
- *Track Select* enables hot tracking. This item is usually cleared.
- *Single Expand* indicates that nodes in the tree will be expanded when they are selected. This item is usually cleared.

Open the Properties dialog box for the tree view control and change the resource ID to IDC_TREE. All other properties should be set to their default values except for the following items, which should be checked:

- Has Lines
- Lines at Root
- Has Buttons

Using ClassWizard, associate a CTreeCtrl member variable with the new tree view control, using the values from Table 18.1.

TABLE 18.1. VALUES USED TO ADD A CTreeCtrl MEMBER VARIABLE FOR CAboutDlg.

Control ID	Variable Name	Category	Type
IDC_TREE	m_tree	Control	CTreeCtrl

Creating an Image List Control

The version of the tree view control contained in the About dialog box displays two bitmaps next to tree view items:

- A notebook icon for root-level items
- A document page icon for second-level items

As discussed in Hour 16, "Using Bitmaps and Image Lists," an image list can consist of a single bitmap that has one or more segments. The bitmap shown in Figure 18.5 contains both images used by the tree view control.

FIGURE 18.5.

Bitmaps displayed in the tree view control.

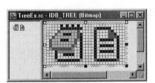

Use the image editor to create the bitmap in Figure 18.5. Use red as a background color for the bitmap to make it easier to draw the bitmap transparently. Use the values from Table 18.2 for the bitmap.

TABLE 18.2. ATTRIBUTES FOR THE IMAGE LIST BITMAP USED IN TREEEX.

Resource ID	Height	Item Width	Total Width
IDB_TREE	14	14	28

Modifying the Dialog Box Class

You must modify the CAboutDlg class in order to handle the tree view control. You must add a CImageList variable that will be used to supply the images displayed next to each item in the tree view control.

Add the source code provided in Listing 18.3 to the implementation section of the CAboutDlg class declaration.

18

INPUT   **LISTING 18.3.** ADDITIONS TO THE CAboutDlg CLASS DECLARATION.

```
// Implementation
protected:
    CImageList   m_imageList;
```

The tree view control is initialized when the CAboutDlg class receives the WM_INITDIALOG message. Using ClassWizard, add a message-handling function for WM_INITDIALOG, and accept the suggested name of OnInitDialog. Add the source code in Listing 18.4 to the OnInitDialog member function. A little cut-and-paste editing can save you some typing here because this source code is similar to the source code used earlier in Listing 18.1.

INPUT   **LISTING 18.4.** THE CAboutDlg::OnInitDialog MEMBER FUNCTION.

```
BOOL CAboutDlg::OnInitDialog()
{
    CDialog::OnInitDialog();
    m_imageList.Create( IDB_TREE, 14, 1, RGB(255,0,0) );
    m_tree.SetImageList( &m_imageList, TVSIL_NORMAL );
    HTREEITEM hChapter;
    hChapter = m_tree.InsertItem( "Chapter 1", 0, 0 );
    m_tree.InsertItem( "What", 1, 1, hChapter );
    m_tree.InsertItem( "Why", 1, 1, hChapter );
    m_tree.InsertItem( "How", 1, 1, hChapter );
    hChapter = m_tree.InsertItem( "Chapter 2", 0, 0 );
    m_tree.InsertItem( "What", 1, 1, hChapter );
    m_tree.InsertItem( "Why", 1, 1, hChapter );
    m_tree.InsertItem( "How", 1, 1, hChapter );
    return TRUE;
}
```

ANALYSIS   There are a few small differences between Listing 18.1 and Listing 18.4. In Listing 18.4, an image list is first created and then associated with the tree view control by calling the SetImageList function. In addition, the InsertItem function uses two extra parameters.

```
m_tree.InsertItem( "How", 1, 1, hChapter );
```

As in Listing 18.1, the first parameter is the text label associated with the tree item. The second parameter is the image index associated with the item when it's not selected; the third parameter is the selected image index. This enables you to specify different images for selected and non-selected items. As before, the last parameter is a handle to the item's parent item, or it is omitted if the item is added at the root level.

Compile and run the TreeEx project. The modified TreeEx About dialog box is shown in Figure 18.6.

Figure **18.6.**

The modified About dialog box from TreeEx.

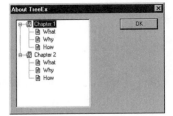

Deleting Items from a Tree View Control

Of course, any control that enables items to be inserted must also enable them to be removed. The `CTreeCtrl::DeleteItem` member function is used to delete an item from the tree view control:

```
BOOL fResult = m_tree.DeleteItem(hTreeItem);
```

> When an item is removed from the tree view control, any child items that are nested below it are also removed.

The return value from `DeleteItem` is `FALSE`, or zero, if the item could not be deleted or nonzero if the item was deleted successfully.

> To delete all the items in a tree view control, use the `CTreeCtrl::DeleteAllItems` member function:
>
> ```
> BOOL fResult = m_tree.DeleteAllItems();
> ```

To show how these functions are used in a real application, add two buttons to the About dialog box. Figure 18.7 shows the About dialog box after adding Remove and Remove All buttons.

18

FIGURE 18.7.

The About dialog box
after adding new
pushbutton controls.

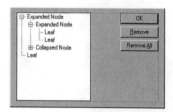

Use the values from Table 18.3 to assign properties to the new controls added to the About dialog box.

TABLE 18.3. PROPERTY VALUES FOR CONTROLS ADDED TO THE ABOUT DIALOG BOX.

Control	Resource ID	Caption
Remove button	IDC_REMOVE	&Remove
Remove All button	IDC_REMOVEALL	Remove &All

Use ClassWizard to add message-handling functions for the new controls, as shown in Table 18.4.

TABLE 18.4. MESSAGE-HANDLING FUNCTIONS USED FOR THE NEW CONTROLS.

Class Name	Object ID	Message	Function
CAboutDlg	IDC_REMOVE	BN_CLICKED	OnRemove
CAboutDlg	IDC_REMOVEALL	BN_CLICKED	OnRemoveall

The source code used to implement the Remove and Removeall functions is provided in Listing 18.5. Add this source code to the CAboutDlg::Remove and CAboutDlg::Removeall functions found in TreeEx.cpp.

INPUT   LISTING 18.5. DELETING ITEMS FROM THE ABOUT TREEEX DIALOG BOX.

```
void CAboutDlg::OnRemove()
{
    HTREEITEM hItem = m_tree.GetSelectedItem();
    if(hItem != NULL)
    {
        VERIFY(m_tree.DeleteItem(hItem));
    }
```

```
    else
    {
        AfxMessageBox("Please select an item first");
    }
}

void CAboutDlg::OnRemoveall()
{
    m_tree.DeleteAllItems();
}
```

Compile and run the TreeEx project. Experiment with removing items from the dialog box. Note that removing a node at the root level also removes all its children.

Performing In-Place Label Editing

Like the list view control, the tree view control offers a built-in edit control that you can use to edit items contained in the control. In order to take advantage of this capability, the tree view control must have its Edit labels property checked.

In addition to setting the tree view control style, there are two messages that relate to label editing:

- TVN_BEGINLABELEDIT, which is sent just before the label editing begins.
- TVN_ENDLABELEDIT, which is sent after editing is completed or after the user has canceled the editing operation.

These messages are handled exactly as they are for a list view control. When you receive TVN_BEGINLABELEDIT, you can prevent a label from being edited by setting *pResult to TRUE, and you can allow editing to proceed by setting *pResult to FALSE. In addition, you can use the TVN_BEGINLABELEDIT message to take control of the tree view's edit control.

The TVN_ENDLABELEDIT message is used exactly like the LVN_ENDLABELEDIT message is used with a list view control.

18

> If you use the newly edited label text in your application, make sure to look out for situations in which the user has canceled the label editing operation. When this happens, the TV_ITEM pszText member variable is set to NULL, or the iItem member variable is set to −1.

Add new message-handling functions for the label editing messages using the values in Table 18.5.

TABLE 18.5. MESSAGE-HANDLING FUNCTIONS USED FOR LABEL EDITING.

Class Name	Object ID	Message	Function
CAboutDlg	IDC_TREE	TVN_BEGINLABELEDIT	OnBeginlabeleditTree
CAboutDlg	IDC_TREE	TVN_ENDLABELEDIT	OnEndlabeleditTree

The source code for these functions is provided in Listing 18.6.

LISTING 18.6. FUNCTIONS USED TO IMPLEMENT SIMPLE DRAG AND DROP.

```
void CAboutDlg::OnBeginlabeleditTree(NMHDR* pNMHDR, LRESULT* pResult)
{
    *pResult = FALSE;
}

void CAboutDlg::OnEndlabeleditTree(NMHDR* pNMHDR, LRESULT* pResult)
{
    *pResult = TRUE;
}
```

Compile and run the TreeEx project. Experiment with editing item labels and removing items in the About dialog box.

Summary

In this hour, you learned about the tree view control and created two examples: a tree view used as an SDI main view and a tree view control in a dialog box.

Q&A

Q How can I allow or deny label editing based on the text the user has entered into a label?

A When you receive the TVN_ENDLABELEDIT message, you can check the value stored in the pszText member of the item structure. If the string is valid, set *pResult to TRUE; otherwise, set it to FALSE to reject the change.

Q How can I force the tree view control to scroll to a particular position?

A You can force a particular item to be visible by calling the
`CTreeCtrl::EnsureVisible` function:

`m_tree.EnsureVisible(hItem);`

The tree view control will scroll if necessary to display the item referred to by
`hItem`. If the item is hidden under a parent, the tree will be expanded to show the
item.

Workshop

The Workshop is designed to help you anticipate possible questions, review what you've
learned, and begin thinking ahead to putting your knowledge into practice. The answers
to the quiz are in Appendix A, "Quiz Answers."

Quiz

1. What messages are sent when a user edits a tree view label?
2. What tree view control property indicates that tree view labels can be edited?
3. Why are two image list indexes specified when adding an item that displays an image to a tree view control?
4. What `CTreeCtrl` member function is used to remove all items in a tree view control?
5. How do you change the properties for a tree view control that is part of the `CTreeView` class?
6. What properties are available specifically for tree view controls, and what are their equivalent window styles?
7. How are individual tree view items referred to?
8. What is the size of the images used by the tree view control?
9. How do you insert an item as the first child under a parent?

Exercises

1. Modify the `CAboutDlg` so that you can add an item to the tree view control.
2. Add an additional item to the `IDB_TREE` image list. Use the new image list item when a top-level tree view control item is selected.

18

HOUR 19

Using ActiveX Controls

ActiveX controls are reusable custom controls written for Windows. In this hour, you will learn about ActiveX controls and how they can be used to add exciting features to your applications without much work. In this hour, you will learn

- How ActiveX controls are used to replace OLE controls and VBX controls
- How you can use ActiveX controls to easily add functionality to your project
- How to use the Microsoft Hierarchical Flex Grid control included with Visual C++

A small example at the end of the hour uses one of the ActiveX controls included with Visual C++.

What Is an ActiveX Control?

NEW TERM An *ActiveX control* is a reusable control that is packaged and available for use in your applications. ActiveX controls use Component Object Model (COM) interfaces for communication to and from the control.

ActiveX controls can be developed for both the 16-bit and 32-bit versions of Windows. In addition, they have features that make them more attractive for distribution, such as support for licensing and localization into different languages.

A wide range of ActiveX controls is available. Later in this hour, you can follow the steps required to use the Microsoft Hierarchical Flex Grid control that is included with Visual C++, which enables you to write simple spreadsheet applications.

Why Use an ActiveX Control?

ActiveX controls are easy to use in your MFC-based applications because they have been designed for reuse. Developer Studio includes the Component and Controls Gallery, a tool that helps you easily integrate ActiveX controls into your MFC programs.

 ActiveX controls communicate over well-defined *interfaces* that are understood by ActiveX controls and the programs that use them. These interfaces are used to pass information and events to and from the control.

Because ActiveX controls use a standard interface that is not specific to any particular programming language, ActiveX controls can be used by a variety of development tools. The ActiveX controls that you use today in a Visual C++ program can also be used with other tools, such as Microsoft Access, Visual FoxPro, and Visual Basic.

ActiveX controls offer more functionality than is available with standard controls offered by Windows. For example, before the release of Windows 95, many vendors of Visual Basic Controls (VBXs) offered controls that were similar to tree view controls; these vendors are now offering ActiveX controls with even newer features that are not available when using standard controls.

How Is an ActiveX Control Used?

NEW TERM An ActiveX *event* is a message that is sent from the control to the application that contains the control.

An ActiveX control always communicates with an ActiveX control container. Control containers understand the ActiveX control interfaces, as shown in Figure 19.1. An ActiveX control container is responsible for providing an environment in which the control can pass events to its owner and receive information from the outside world. The ActiveX control sends events to the ActiveX container when an event occurs inside the control. Mouse clicks, pressed buttons, and expiring timers are examples of events. The ActiveX container provides information to the control such as the natural or "ambient" background color and the default font.

FIGURE 19.1.

Messages sent to and from an ActiveX control in an MFC program.

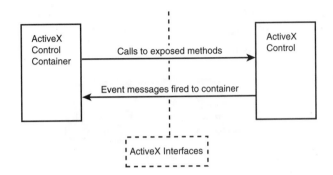

NEW TERM   When an ActiveX control container must communicate with an ActiveX control, it interacts with a set of properties and methods that are exposed by the ActiveX control. An ActiveX *property* is an attribute that is applied to the control, such as a color or the height of a button. An example of an ActiveX property is the font or background color used by a control.

NEW TERM   An ActiveX *method* is a function that is exposed by the control and is called by the control's container. An example of an ActiveX method is a function that sorts the items in a list control.

> Every class derived from CWnd in an MFC application can be used as an ActiveX control container. The MFC class COleControl is used as a base class for all ActiveX controls created using MFC.

19

Using the Components and Controls Gallery

The Components and Controls Gallery is used to store reusable components that can be used in your MFC-based Windows projects. If you develop a class that you would like to reuse in future projects, you can add the class to the Gallery by following these steps:

1. Open the project that contains the class to be reused.
2. Open the ClassView in the project workspace.
3. Right-click on the class name, and select Add to Gallery from the shortcut menu.

The most frequently used components stored in the Components and Controls Gallery are ActiveX controls. To display all the ActiveX controls available on your machine, open the Components and Controls Gallery by selecting Project | Add to Project | Components and Controls from the main menu.

After the Component Gallery dialog box is displayed, select Registered ActiveX Controls from the list box; this displays all the available ActiveX controls. Figure 19.2 shows this dialog box with the controls on my system.

FIGURE 19.2.

Displaying ActiveX controls in the Component and Controls Gallery.

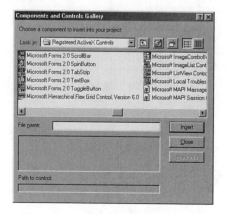

Adding an ActiveX Control to the Dialog Editor

Before using an ActiveX control in a dialog box, you must insert the control into the dialog editor's control palette. To add an ActiveX control to the dialog editor, follow these steps:

1. Select one of the displayed ActiveX control icons.
2. From the Components and Controls Gallery dialog box, click the Insert button.
3. A message box will be displayed asking if you would like to insert the component. Click OK.
4. A list box containing classes that will be added to your project is displayed inside the Confirm Classes dialog box. Click OK to add the classes to your project.
5. Click Close to dismiss the Components and Controls Gallery dialog box.

The ActiveX control you selected is now included in the dialog editor's control palette. Open a dialog box for editing, and you see the new control palette, including the new ActiveX control.

You can use the new ActiveX control as you would any other control. To add it to a dialog box resource, drag and drop the control on the dialog box, or select the ActiveX control's icon and click on the dialog box resource.

Using ClassWizard to Configure an ActiveX Control

Before you can use the ActiveX control, it must be integrated into your project. As with any other control added to a dialog box, use ClassWizard to add message-handling functions and associate the control with an MFC object.

When adding a member variable associated with an ActiveX control, you can use ClassWizard as you would if the control were a button, list box, or another standard Windows control. Unlike standard Windows controls, each ActiveX control has a large number of properties that are exposed as variables.

An Example Using an ActiveX Custom Control

As an example of using an ActiveX control in an MFC-based project, you will now use the Microsoft Hierarchical Flex Grid control in a dialog box-based application. The grid control is used to create a small spreadsheet in the main dialog box.

To get started with the sample project, use AppWizard to create a dialog box-based application named CustomCtrl. In contrast to most of the book's other AppWizard examples, for this project you must keep one of the default options offered by the wizard. On the second AppWizard page, make sure the ActiveX Controls check box is selected. Selecting this option causes AppWizard to configure the project to be ActiveX control-ready.

What Is a Grid Control?

19

NEW TERM A *grid control* is a popular reusable control that is similar to a spreadsheet. Many suppliers of Visual Basic controls offer grid controls, and Visual C++ includes the Microsoft Hierarchical Flex Grid control.

As you can probably guess by its name, a grid control is divided into a series of rectangles, or grids. Vertical lines separate the controls into columns, and horizontal lines divide the control into rows. The intersection of a row and column is known as a cell.

A grid control can contain a mixture of images and text. In most cases, text is used. You cannot directly edit the individual cells in a grid control. The grid control is strictly a read-only window, although there are ways to simulate cell editing that are discussed later this hour.

The most common use for a grid control is creating a small spreadsheet. If you want to display a small budget or other information, a grid control is ideal. In addition, you can use a grid control whenever you must arrange information into rows and columns. For example, a calendar dialog box might use a grid control to provide access to the individual days of the month.

A grid control spares you the work of creating and maintaining a large number of smaller controls. The grid control tracks the active cells, as well as the size and contents of each cell. When you need access to a particular cell, the grid control can provide that information through a function call. At a minimum, grid controls enable you to do the following:

- Retrieve current row, cell, and column information.
- Set attributes for the current cell, such as font, size, and contents.
- Retrieve the attributes of the current cell.

Adding an ActiveX Control to the Dialog Editor

To add a grid ActiveX control to the CustomCtrl project's main dialog box, you must first add the grid control to the dialog editor's control palette by following these steps:

1. Open the Components and Controls Gallery by selecting Project | Add to Project | Components and Controls from the menu.
2. Display the available ActiveX controls by clicking Registered ActiveX Controls from the list box.
3. Select the control you want to add. In this case select the Microsoft ~~Hierarchical~~ Flex Grid Control, Version 6.0 icon.
4. Click the Insert button; then click OK on the message box.
5. The list of classes that will be added to the project will be displayed. Accept these classes by clicking OK.
6. Close the Components and Controls Gallery dialog box.

Adding a Grid Control to the Main Dialog Box

Before adding the grid control to the main dialog box, you must first load the dialog box resource into the dialog editor. Open the ResourceView in the project workspace. Open the dialog box resource folder and double-click the IDD_CUSTOMCTRL_DIALOG icon. This opens the dialog box resource inside the Developer Studio dialog editor.

To add a grid control, drag and drop the grid control from the control palette to the dialog box resource. For this example, you must also add an edit control with a resource ID of IDC_EDIT and a pushbutton control with an ID of IDC_CALC to the dialog box. The finished main dialog box resource is shown in Figure 19.3.

FIGURE 19.3.

The main dialog box resource for the CustomCtrl project.

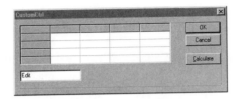

The properties for the ActiveX grid control are provided in Table 19.1.

TABLE 19.1. PROPERTIES USED FOR THE ACTIVEX GRID CONTROL.

Property	Value
ID	IDC_GRID
Rows	5
Columns	5
Fixed Rows	1
Fixed Cols	1
ScrollBars	None

Initializing the Grid Control

Before adding the source code used to initialize the grid control, add member variables to the CCustomCtrlDlg class associated with the grid and edit controls. Using ClassWizard, add the member variables using the values from Table 19.2.

TABLE 19.2. VALUES USED FOR THE GRID AND EDIT CONTROL MEMBER VARIABLES.

Class Name	Resource ID	Category	Type	Variable Name
CCustomCtrlDlg	IDC_EDIT	Control	CEdit	m_edit
CCustomCtrlDlg	IDC_GRID	Control	CMSHFlexGrid	m_grid

Due to the way in which the Developer Studio tools are integrated with ActiveX controls, ClassWizard knows all about the Microsoft Hierarchical Flex Grid control and creates the CMSHFlexGrid class to interact with the control.

Other ActiveX controls will have similar classes created when they are added to a Visual C++ project.

19

The main dialog box class, CCustomCtrlDlg, uses three new member variables to interact with the grid control.

- m_nRow is used to store the current cell row when a cell is being edited.
- m_nCol is used to store the current cell column when a cell is being edited.
- m_bEditing is set to TRUE when a cell is being edited and FALSE otherwise.

Add the declarations for these variables to the CCustomCtrlDlg class, as shown in Listing 19.1. Add the source code to the implementation section, just after the // Implementation comment.

INPUT   **LISTING 19.1.** MODIFICATIONS TO THE CCustomCtrlDlg CLASS DECLARATION.

```
// Implementation
protected:
    BOOL     m_bEditing;
    int      m_nRow;
    int      m_nCol;
```

The grid control must be initialized during the main dialog box's OnInitDialog member function. Add the source code from Listing 19.2 to the CCustomCtrlDlg::OnInitDialog member function, just after the // TODO comment.

INPUT   **LISTING 19.2.** INITIALIZING THE ACTIVEX GRID CONTROL IN OnInitDialog.

```
// TODO: Add extra initialization here
m_bEditing = FALSE;
m_nRow = 1;
m_nCol = 1;
char*    arCols[4] = { "Jan", "Feb", "Mar", "Apr" };
char*    arRows[4] = { "Gas", "Phone", "MSN", "Total" };
m_grid.SetRow( 0 );
for( int nCol = 0; nCol < 4; nCol++ )
{
    m_grid.SetCol( nCol + 1 );
    m_grid.SetText( arCols[nCol] );
}
m_grid.SetCol( 0 );
for( int nRow = 0; nRow < 4; nRow++ )
{
    m_grid.SetRow( nRow + 1 );
    m_grid.SetText( arRows[nRow] );
}
```

The source code added to the OnInitDialog function first initializes the new member variables added in Listing 19.1. The remaining code initializes the grid control.

The first for loop in Listing 19.2 sets the column headings to the first four months of the year. The next for loop sets the text used as row titles in the grid control. This short snippet of code shows how a grid control is typically used: Select a cell and then set or retrieve the text stored in that cell.

Detecting Grid Control Events

When an event occurs in the grid control, the control fires an event message to its container. The MFC framework translates this event message into a function call. To define the Click event message that is handled by the main dialog box, you use ClassWizard to add a message-handling function for the message, as shown in Table 19.3.

TABLE 19.3. ACTIVEX EVENT MESSAGES HANDLED BY THE CCustomCtrlDlg CLASS.

Object ID	Class Name	Message	Function
IDC_GRID	CCustomCtrlDlg	Click	OnClickGrid

Add the source code for the CCustomCtrlDlg::OnClickGrid function provided in Listing 19.3.

INPUT   LISTING 19.3. HANDLING A MOUSE CLICK EVENT FROM THE ACTIVEX GRID CONTROL.

```
void CCustomCtrlDlg::OnClickGrid()
{
    CString szText = m_grid.GetText();
    if( m_bEditing == FALSE )
    {
        // Save the current grid position and set the edit flag.
        m_nRow = m_grid.GetRow();
        m_nCol = m_grid.GetCol();
        m_bEditing = TRUE;
        // Get the current grid text, and display it in the edit
        // control.
        szText = m_grid.GetText();
        m_edit.SetWindowText( szText );
        m_edit.ShowWindow( SW_SHOW );
        m_edit.SetFocus();
        m_edit.SetSel( 0, -1 );
    }
```

19

continues

LISTING 19.3. CONTINUED

```
        else
        {
            // Roll up the edit control, and update the previous
            // grid position. You must save the current position,
            // go back to the old position, and then return to the
            // current position.
            int nCurrentRow = m_grid.GetRow();
            int nCurrentCol = m_grid.GetCol();
             m_grid.SetRow( m_nRow );
             m_grid.SetCol( m_nCol );
             m_grid.SetFocus();

             CString szEntry;
             m_edit.GetWindowText( szText );
            szEntry.Format("%01.2f", atof(szText) );

            m_edit.ShowWindow( SW_HIDE );
            m_grid.SetText( szEntry );
            m_bEditing = FALSE;
            m_grid.SetRow( nCurrentRow );
            m_grid.SetCol( nCurrentCol );        }
        }
```

If the program receives a Click event, the m_bEditing flag is checked to see whether a cell is currently being edited. If not, the current row and column are collected from the grid control. This information is used later when the editing job is finished. The text stored in the current grid cell is retrieved and displayed in the edit control. Finally, the edit control text is selected, which makes it easy for a user to overwrite the current contents.

If a cell is being edited, the text contained in the edit control is stored in the grid. However, it must be stored in the cell that was originally clicked to open the edit control. This cell position was stored when the edit control was opened and is now used to reset the current row and column. The edit control text is reformatted into a standard dollars-and-cents format and stored in the original cell position.

The GetRow and GetCol functions provided by CGridCtrl are examples of ActiveX control methods that are exposed by the grid control. For a complete list of exposed methods, open the project workspace view and click the ClassView tab. Open the CGridCtrl class icon, and you see a list of the available member functions.

Recalculating the Grid Control Contents

Each column in the spreadsheet is recalculated when you click the Calculate button. Add a message-handling function to the CCustomCtrlDlg class that handles messages from the Calculate button, using the values from Table 19.4.

TABLE **19.4.** MESSAGES HANDLED BY THE CCustomCtrlDlg CLASS.

Object ID	Class Name	Message	Function
IDC_CALC	CCustomCtrlDlg	BN_CLICKED	OnCalc

Add the source code in Listing 19.4 to the CCustomCtrlDlg::OnCalc member function.

INPUT   LISTING **19.4.** RECALCULATING THE CONTENTS OF THE ACTIVEX GRID CONTROL.

```
void CCustomCtrlDlg::OnCalc()
{
    // Close current editing job, if any.
    if( m_bEditing != FALSE )
    {
        CString szEntry, szText;
        m_edit.GetWindowText( szText );
        szEntry.Format("%01.2f", atof(szText) );
        m_edit.ShowWindow( SW_HIDE );
        m_grid.SetText( szEntry );
        m_bEditing = FALSE;
    }
    for( int nCol = 1; nCol < 5; nCol++ )
    {
        double  dTotal = 0.0;
        m_grid.SetCol( nCol );
        for( int nRow = 1; nRow < 4; nRow++ )
        {
            m_grid.SetRow( nRow );
            CString szCell = m_grid.GetText();
            dTotal += atof( szCell );
        }
        CString szTotal;
        szTotal.Format( "%01.2f", dTotal );
        m_grid.SetRow( 4 );
        m_grid.SetText( szTotal );    }
}
```

19

Compile and run the CustomCtrl example. The grid control is initially empty. Clicking on a cell displays the edit control, which enables you to enter or change the cell's contents. If you click on the cell again, the value from the edit control is moved into the cell, and the edit control is hidden. Clicking the Calculate button totals each column in the grid control and hides the edit control. Figure 19.4 shows the CustomCtrl main dialog box with some of the grid cells filled in.

FIGURE 19.4.

The CustomCtrl project after adding items to the grid control.

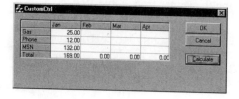

Summary

In this hour, you learned about ActiveX controls and the Developer Studio tools that are used with them. As part of the discussion, you created an example that used an ActiveX grid control as a small spreadsheet.

Q&A

Q How can I determine which events are provided by an ActiveX control?

A After the ActiveX control is added to your project, you can use ClassWizard to examine the events that are generated by the control.

Q How can I reuse controls installed on my computer by other applications?

A Most commercial controls are licensed; they can't be used to design new applications without the proper ActiveX licensing file. Some controls can be used for evaluation purposes, even without a license—to be sure, contact the control vendor.

Workshop

The Workshop is designed to help you anticipate possible questions, review what you've learned, and begin thinking ahead to putting your knowledge into practice. The answers to the quiz are in Appendix A, "Quiz Answers."

Quiz

1. Where are reusable components stored in Developer Studio?

2. What are some other development tools that support the creation and use of ActiveX controls?

3. What are some examples of events sent from an ActiveX control?

4. What are some examples of properties exposed by ActiveX controls?

5. What ActiveX control is often used to model a small spreadsheet?

6. True or False: You can edit directly in a grid cell.

7. What AppWizard option must be selected to allow an ActiveX control to work properly?

8. What is an ActiveX method?

9. True or False: ActiveX controls can be developed only for 32-bit systems.

Exercises

1. Modify the CustomCtrl project so that 12 months are displayed in the grid and totals are provided for each row as well as for columns.

2. Modify the CustomCtrl project so that the grid is recalculated automatically.

19

Part VI

Advanced MFC Programming

Hour

HOUR 20

Dynamic HTML

One of the new features introduced in Visual C++ 6 is support for writing applications that support Dynamic HTML. In this chapter, you will learn

- The support offered for Web browsing by Visual C++ and the MFC class library
- The MFC classes used to implement a view that acts as a simple Web browser
- How to embed Dynamic HTML scripts into your application as a resource

In this hour you will also build WWWTest, a sample program that will help illustrate how the MFC Web-browsing view class is used in an application.

What Is Dynamic HTML?

Dynamic HTML (Hypertext Markup Language) is a scripting language used to create Web pages. The latest versions of Internet Explorer and Netscape Navigator support Dynamic HTML, which is also known as DHTML. You can use Dynamic HTML to create interactive documents that have many of the same features as an application. You can easily create buttons and visual effects, and interact with a remote host.

A simple DHTML document that highlights text when the mouse moves over the text is provided in Listing 20.1.

LISTING 20.1. A SIMPLE DYNAMIC HTML DOCUMENT.

```
<html>
<body>

<div onmouseover="onEnterHighlight(this);"
     onmouseout="onExitHighlight(this);">
This text will change color under the mouse
</div>

<script>
function onEnterHighlight(theElement)
{
   theElement.style.color = 'red';
}

function onExitHighlight(theElement)
{
   theElement.style.color = 'black';
}

</script>

</body>
</html>
```

When the document in Listing 20.1 is loaded in Internet Explorer or another browser that supports Dynamic HTML, it causes one line of text to be displayed to a user. The following line is located between the `<div>` and `</div>` tags, creating an element that can be treated like an object:

`This text will change color under the mouse`

Dynamic HTML enables you to define special behavior and properties for the elements within a document. In this example, two events are handled:

- `onmouseover` is generated when the mouse moves over the text. When this event is received, the `onEnterHighlight` script function is called, which changes the color of the element to red.

- `onmouseout` is generated when the mouse moves away from the element. When this event is received, the `onExitHighlight` script function is called, which changes the color of the element to black.

For more information on Dynamic HTML, including event handling and properties, visit the Microsoft SiteBuilder Web site at

```
http://www.microsoft.com/workshop/author/dhtml
```

Visual C++ Support for Dynamic HTML

You can use two Visual C++ components to create an interactive application that uses Dynamic HTML:

- The Microsoft WebBrowser control
- The MFC `CHtmlView` class

You must have Internet Explorer 4.0 installed to use either of these components. Both of these components help you leverage the Internet Explorer in your own applications. The WebBrowser control is an ActiveX component that provides access to the browsing components in Internet Explorer.

The `CHtmlView` class wraps the WebBrowser control into an easy-to-use package that fits nicely into the MFC Document/View architecture. The primary function of the `CHtmlView` class is to give your application easy access to functions provided by the WebBrowser control and Internet Explorer.

Navigating

`CHtmlView` includes two functions for navigating to HTML documents. You can easily navigate to a location on your computer, a local network, or the Internet by using the `Navigate` and `Navigate2` functions. The `Navigate` function looks like this:

```
Navigate( "http://www.samspublishing.com",
          navOpenInNewWindow,
          "main",
          NULL,
          NULL,
          0);
```

`20`

`Navigate` has six parameters:

- The location that should be navigated to
- An optional browser navigation constant, discussed later
- An optional target frame for the navigation

- Optional header information that is be sent to the server; this parameter is ignored unless the location is an HTTP URL

- Optional data sent to the server during a POST transaction

- An optional parameter that contains the length of the data in the previous parameter

One version of Navigate2 takes exactly the same parameters as Navigate:

```
Navigate2( "http://www.samspublishing.com",
          navOpenInNewWindow,
          "main",
          NULL,
          NULL,
          0);
```

Only the first parameter is actually required for the Navigate and Navigate2 functions. You can get default behavior simply by providing the new location:

```
Navigate("http://www.samspublishing.com");
```

You can use the following values as browser navigation constants for the Navigate and Navigate2 functions:

- navOpenInNewWindow specifies that the location should be opened in a new instance of Internet Explorer.

- navNoHistory specifies that the new location should not be added to the history list.

- navAllowAutosearch specifies that an automatic search should be attempted if the location can't be found. Autosearch will attempt to find the location by appending common root domains to the location. If autosearch fails, the location is passed to the search engine configured by the user.

- navBrowserBar specifies that the current Explorer bar should navigate to the location.

Useful CHtmlView Class Member Functions

The CHtmlView class includes several member functions that can be used to control navigation. In addition to Navigate and Navigate2, the following are the most commonly used member functions:

- GoBack is used to navigate to the previous location in the history list, if any.

- GoHome is used to navigate to the home URL.

- GoForward is used to navigate to the next location in the history list, if any.

- Stop is used to halt the download of a document.

- Refresh is used to force the current document to be reloaded.

- `LoadFromResource` is used to load a document that has been stored as a resource.
- `Navigate`, discussed earlier, is used to navigate to a specific URL.
- `Navigate2`, also discussed earlier, is used to navigate to a specific URL or special file, such as `Desktop` or `My Computer`.

Except for the `Navigate` and `Navigate2` functions, the functions just listed have no parameters. For example, to refresh the current page, you can simply call the `Refresh` function:

```
void CMyHtmlView::OnUpdate()
{
    Refresh();
}
```

Adding Dynamic HTML to Your Programs

So were do you find a DHTML document to use in your application? There are three ways to introduce DHTML into your programs:

- A Dynamic HTML document can be embedded in your application's resource file, just like other resources such as dialog boxes, icons, and menus.
- A Dynamic HTML document can be loaded from a file on your computer.
- The document can be downloaded from a remote location on the Internet or other network.

> If your application needs a specific Dynamic HTML document that must be accessible at all times, store it as an HTML resource.

Using MFC and Dynamic HTML

For the examples in this hour, create an SDI project named WWWTest using AppWizard. In AppWizard step six, a checkered flag is displayed along with a list box that contains classes generated for the application. Follow these steps to use the `CHtmlView` class as the view for WWWTest:

1. Select the view class in the Class list box, in this case `CWWWTestView`.
2. Select `CHtmlView` from the Base Class combo box.
3. Click the Finish button to end the AppWizard process and display the New Project Information dialog box.
4. Click OK to generate the code for the WWWTest project.

20

Simple Navigation Using `CHtmlView`

When the WWWTest project is generated by AppWizard, a default implementation of
the `OnInitialUpdate` function in the `CWWWTestView` class is provided, as shown in
Listing 20.2. This function will navigate to the Microsoft Visual C++ home page and
display the page in the view.

LISTING 20.2. NAVIGATING TO AN INTERNET HTML DOCUMENT.

```
void CWWWTestView::OnInitialUpdate()
{
    CHtmlView::OnInitialUpdate();
    Navigate2(_T("http://www.microsoft.com/visualc/"),NULL,NULL);
}
```

Build and launch the WWWTest project. If you have a connection to the Internet the
Microsoft home page displays. You can navigate through the Microsoft Web site, just as
with Internet Explorer or any other browser.

Navigating to a Source File

You can also use `CHtmlView` to interact with Dynamic HTML documents located on your
local hard drive. To navigate to a file on your local computer, pass the file path as a parameter to the `Navigate` or `Navigate2` functions.

Listing 20.3 contains a Dynamic HTML page that includes a button control. When the
button control is clicked, some of the text on the page is hidden. Save the contents of
Listing 20.3 as `C:\Simple.htm`.

INPUT **LISTING 20.3.** AN INTERACTIVE DYNAMIC HTML PAGE.

```
<html>
<body>
This example uses DHTML to hide text that has the span attribute.

<!--- Define the button control   ---!>
<p>
    <button style="cursor: hand"
        onclick="onOffToggle(document.all.toggledLine);"
        onmouseover="onEnterHighlight(this);"
        onmouseout="onExitHighlight(this);">DHTML Toggle
    </button>
</p>
```

```
Click the button to hide the blue text on the line below.<br>

<!--- Define a span as the first part of a line of text  ---!>
<span style="color: blue"
    id=toggledLine>
    Should I stay or should I go?
</span> I'm staying, no matter what!<br>

<script>
<!---  onOffToggle: toggles an element's display property  ---!>
function onOffToggle(theElement)
{
  if(theElement.style.display == "none"){
    theElement.style.display = "";
  }else{
    theElement.style.display = "none";
  }
}

<!---  OnEnterHighlight: highlights an element  ---!>
function onEnterHighlight(theElement)
{
  theElement.style.color = 'red';
}

<!---  OnEnterHighlight: clears highlights from an element ---!>
function onExitHighlight(theElement)
{
  theElement.style.color = 'black';
}

</script>

</body>
</html>
```

To modify the WWWTest project so that Simple.htm is loaded when its view is initially displayed, replace the OnInitialUpdate function in CWWWTestView with the function provided in Listing 20.4.

20

INPUT

LISTING 20.4. NAVIGATING TO A DYNAMIC HTML DOCUMENT ON THE LOCAL COMPUTER.

```
void CWWWTestView::OnInitialUpdate()
{
    CHtmlView::OnInitialUpdate();
    Navigate2("c:\\simple.htm", NULL, NULL);
}
```

Build and run the WWWTest project. Figure 20.1 shows the WWWTest project displaying the Simple.htm page.

FIGURE 20.1.

*Displaying a Dynamic
HTML page in an
MFC application.*

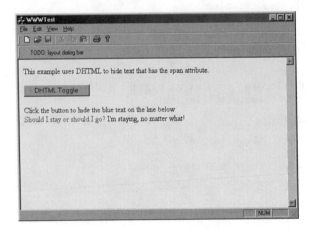

Navigating to the User's Home Page

In addition to the navigation capabilities discussed earlier, the CHtmlView class allows
you easy access to the configuration information used by Internet Explorer. For example,
you can navigate to the home page defined by the user by calling the
CHtmlView::GoHome member function.

To enable the WWWTest program to navigate to the predefined home page, you must
first add a new menu item to the WWWTest project. Add a menu item to the View menu,
using the values from Table 20.1.

TABLE 20.1. A NEW MENU ITEM FOR THE VIEW MENU.

Menu ID	Caption	Event	Function Name
ID_VIEW_HOME	Home	COMMAND	OnViewHome

Use the values from Table 20.1 to add a menu-handling function to the CWWWTestView class
named OnViewHome. Add the source code from Listing 20.5 to the OnViewHome function.

INPUT **LISTING 20.5.** NAVIGATING TO THE USER'S HOME PAGE.

```
void CWWWTestView::OnViewHome()
{
    GoHome();
}
```

Build and run the WWWTest project. Navigate to the local computer's home page by selecting Home from the View menu.

Using a Dynamic HTML Document Resource

A Dynamic HTML document can be stored as one of your application's resources, just like menus, dialog boxes, and icons. Storing a page as a resource often makes it easier to use in your application because you can refer to the resource with a symbol name instead of providing a path or location.

You add an HTML resource to a project much like any other resource:

1. Right-click the resource tree and select Insert from the shortcut menu. An Insert Resource dialog box displays.

2. Select HTML as the resource type, and click the button labeled New to close the dialog box.

3. A blank HTML document will be added to the resource tree, and the document will be opened for editing.

To modify a property for an HTML resource such as the Resource ID, right-click anywhere in the HTML document while it's loaded in the editor, and select Properties from the shortcut menu.

Add a new HTML resource to the WWWTest project, using the steps outlined previously. Name the resource IDR_VISUALC_LINKS. Add the source code from Listing 20.6 to the resource.

INPUT

LISTING 20.6. AN HTML PAGE THAT DISPLAYS USEFUL LINKS FOR VISUAL C++ PROGRAMMING.

```
<html>
<body>

<h3>Useful Visual C++ Programming Links</h3>
<br>
<ul>
<li><A HREF = "http://www.microsoft.com/msdn">
      Microsoft Developer's Network
   </A>
</li>
<li><A HREF = "http://www.microsoft.com/visualc">
      Visual C++ Start Page
   </A>
```

20

continues

LISTING 20.6. CONTINUED

```
</li>
<li><A HREF = "http://www.mcp.com">
      Macmillan Computer Publishing
    </A>
</li>
<li><A HREF = "http://www.numega.com">
      NuMega Technologies
    </A>
</li>
<li><A HREF = "http://www.codevtech.com">
      Codev Technologies
    </A>
</li>
</ul>

</body>
</html>
```

To use the IDR_VISUALC_LINKS resource when the WWWTest project is run, you use the LoadFromResource function. You pass to this function the ID of the HTML resource you want loaded. To see this in action, replace the OnInitialUpdate function in CWWWTestView with the function provided in Listing 20.7.

INPUT **LISTING 20.7.** NAVIGATING TO A DYNAMIC HTML RESOURCE.

```
void CWWWTestView::OnInitialUpdate()
{
    CHtmlView::OnInitialUpdate();
    LoadFromResource(IDR_VISUALC_LINKS);
}
```

Build and run the WWWTest project. The contents of the HTML resource will be displayed in the WWWTest application's view, as shown in Figure 20.2.

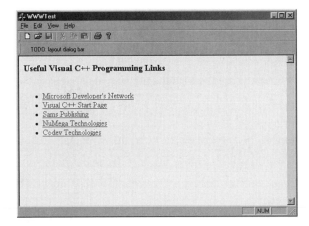

Summary

In this hour you learned about the support that Visual C++ includes for Dynamic HTML. You learned how to use AppWizard to create an application that uses CHtmlView as its view class, and how to use member functions found in CHtmlView to add browser-like functionality to your programs.

Q&A

Q Why are file paths that contain backslashes written with two backslashes where I would expect to see only one?

A The backslash is a special character in C and C++ programming. To indicate that a backslash is required, you must use two backslashes together.

Q Why don't the examples in this hour work on a machine that doesn't have Internet Explorer installed?

A The WebBrowser control and CHtmlView use Internet Explorer to provide the Web browser functions discussed this hour. If Internet Explorer isn't installed, those functions aren't available.

Workshop

The Workshop is designed to help you anticipate possible questions, review what you've learned, and begin thinking ahead to putting your knowledge into practice. The answers to the quiz are in Appendix A, "Quiz Answers."

20

Quiz

1. What MFC class is used to manage Dynamic HTML documents?
2. What function is used to load a Web page?
3. What function is used to load the previous document in the history list?
4. What function is used to navigate to the home page configured for Internet Explorer?
5. What function is used to load a Web page stored as a resource?
6. What function is used to load the next document in the history list?
7. What event is generated for a Dynamic HTML element when the mouse moves over the element?
8. What event is generated for a Dynamic HTML element when the mouse moves away from the element?
9. How do you get access to the properties for an HTML resource?

Exercises

1. Change the WWWTest example so that a new menu item causes the view to navigate to the Microsoft Internet Explorer WWW page at

   `http://www.microsoft.com/ie`

2. Add a menu item to the WWWTest example that allows you to move to the previous document in the history list.

Hour 21

Printing

There are two primary output devices in Windows: the screen and the printer. In this hour, you will learn

- The support provided for printing using the Document/View architecture
- The differences between printer and screen display output
- How to manage GDI resources used for printing

You also will create a sample program to learn how printing for a Document/View application is done.

What Is Printing in a Windows Program?

Programs written for Windows should be hardware independent. This extends to the printer, where all output is performed through device contexts, much as displays to the screen are performed.

Many programs written for Windows need no hard-copy output. However, many programs can be improved by providing reports or other information in a printout. The Document/View architecture and MFC class library provide standard printing functionality to all SDI and MDI applications.

Historically, printing in a program written for Windows has been a nightmare. Using the traditional SDK approach, seemingly dozens of function calls and structures must be used to send output to a printer. Because Windows supports literally hundreds of printers, ensuring that printed output is printed correctly can be difficult.

The Document/View architecture and the MFC class library help make creating hard-copy printouts in a Windows program much easier. You can use the Common Print dialog box and reuse functions in your view class to display information on the screen.

Printing in an MFC program is almost effortless. If your program uses the Document/View architecture and does all its drawing in the OnDraw function, you might not need to do anything to get basic printing to work. The source code provided in Listing 21.1 is an example of a simple OnDraw function that can be used for both screen and printer output.

LISTING 21.1. A SIMPLE OnDraw FUNCTION THAT WORKS FOR THE SCREEN AND THE PRINTER.

```
void CPrintView::OnDraw(CDC* pDC)
{
    CString szMsg = "Hello printer and view example.";
    pDC->TextOut( 0, 50, szMsg );
}
```

Using the view's OnDraw member function is an easy way to take advantage of the hardware independence offered by Windows. If your code is portable enough to run on a variety of screen displays, you probably will get an acceptable printout using most printers available for Windows.

On the other hand, there are many cases in which you might want to get more involved in the printing. For example, if your view is not WYSIWYG, the printed output might not be suitable. If your view is a form view, for example, you might want to print your document's data in another form, such as a list of items in the entire document or detailed information about an item in the current form.

When you customize the view functions that are responsible for printing, you can also offer nice user interface elements such as headers, footers, page numbers, or special fonts.

Understanding the MFC Printing Routines

The following CView routines are used to print a view:

- OnPreparePrinting, called before the Common Print dialog box is displayed
- OnBeginPrinting, where GDI resources specific to using the printer should be allocated
- OnPrepareDC, called once per page just before the printout begins
- OnPrint, called to actually draw to the printer's device context (DC)
- OnEndPrinting, called once after all pages have been printed or after the job is canceled; this is where GDI resources specific to using the printer are released

These member functions are called by the MFC framework as the print routine progresses. The relationship between these routines is shown in Figure 21.1.

FIGURE 21.1.

CView *member functions called when printing a document.*

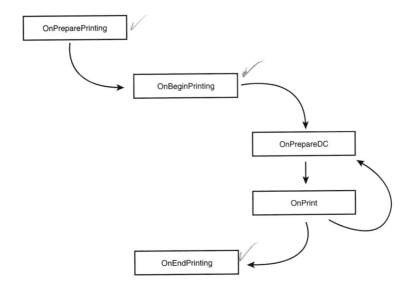

As shown in Figure 21.1, only the OnPrepareDC and OnPrint member functions are called for every page sent to the printer. The other functions are used to initiate variables in preparation of the printout or to clean up and free resources after the printout has been completed.

When AppWizard creates a view class for your program, the OnPreparePrinting, OnBeginPrinting, and OnEndPrinting functions are automatically provided for you. You can add the other member functions with ClassWizard if you must override the basic functionality.

21

Creating an MFC Printing Example

As an example of the MFC print functions, create a small program that displays information to the screen and the printer. To begin, create an SDI project named MFCPrint using ClassWizard.

With ClassWizard, add two message-handling functions for the CMFCPrintView class: OnPrepareDC and OnPrint. You'll find out more about OnPrepareDC and OnPrint in the next few sections. The other printing functions have already been included in the CMFCPrintView class by AppWizard.

Add five new member variables and two new functions to the implementation section of the CMFCPrintView class, as shown in Listing 21.2.

INPUT   **LISTING 21.2.** NEW CPrintView MEMBER VARIABLES.

```
protected:
    int     m_nCurrentPrintedPage;
    CFont*  m_pFntBold;
    CFont*  m_pFntBanner;
    CFont*  m_pFntHighlight;
    void PrintHeader(CDC* pDC);
    void PrintFooter(CDC* pDC);
```

These new member variables and functions are used during the printout.

Checking the Current State of a Printout

The CPrintInfo class is used to store information about the current state of a printout. A pointer to a CPrintInfo object is passed as a parameter to functions involved in the printout. You can access attributes of the CPrintInfo object for information about the printout, or in some cases you can change the attributes to customize the printout. Here are the most commonly used CPrintInfo members:

- m_bPreview is a flag that is set to TRUE if the document is being previewed.
- m_bContinuePrinting is a flag that is set to FALSE to stop the print loop.
- m_nCurPage contains the currently printing page number.
- m_rectDraw contains the current printout rectangle.
- SetMinPage sets the document's first page number.
- SetMaxPage sets the document's last page number.
- GetMinPage returns the value previously set as the document's first page number.

- GetMaxPage returns the value previously set as the document's last page number.
- GetFromPage returns the number of the first page being printed.
- GetToPage returns the number of the last page being printed.

Some of these members are used in a particular function. As you learn about each function in the next few sections, commonly used CPrintInfo members will be discussed.

Using the OnPreparePrinting Function

AppWizard generates the OnPreparePrinting function for a project's initial view class. This function is called before the Common Print dialog box is displayed, and it gives you an opportunity to change the values displayed in the Print dialog box.

If your document has more than one page, you should calculate the number of pages, if possible. This allows the maximum number of pages to be displayed in the Print dialog box. You can set the number of pages by calling the CPrintInfo::SetMaxPages function:

```
pInfo->SetMaxPages( 2 );
```

> You should not allocate resources in the CPrintInfo::SetMaxPages function because you are not notified if the user cancels the Print dialog box.

Using the OnBeginPrinting Function

The OnBeginPrinting function is called after the user has pressed OK in the Print dialog box in order to start the printout. This function is the proper place to allocate resources such as fonts, brushes, and pens that might be needed for the printout. In the example you work with later, this function is used to create CFont objects.

The OnBeginPrinting function is called only once for each printout. If this function is called, the OnEndPrinting function is called after the printout is finished in order to give you a chance to free resources allocated in the OnBeginPrinting function.

Using the OnPrepareDC Function

The OnPrepareDC function is called just before a page is printed or displayed in the view. If OnPrepareDC is called with the CPrintInfo pointer set to NULL, the document is not being printed.

21

This function often is overridden for multiple-page documents in order to continue the printout over multiple pages. To print another page, set the CPrintInfo::m_bContinue member variable to TRUE:

```
pInfo->m_bContinuePrinting = TRUE;
```

> By default, only one page will be printed unless you override OnPrepareDC and set m_bContinuePrinting to TRUE.

Using the OnPrint Function

The OnPrint function is the printing counterpart to OnDraw. In fact, many programs can just use the default version of OnPrint, which calls OnDraw. However, most printouts can benefit from providing page numbers, headers, footers, or special fonts that aren't displayed in the view.

NEW TERM   A *twip* is 1/20 of a point. A *point*, in turn, is almost exactly 1/72 of an inch. This works out to about 1,440 twips per inch.

When printing, the MM_TWIPS mapping mode is used. The really odd thing about MM_TWIPS is that the mapping mode begins with the upper-left corner at (0,0) and runs in a negative direction down the page, making the point one inch below the origin (0,–1440). Like other modes, the mapping mode extends in a positive direction to the right side of the page.

The OnPrint function is called once for every page. If you're printing data that is arranged so that the page number can easily be determined, it's a good idea to use the CPrintInfo parameter to determine the current page number.

> Remember, the user might ask for a range of pages to be printed, not just the entire document. No built-in MFC function will take you directly to the proper page in your document. If the user has selected a range, you must calculate the proper place to start printing yourself.

Using the OnEndPrinting Function

The OnEndPrinting function is called after the printout is finished. This function is not used to print footers or other information at the end of the print job. This function can be called because the job was completed successfully or because it has failed; you don't really know. The purpose of this function is to release any resources that were allocated in the OnBeginPrinting function.

Querying the Printing Device Context

Unlike video displays, printing devices offer a wide variation in their capabilities. It's a good idea to examine the capabilities of a printout device before attempting graphics functions.

As shown in Listing 21.3, you can use the CDC::GetDeviceCaps function to retrieve information about a selected output device.

LISTING 21.3. USING GetDeviceCaps TO DETERMINE WHETHER BitBlt IS
INPUT SUPPORTED.

```
int nRasterFlags = pDC->GetDeviceCaps(RASTERCAPS);
if(nRasterCaps & RC_BITBLT)
{
    // BitBlt is allowed
}
else
{
    // BitBlt is not allowed
}
```

GetDeviceCaps accepts an index as a parameter. This index specifies the type of information returned from the function. In Listing 21.3, the RASTERCAPS index results in a return value that contains flags which indicate the raster capabilities of the device. If the RC_BITBLT flag is set, the BitBlt function can be applied to that device.

> You can use this function for any type of device—not just printers. This function can be used to return all types of information. Check the online documentation for details.

Adding Printing Functionality to the MFCPrint Example

21

The remaining part of this hour is used to add printing functionality to the MFCPrint example, using the functions discussed in the earlier sections. The OnPreparePrinting function supplied by AppWizard isn't changed for this example.

Initializing and Destroying Resources for Printing

The member variables added to the CMFCPrintView class must be initialized in the CMFCPrintView constructor, and any allocated resources must be released in the destructor. The source code for the constructor and destructor is provided in Listing 21.4.

INPUT   LISTING **21.4.** THE CONSTRUCTOR AND DESTRUCTOR FOR CMFCPrintView.

```
CMFCPrintView::CMFCPrintView()
{
    COLORREF clrBlack = GetSysColor(COLOR_WINDOWFRAME);
    m_pFntBold = NULL;
    m_pFntBanner = NULL;
    m_pFntHighlight = NULL;
}

CMFCPrintView::~CMFCPrintView()
{
    // The fonts must be released explicitly
    // since they were created with new.
    delete m_pFntBold;
    delete m_pFntBanner;
    delete m_pFntHighlight;
}
```

The usual practice with GDI objects is to defer actually creating the object until it is needed. The constructor for CMFCPrintView sets each of the CFont pointer variables to NULL; these objects are created dynamically using the new operator when the print job begins.

The destructor for CMFCPrintView deletes the dynamically allocated CFont objects. Under normal execution, these pointers do not need to be freed because resources are released at the end of a print job. However, this code protects you in case of abnormal program termination, and because it is always safe to delete a pointer with a value of NULL or zero, no harm will come to your program in the normal case.

Allocating Resources for Printing

As you learned earlier, the OnBeginPrinting function is called just before printing begins. Add the source code in Listing 21.5 to the OnBeginPrinting function. This version of OnBeginPrinting creates three new fonts that are used in the printout. (You learned about creating fonts in Hour 13, "Fonts.")

> To prevent compiler warnings about unused variables, AppWizard comments
> out the pDC and pInfo parameters. If you use these parameters, you must
> remove the comments, as shown in Listing 21.5.

INPUT   **LISTING 21.5.** ALLOCATING NEW FONTS IN THE OnBeginPrinting FUNCTION.

```
void CMFCPrintView::OnBeginPrinting(CDC* pDC, CPrintInfo* pInfo)
{
    ASSERT( m_pFntBold == 0 );
    ASSERT( m_pFntBanner == 0 );
    ASSERT( m_pFntHighlight == 0 );

    m_nCurrentPrintedPage = 0;
    pDC->SetMapMode( MM_TWIPS );

    // Create the bold font used for the fields. TimesRoman,
    // 12 point semi-bold is used.
    m_pFntBold = new CFont;
    ASSERT( m_pFntBold );
    m_pFntBold->CreateFont( -240,
                            0,
                            0,
                            0,
                            FW_SEMIBOLD,
                            FALSE,
                            FALSE,
                            0,
                            ANSI_CHARSET,
                            OUT_TT_PRECIS,
                            CLIP_DEFAULT_PRECIS,
                            DEFAULT_QUALITY,
                            DEFAULT_PITCH | FF_ROMAN,
                            "Times Roman" );
    // Create the normal font used for the Headline banner.
    // TimesRoman, 18 point italic is used.
    m_pFntBanner = new CFont;
    ASSERT( m_pFntBanner );
    m_pFntBanner->CreateFont( -360,
                              0,
                              0,
                              0,
                              FW_NORMAL,
                              TRUE,
                              FALSE,
                              0,
                              ANSI_CHARSET,
```

21

continues

LISTING 21.5. CONTINUED

```
                                          OUT_TT_PRECIS,
                                          CLIP_DEFAULT_PRECIS,
                                          DEFAULT_QUALITY,
                                          DEFAULT_PITCH | FF_ROMAN,
                                          "Times Roman" );
        // Create the normal font used for the Headline highlight.
        // This is the text used under the headline banner, and in
        // the footer. TimesRoman, 8 point is used.
        m_pFntHighlight = new CFont;
        ASSERT( m_pFntHighlight );
        m_pFntHighlight->CreateFont( -160,
                                      0,
                                      0,
                                      0,
                                      FW_NORMAL,
                                      TRUE,
                                      FALSE,
                                      0,
                                      ANSI_CHARSET,
                                      OUT_TT_PRECIS,
                                      CLIP_DEFAULT_PRECIS,
                                      DEFAULT_QUALITY,
                                      DEFAULT_PITCH | FF_ROMAN,
                                      "Times Roman" );
        CView::OnBeginPrinting(pDC, pInfo);
    }
```

Printing Multiple Pages

The OnPrepareDC function is called just before each page is printed. The default version
of this function allows one page to be printed. By modifying the bContinuePrinting
flag, you can use this function to continue the printout. Add the source code provided in
Listing 21.6 to the OnPrepareDC function.

INPUT   **LISTING 21.6.** THE OnPrepareDC FUNCTION.

```
void CMFCPrintView::OnPrepareDC(CDC* pDC, CPrintInfo* pInfo)
{
    CView::OnPrepareDC(pDC, pInfo);
    if( pInfo )
    {
        if(pInfo->m_nCurPage < pInfo->GetToPage())
            pInfo->m_bContinuePrinting = TRUE;
```

```
        else
            pInfo->m_bContinuePrinting = FALSE;
    }
}
```

The OnPrepareDC function is called by the MFC framework to give you a chance to modify the device context that is used for the printout. You should not try to do any printing in this function—you should perform that work in the OnPrint function, which is discussed in the next section.

Printing the Actual Report in the OnPrint Function

The default implementation of OnPrint calls the OnDraw member function. For this example, add the source code from Listing 21.7 to OnPrint, which sends a header followed by several rows of text and a footer to the printer.

INPUT   **LISTING 21.7.** PRINTING A HEADER AND TEXT USING THE OnPrint FUNCTION.

```
void CMFCPrintView::OnPrint(CDC* pDC, CPrintInfo* pInfo)
{
    CPoint      pt( 5000, -7000 );
    TEXTMETRIC  tm;

    //Because the DC has been modified, it's always a good idea to reset
    //the mapping mode, no matter which one you use. In our case, because
    //we use MM_TWIPS, we have to reset the mapping mode for each page.
    pDC->SetMapMode( MM_TWIPS );
    PrintHeader( pDC );
    CFont* pOldFont = pDC->SelectObject( m_pFntBold );
    pDC->GetTextMetrics( &tm );
    int cyText = tm.tmHeight + tm.tmExternalLeading;

    m_nCurrentPrintedPage++;
    pDC->TextOut( pt.x, pt.y, "Hello Printer!!!" );

    pt.y += cyText;
    CString  szPageInfo;
    szPageInfo.Format( TEXT("Page number %d"),
    m_nCurrentPrintedPage );
    pDC->TextOut( pt.x, pt.y, szPageInfo );

    pDC->SelectObject( pOldFont );
    PrintFooter( pDC );
}
```

21

The OnPrint function is called once per page. In MFCPrint, the OnPrint function prints the header, prints a message in the middle of the page, then prints the footer. The current position on the page is stored in pt, a CPoint object.

Listing 21.8 provides the source code used to print the header and footer. Add these two functions to the MFCPrintView.cpp source file.

INPUT **LISTING 21.8.** PRINTING THE HEADER AND FOOTER.

```
void CMFCPrintView::PrintFooter( CDC* pDC )
{
    ASSERT( pDC );
    TEXTMETRIC  tm;
    CPoint   pt( 0, -14400 );

    //Select the smaller font used for the file name.
    ASSERT( m_pFntHighlight );
    CFont* pOldFont = pDC->SelectObject( m_pFntHighlight );
    ASSERT( pOldFont );
    pDC->GetTextMetrics( &tm );
    int cyText = tm.tmHeight + tm.tmExternalLeading;

    pt.y -= cyText;
    pDC->TextOut( pt.x, pt.y, TEXT("Every page needs a footer") );
    // Restore GDI objects.
    pDC->SelectObject( pOldFont );
}
void CMFCPrintView::PrintHeader( CDC* pDC )
{
    ASSERT( pDC );
    TEXTMETRIC  tm;
    CPoint       pt( 0, 0 );

    // Select the banner font, and print the headline.
    CFont* pOldFont = pDC->SelectObject( m_pFntBanner );
    ASSERT( pOldFont );
    pDC->GetTextMetrics( &tm );
    int cyText = tm.tmHeight + tm.tmExternalLeading;
    pt.y -= cyText;
    pDC->TextOut( pt.x, pt.y, " Teach Yourself Visual C++ in 24 Hours" );
    // We move down about 1/2 line, and print the report type using the
    // smaller font.
    VERIFY( pDC->SelectObject( m_pFntHighlight ) );
    pDC->GetTextMetrics( &tm );
    cyText = tm.tmHeight + tm.tmExternalLeading;
    pt.y -= (cyText / 2);
    pDC->TextOut( pt.x, pt.y, "Printing Demonstration" );
    // Restore GDI objects.
    pDC->SelectObject( pOldFont );
}
```

In Listing 21.8, the source code used to create the header and footer are placed into separate functions. This helps keep the functions small and reusable—they can be used in other programs without much modification.

Releasing Resources After Printing

The OnEndPrinting function is called once per print job, but only if the OnBeginPrinting function has been called. Use this function to release the resources allocated in OnBeginPrinting.

> The destructor is called when the CMFCPrintView instance is destroyed. Normally, the resources are released in OnEndPrinting. If there's a GPF or other application error, OnEndPrinting won't be called, so you must also clean up in the destructor.

> You must match all your allocations made in OnBeginPrinting with deallocations in OnEndPrinting. If you don't, you will get a memory or resource leak.

Listing 21.9 is the source code for the OnEndPrinting function used in MFCPrintView. As in the OnBeginPrinting function presented in Listing 21.5, AppWizard comments out the pDC and pInfo parameters. If you use these parameters, you must remove the comments.

INPUT   **LISTING 21.9.** RELEASING RESOURCES IN THE OnEndPrinting FUNCTION.

```
void CMFCPrintView::OnEndPrinting(CDC* pDC, CPrintInfo* pInfo)
{
    delete m_pFntBold;
    delete m_pFntBanner;
    delete m_pFntHighlight;
    // Because the destructor also deletes these fonts, we have
    // to set pointers to 0 to avoid dangling pointers and exceptions
    // generated by invoking delete on a non-valid pointer.
    m_pFntBold = NULL;
    m_pFntBanner = NULL;
    m_pFntHighlight = NULL;
    CView::OnEndPrinting(pDC, pInfo);
}
```

21

Compile and run the MFCPrint project, and send the output to the printer using either the File menu or the toolbar icon. Send the sample printout pages to the printer.

Summary

In this hour you learned about the print functions and support offered by MFC and the Document/View architecture. You learned the steps that you must go through to print a report; these included initializing your printing information, setting up your print device contexts, printing your actual information, and cleaning up after your report is completed.

Q&A

Q How can I draw graphics such as rectangles and ellipses on my printouts?

A The same way that you draw them to the screen—you can use all the basic GDI functions when printing, including `Ellipse` and `Rectangle`.

Q How can I change my printout to have landscape instead of portrait orientation?

A To change the page orientation to landscape, you must change a printing attribute attached to the device context. Due to minor differences in the way in which Windows 95, Windows 98, and Windows NT handle printing details, this must be done for each page during the `OnPrepareDC` function. Add the following code at the top of `CMFCPrintView::OnPrepareDC`:

```
if(pDC->IsPrinting())
{
    LPDEVMODE   pDevMode;
    pDevMode = pInfo->m_pPD->GetDevMode();
    pDevMode->dmOrientation = DMORIENT_LANDSCAPE;
    pDC->ResetDC(pDevMode);
}
```

Workshop

The Workshop is designed to help you review what you've learned and begin thinking ahead to putting your knowledge into practice. The answers to the quiz are in Appendix A, "Quiz Answers."

Quiz

1. How can you determine whether a printer supports `BitBlt` operations?
2. What five MFC view functions are most commonly overridden for printing?
3. Which MFC view functions are called once for every printed page, and which functions are called once per print job?
4. What class is used to store information about the state of a print job?

5. Which view function is used to allocate resources used to render the printout?

6. Approximately how many twips are in an inch?

7. What CPrintInfo member variable must be set for multiple page printouts?

8. When using the MM_TWIPS mapping mode, which direction is positive: up or down?

9. When using the MM_TWIPS mapping mode, which direction is positive: left or right?

10. Which MFC view function should be used to release resources allocated for printing?

Exercises

1. Modify the MFCPrint project so that it prints the page number at the foot of each page.

2. Modify the MFCPrint project so that it prints the time at the top of each page.

21

Hour **22**

Using MFC to Save Program Data

MFC programs use a process known as *serialization* to read and write application data to files. In this hour, you will learn about

- Persistence and serialization
- Serialization support in commonly used MFC classes
- Macros and other MFC features that are used when implementing serialization

You also will create an example that uses serialization in a Document/View application.

What Are Persistence and Serialization?

NEW TERM The property of an object to be stored and loaded is *persistence*, which is also defined as the capability of an object to save and reload its data between executions.

NEW TERM   *Serialization* is the process of storing the state of an object for the purpose of loading it at another time. Serialization is the way in which classes derived from CDocument store and retrieve data from an archive, which is usually a file. Figure 22.1 shows the interaction between a serialized object and an archive.

FIGURE 22.1.

Serializing an object to and from an archive.

When an object is serialized, information about the object's type is written to the storage along with information and data about the object. When an object is deserialized, the same process happens in reverse, and the object is loaded and created from the input stream.

Why Use Serialization?

The goal behind serialization is to make the storage of complex objects as simple and reliable as the storage of the basic data types available in C++. You can store a basic type, such as an int, in a file in the following way:

```
int nFoo = 5;
fileStream << nFoo;
```

If a file contains an int value, it can be read from the stream in the following way:

```
fileStream >> nFoo;
```

A persistent object can be serialized and deserialized using a similar syntax, no matter how complicated the object's internal structure. Using serialization to store objects is much more flexible than writing specialized functions that store data in a fixed format.

Persistent objects also help you easily write programs that are saved to storage. An object that is serialized might be made up of many smaller objects that are also serialized. Because individual objects are often stored in a collection, serializing the collection also serializes all objects contained in the collection.

A Document/View Serialization Example

Using AppWizard, create an MDI project named Customers. This project will use serialization to store a very simple list of customer names and email addresses, using a persistent class named CUser. This project will serve as the basis for examples and source code used in the remainder of this hour.

The MFC Classes Used for Serialization

You use two MFC classes to serialize objects:

- CArchive is almost always a file and is the object that other persistent objects are serialized to or from.
- CObject defines all the interfaces used to serialize objects to or from a CArchive object.

Objects are serialized in one of two ways. As a rule of thumb, if an object is derived from CObject, that object's Serialize member function is called in the following way:

```
myObject.Serialize( ar );
```

If the object isn't derived from CObject—such as a CRect object—you should use the insertion operator in the following way:

```
ar << rcWnd;
```

This insertion operator is overloaded in much the same way it is for cout and cin, which were used in the first two hours for console-mode input and output.

Using the CObject Class

You must use the CObject class for all classes that use the MFC class library's built-in support for serialization. The CObject class contains virtual functions that are used during serialization. The most commonly used virtual function in CObject is Serialize, which is called to serialize or deserialize the object from a CArchive object. This function is declared as virtual so that any persistent object can be called through a pointer to CObject in the following way:

```
CObject* pObj = GetNextObject();
pObj->Serialize( ar );
```

As discussed later in the section "Using the Serialization Macros," when you're deriving a persistent class from CObject, you must use two macros to help implement the serialization functions.

The CArchive Class

The CArchive class is used to model a generic storage object. In most cases, a CArchive object is attached to a disk file. In some cases, however, the object might be connected to an object that only seems to be a file, like a memory location or another type of storage.

When a CArchive object is created, it is defined as used for either input or output but never both. You can use the IsStoring and IsLoading functions to determine whether a CArchive object is used for input or output, as shown in Listing 22.1.

LISTING 22.1. USING THE CArchive::IsStoring FUNCTION TO DETERMINE THE SERIALIZATION DIRECTION.

```
CMyObject;Serialize( CArchive& ar )
{
    if( ar.IsStoring() )
        // Write object state to ar
    else
        // Read object state from ar}
```

Using the Insertion and Extraction Operators

The MFC class library overloads the insertion and extraction operators for many commonly used classes and basic types. You often use the insertion operator, <<, to serialize—or store—data to the CArchive object. You use the extraction operator, >>, to deserialize—or load—data from a CArchive object.

These operators are defined for all basic C++ types, as well as a few commonly used classes not derived from CObject, such as the CString, CRect, and CTime classes. The insertion and extraction operators return a reference to a CArchive object, enabling them to be chained together in the following way:

```
archive << m_nFoo << m_rcClient << m_szName;
```

When used with classes that are derived from CObject, the insertion and extraction operators allocate the memory storage required to contain an object and then call the object's Serialize member function. If you don't need to allocate storage, you should call the Serialize member function directly.

Using the Serialization Macros

There are two macros that you must use when creating a persistent class based on CObject. Use the DECLARE_SERIAL macro in the class declaration file and the IMPLEMENT_SERIAL macro in the class implementation file.

Declaring a Persistent Class

The DECLARE_SERIAL macro takes a single parameter: the name of the class to be serialized. An example of a class that can be serialized is provided in Listing 22.2. Save this source code in the Customers project directory in a file named Users.h.

> A good place to put the DECLARE_SERIAL macro is on the first line of the class declaration, where it serves as a reminder that the class can be serialized.

INPUT   **LISTING 22.2.** THE CUser CLASS DECLARATION.

```
#pragma once
class CUser : public CObject
{
    DECLARE_SERIAL(CUser);
public:
    // Constructors
    CUser();
    CUser( const CString& szName, const CString& szAddr );
    // Attributes
    void Set( const CString& szName, const CString& szAddr );
    CString GetName() const;
    CString GetAddr() const;
    // Operations
    virtual void Serialize( CArchive& ar );
    // Implementation
private:
    // The user's name
    CString m_szName;
    // The user's e-mail addresss
    CString m_szAddr;
};
```

Defining a Persistent Class

The IMPLEMENT_SERIAL macro takes three parameters and is usually placed before any member functions are defined for a persistent class. The parameters for IMPLEMENT_SERIAL are the following:

- The class to be serialized
- The immediate base class of the class being serialized
- The schema, or version number

The schema number is a version number for the class layout used when you're serializing and deserializing objects. If the schema number of the data being loaded doesn't match the schema number of the object reading the file, the MFC library will generate an error. The schema number should be incremented when changes are made that affect serialization, such as adding a class member or changing the serialization order.

The member functions for the CUser class, including the IMPLEMENT_SERIAL macro, are provided in Listing 22.3. Save this source code in the Customers project directory as Users.cpp.

INPUT **LISTING 22.3.** THE CUser MEMBER FUNCTIONS.

```
#include "stdafx.h"
#include "Users.h"

IMPLEMENT_SERIAL( CUser, CObject, 1 );
CUser::CUser() { }
CUser::CUser( const CString& szName, const CString& szAddr )
{
    Set( szName, szAddr );
}
void CUser::Set( const CString& szName, const CString& szAddr )
{
    m_szName = szName;
    m_szAddr = szAddr;
}
CString CUser::GetName() const
{
    return m_szName;
}
CString CUser::GetAddr() const
{
    return m_szAddr;}
```

Overriding the Serialize Function

Every persistent class must implement a Serialize member function, which is called in order to serialize or deserialize an object. The single parameter for Serialize is the CArchive object used to load or store the object. The version of Serialize used by the CUser class is shown in Listing 22.4; add this function to the Users.cpp source file.

INPUT   **LISTING 22.4.** THE CUser::Serialize MEMBER FUNCTION.

```
void CUser::Serialize( CArchive& ar )
{
    if( ar.IsLoading() )
    {
        ar >> m_szName >> m_szAddr;
    }
    else
    {
        ar << m_szName << m_szAddr;
    }
}
```

Creating a Serialized Collection

You can serialize most MFC collection classes, enabling large amounts of information to be stored and retrieved easily. For example, you can serialize a CArray collection by calling its Serialize member function.

By default, the template-based collection classes perform a bitwise write when serializing a collection and a bitwise read when deserializing an archive. This means that the data stored in the collection is literally written, bit by bit, to the archive. Bitwise serialization is a problem when you use collections to store pointers to objects. For example, the Customers project uses the CArray class to store a collection of CUser objects. The declaration of the CArray member is as follows:

```
CArray<CUser*, CUser*&>    m_setOfUsers;
```

Because the m_setOfUsers collection stores CUser pointers, storing the collection using a bitwise write will only store the current addresses of the contained objects. This information becomes useless when the archive is deserialized.

Usually, you must implement a helper function to assist in serializing a template-based collection. Helper functions don't belong to a class; they are global functions. The helper function used when serializing a template is SerializeElements. Figure 22.2 shows how you call the SerializeElements function to help serialize items stored in a collection.

FIGURE 22.2.

The
SerializeElements
helper function.

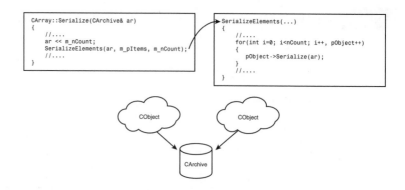

A version of SerializeElements used with collections of CUser objects is provided in Listing 22.5. Add this source code to the bottom of the CustomersDoc.cpp source file.

INPUT   **LISTING 22.5.** THE SerializeElements FUNCTION.

```
void AFXAPI SerializeElements( CArchive&    ar,
                               CUser**      pUser,
                               int          nCount )
{
    for( int i = 0; i < nCount; i++, pUser++ )
    {
        if( ar.IsStoring() )
        {
            CUser *pStoredUser = *pUser;
            pStoredUser->Serialize(ar);
        }
        else
        {
            CUser* pNewUser = new CUser;
            pNewUser->Serialize(ar);
            *pUser = pNewUser;
        }
    }
}
```

The SerializeObjects function has three parameters:

- A pointer to a CArchive object, as with Serialize.
- The address of an object stored in the collection. In this example, pointers to CUser are stored in a CArray, so the parameter is a pointer to a CUser pointer.
- The number of elements to be serialized.

22

In this example, when you're serializing objects to the archive, each CUser object is individually written to the archive. When you're deserializing objects, a new CUser object is created, and that object is deserialized from the archive. The collection stores a pointer to the new object.

How Are Document/View Applications Serialized?

As discussed in Hour 9, "The Document/View Architecture," data stored in a Document/View application is contained by a class derived from CDocument. This class also is responsible for controlling the serialization of all data contained by the document class. This includes tracking modifications to the document so that the program can display a warning before the user closes an unsaved document.

There are five phases in a document's life cycle:

- Creating a new document
- Modifying the document
- Storing, or serializing, the document
- Closing the document
- Loading, or deserializing, the document

You learned about most of these phases in earlier hours. The following sections discuss how each phase affects document serialization.

Creating a New Document

As discussed in Hour 9, you create MDI and SDI documents differently. An MDI application creates a new CDocument class for every open document, whereas an SDI program reuses a single document.

Both SDI and MDI applications call the OnNewDocument function to initialize a document object. The default version of OnNewDocument calls the DeleteContents function to reset any data contained by the document.

> If you need special behavior when your document is created, you should override DeleteContents. Use ClassWizard to add the function to your Document class.

Storing a Document

When the user saves a document by selecting File | Save, the CWinApp::OnFileSave function is called. This function is almost never overridden; it's a good idea to leave it alone because it calls the CDocument::OnOpenDocument function to serialize the document's data. The default version of OnOpenDocument creates a CArchive object and passes it to the document's Serialize member function. Usually, you serialize the data contained in the document in the same way that other member data was serialized earlier this hour. After the document's data has been serialized, the document is marked as unmodified. The steps involved in storing a document are shown in Figure 22.3.

FIGURE 22.3.

The major functions called when you save a document.

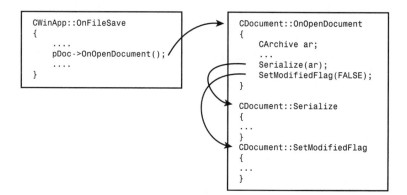

When the user selects Save As from the File menu, a Common File dialog box collects filename information. After the user selects a filename, the program calls the same CDocument functions, and the serialization process works as described previously.

Closing a Document

When the user closes a document, the MFC Document/View framework calls the document object's OnCloseDocument member function, as shown in Figure 22.4. The default version of this function checks the document for unsaved changes by calling the IsModified function. If the user did not modify the document object, DeleteContents is called to free the data stored by the document, and all views for the document are closed.

FIGURE 22.4.

The major functions called when you close a document.

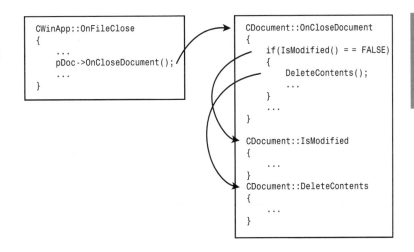

22

If the document has been modified, OnOpenDocument asks the user whether the document's unsaved changes should be saved. If the user elects to save the document, the Serialize function is called. The document is then closed by calling DeleteContents and closing all views for the document.

Loading a Document

When you're loading a document, the MFC framework calls the document object's OnOpenDocument function. The default version of this function calls the DeleteContents member function and then calls Serialize to load, or deserialize, the archive. The default version of OnOpenDocument, shown in Figure 22.5, is sufficient for almost any application.

FIGURE 22.5.

The major functions called when you load a document.

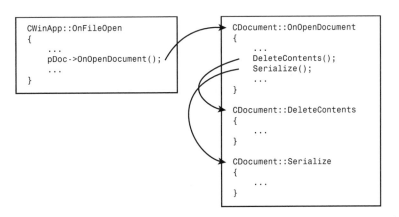

Modifying the Document Class

The document class used in the Customers project has one new data member, a CArray object that stores a collection of CUser pointers representing a customer list. The document class also has two member functions used to access the array of CUser pointers. Add declarations for m_setOfUsers and two member functions to the CCustomersDoc class, as shown in Listing 22.6.

INPUT

LISTING 22.6. ADDING A CArray MEMBER VARIABLE TO THE CCustomersDoc CLASS.

```
// Attributes
public:
    int    GetCount() const;
    CUser* GetUser( int nUser ) const;
protected:
    CArray<CUser*, CUser*&> m_setOfUsers;
```

You should make two other changes to the CustomersDoc.h header file. First, because the CArray template m_setOfUsers is declared in terms of CUser pointers, you must add an #include statement for the Users.h file. Second, you use a version of the SerializeElements helper function so you need a declaration of that global function. Add the source code provided in Listing 22.7 to the top of CustomersDoc.h, just before the CCustomersDoc class declaration.

INPUT   **LISTING 22.7.** CHANGES TO THE CustomersDoc.h HEADER FILE.

```
#include "Users.h"
    void AFXAPI SerializeElements( CArchive& ar,
                                   CUser**   pUser,
                                   int       nCount );
```

Because the CCustomerDoc class contains a CArray member variable, the template collection declarations must be included in the project. Add an #include statement to the bottom of the StdAfx.h file, just before the last #endif directive:

```
#include "afxtempl.h"
```

Creating a Dialog Box

The dialog box used to enter data for the Customers example is similar to dialog boxes you created for previous examples. Create a dialog box that contains two edit controls, as shown in Figure 22.6.

FIGURE 22.6.

The dialog box used in the Customers sample project.

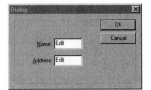

22

Give the new dialog box a resource ID of IDD_USER_DLG. The two edit controls are used to add usernames and email addresses to a document contained by the CCustomerDoc class. Use the values from Table 22.1 for the two edit controls.

TABLE 22.1. EDIT CONTROLS CONTAINED IN THE IDD_USER_DLG DIALOG BOX.

Edit Control	Resource ID
Name	IDC_EDIT_NAME
Address	IDC_EDIT_ADDR

Using ClassWizard, add a class named CUsersDlg to handle the new dialog box. Add two CString variables to the class using the values from Table 22.2.

TABLE 22.2. NEW CString MEMBER VARIABLES FOR THE CUsersDlg CLASS.

Resource ID Type	Name	Category	Variable
IDC_EDIT_NAME	m_szName	Value	CString
IDC_EDIT_ADDR	m_szAddr	Value	CString

Adding a Menu Item

Use the values from Table 22.3 to add a menu item and message-handling function to the CCustomersDoc class. Add the new menu item, labeled Add User..., to the Edit menu in the IDR_CUSTOMTYPE menu resource. In this example, the menu item is handled directly by the document class. However, the menu item can also be handled by a view class or CMainFrame.

TABLE 22.3. NEW MEMBER FUNCTIONS FOR THE CCustomersDoc CLASS.

Menu ID Name	Caption	Message	Function
ID_EDIT_USER	Add User...	COMMAND	OnEditUser

Listing 22.8 contains the source code for the `OnEditUser` function, which handles the message sent when the user selects the new menu item. If the user clicks OK, the contents of the dialog box are used to create a new `CUser` object, and a pointer to the new object is added to the `m_setOfUsers` collection. The `SetModifiedFlag` function is called to mark the document as changed. Add the source code provided in Listing 22.8 to the `CCustomersDoc::OnEditUser` member function.

INPUT **LISTING 22.8.** ADDING A NEW CUser OBJECT TO THE DOCUMENT CLASS.

```
void CCustomersDoc::OnEditUser()
{
    CUsersDlg    dlg;
    if( dlg.DoModal() == IDOK )
    {
        CUser*  pUser = new CUser( dlg.m_szName, dlg.m_szAddr );
        m_setOfUsers.Add( pUser );
        UpdateAllViews( NULL );
        SetModifiedFlag();
    }
}
```

Add the source code provided in Listing 22.9 to the `CustomersDoc.cpp` source file. These functions provide access to the data contained by the document. The view class, `CCustomerView`, calls the two `CCustomersDoc` member functions provided in Listing 22.9 when updating the view window.

INPUT **LISTING 22.9.** DOCUMENT CLASS MEMBER FUNCTIONS USED FOR DATA ACCESS.

```
int CCustomersDoc::GetCount() const
{
    return m_setOfUsers.GetSize();
}

CUser* CCustomersDoc::GetUser( int nUser ) const
{
    CUser* pUser = 0;
    if( nUser < m_setOfUsers.GetSize() )
        pUser = m_setOfUsers.GetAt( nUser );
    return pUser;
}
```

Every document needs a `Serialize` member function. The `CCustomersDoc` class has only one data member so its `Serialize` function deals only with `m_setOfUsers`, as shown in Listing 22.10. Add this source code to the `CCustomersDoc::Serialize` member function.

22

INPUT **LISTING 22.10.** SERIALIZING THE CONTENTS OF THE DOCUMENT CLASS.

```
void CCustomersDoc::Serialize(CArchive& ar)
{
    m_setOfUsers.Serialize( ar );
}
```

Add two #include statements to the CustomersDoc.cpp file so that the CCustomersDoc class can have access to declarations of classes used by CCustomersDoc. Add the source code from Listing 22.11 near the top of the CustomersDoc.cpp file, just after the other #include statements.

INPUT **LISTING 22.11.** INCLUDE STATEMENTS USED BY THE CCustomersDoc CLASS.

```
#include "Users.h"
#include "UsersDlg.h"
```

Modifying the View

The view class, CCustomersView, displays the current contents of the document. When the document is updated, the view is repainted and displays the updated contents. You must update two functions in the CCustomersView class: OnDraw and OnUpdate.

AppWizard creates a skeleton version of the CCustomersView::OnDraw function. Add the source code from Listing 22.12 to OnDraw so that the current document contents are displayed in the view.

INPUT **LISTING 22.12.** USING OnDraw TO DISPLAY THE CURRENT DOCUMENT'S CONTENTS.

```
void CCustomersView::OnDraw(CDC* pDC)
{
    CCustomersDoc* pDoc = GetDocument();
    ASSERT_VALID(pDoc);
    // Calculate the space required for a single
    // line of text, including the inter-line area.
    TEXTMETRIC  tm;
    pDC->GetTextMetrics( &tm );
    int nLineHeight = tm.tmHeight + tm.tmExternalLeading;
    CPoint  ptText( 0, 0 );
    for( int nIndex = 0; nIndex < pDoc->GetCount(); nIndex++ )
    {
        CString szOut;
        CUser* pUser = pDoc->GetUser( nIndex );
        szOut.Format( "User = %s, email = %s",
```

continues

LISTING 22.12. CONTINUED

```
            pUser->GetName(),
            pUser->GetAddr() );
        pDC->TextOut( ptText.x, ptText.y, szOut );
        ptText.y += nLineHeight;
    }
}
```

As with most documents, the CCustomersDoc class calls UpdateAllViews when it is
updated. The MFC framework then calls the OnUpdate function for each view connected
to the document.

Use ClassWizard to add a message-handling function for CCustomersView::OnUpdate
and add the source code from Listing 22.13 to it. The OnUpdate function invalidates the
view; as a result, the view is redrawn with the updated contents.

INPUT **LISTING 22.13.** INVALIDATING THE VIEW DURING OnUpdate.

```
void CCustomersView::OnUpdate( CView* pSender,
                              LPARAM lHint,
                              CObject* pHint)
{
    InvalidateRect( NULL );
}
```

Add an #include statement to the CustomersView.cpp file so that the view can use the
CUser class. Add the #include statement beneath the other #include statements in
CustomersView.cpp.

```
#include "Users.h"
```

Compile and run the Customers project. Add names to the document by selecting Add
User from the Edit menu. Figure 22.7 shows an example of the Customers project running with a few email addresses.

FIGURE 22.7.

The Customers example with some email addresses.

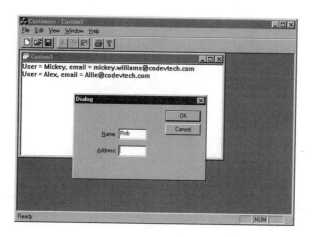

22

Serialize the contents of the document by saving it to a file, and close the document. You can reload the document by opening the file.

Summary

In this hour, you learned about serialization and persistence and how they are used in a Document/View application. You also learned about the CDocument functions used for serialization and created a small Document/View serialization example.

Q&A

Q I'm having a problem using serialization with classes that have a pure virtual function in a base class. What's wrong?

A Classes that have at least one pure virtual function are known as abstract base classes. The MFC serialization process is incompatible with abstract base classes. You can never have an instance of an abstract class; because each serialized object is created as it is read from an instance of CArchive, MFC will attempt to create an abstract class. This isn't allowed by the C++ language definition.

Q Does it matter where I put the DECLARE_SERIAL macro in my class declaration? I added the macro to my source file, and now I receive compiler errors.

A The serialization macros can go anywhere, but you must be sure to specify the access allowed for the class declaration after the macro. Place a public, private, or protected label immediately after the macro and your code should be fine.

Workshop

The Workshop is designed to help you anticipate possible questions, review what you've learned, and begin thinking ahead to putting your knowledge into practice. The answers to the quiz are in Appendix A, "Quiz Answers."

Quiz

1. What is persistence?
2. What is serialization?
3. What is the difference between serialization and deserialization?
4. What MFC class is used to represent a storage object?
5. What virtual function is implemented by all persistent classes?
6. What is the name of the helper function that assists in serializing a template collection that contains pointers?

Exercises

1. Modify the CUser class so that it also contains the postal address for a user persistently. Modify the Customers project to use the new version of the CUsers class.
2. Modify the Customers project so that the number of items stored in a document is displayed when the application starts or a file is opened.

HOUR 23

Form Views

In this hour you learn more about MFC and Document/View, expanding on the material covered in Hour 9, "The Document/View Architecture." In this hour, you will learn about

- Form views, a convenient way to use controls in your views, much like dialog boxes
- Other views that can be used in an MFC application such as edit views and scroll views
- The MFC CFormView class that supports form views

In this hour, you will also modify the DVTest project from Hour 9 so that it includes a form view.

What Is a Form View?

NEW TERM A *form view* is a view that can contain controls, much like a dialog box. You usually add controls to a form view using a dialog resource, the same way you build dialog boxes. However, unlike dialog boxes a form view is never modal; in fact, several form views can be open simultaneously, just like other views.

The most common reason to use a form view is because it's an easy-to-use view that looks like a dialog box. With practice you can create a form view in a few minutes. You can add controls used in a form view to the form view's dialog resource, just as you add controls to a resource used by a normal dialog box. After you add the controls, you can associate them with MFC objects and class member variables, just as you associate controls with dialog boxes.

Using form views enables you to easily adapt the DDX and DDV routines used by dialog boxes to a view. Unlike a modal dialog box, several different form views can be open at once, making your program much more flexible. Like other views, a form view has access to all the Document/View interfaces, giving it direct access to the document class.

It's common for a form view to be one of several possible views for a document. In an MDI application, it's common to have more than one view for each document type. For example, a form view can be used as a data entry view, and another type of view can be used for display purposes. Figure 23.1 presents a class diagram showing some of the classes derived from CView.

FIGURE 23.1.

The MFC view classes.

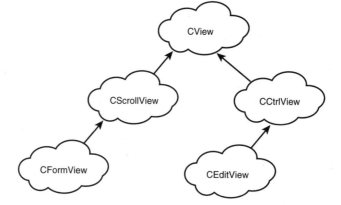

There are several other types of views, each derived from the MFC CView base class. Table 23.1 lists the view classes that can be used in your MFC applications.

TABLE 23.1. MFC VIEWS AND THE ASSOCIATED VIEW CLASS.

View	Class	Description
Scroll view	CScrollView	View with scrollbars
Edit view	CEditView	View with an edit control
Rich Edit view	CRichEditView	View with a rich edit control

View	Class	Description
List view	CListView	View with a list view control
Tree view	CTreeView	View with a tree view control
Form view	CFormView	View that works as a dialog box

Two of the most commonly used views are the scroll and edit views. These two views are covered in the following sections.

Scroll Views

New Term A *scroll view* is a view that can be larger than its visible area. In a scroll view, the invisible part of the view can be made visible using scrollbars associated with the view. An easy way to visualize how scrolling works is to imagine a large virtual view, hidden except for a small window used as a viewport, as shown in Figure 23.2.

Figure 23.2.

Scrolling a view using the CScrollView *class.*

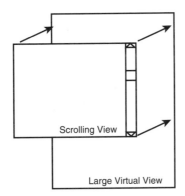

Scrolling View

Large Virtual View

Only a portion of the entire view is visible in Figure 23.2. The view window scrolls to different parts of the document; the underlying large view retains its original position. Although you can implement scrolling yourself for any class derived from CView, much of the work is done for you if you use CScrollView.

Edit Views

New Term The *edit view* is a view that consists of an edit control. The edit view automatically supports printing, using the Clipboard cut, paste, and copy functions, and Find and Replace. The edit view is supported by the CEditView class, so it can be associated with a document just like any other view.

The edit view does not support true what-you-see-is-what-you-get (WYSIWYG) editing; only one font is supported for the entire view, and the display is not always 100 percent accurate with regard to a printed page.

Using a Form View

To illustrate how form views are used, add a form view to a project that was built using AppWizard. To reduce the amount of code that must be entered, you can reuse the DVTest project built in Hour 9. To recap, the DVTest project stored a collection of names in its document class. In this hour, you will associate a form view with the document and use it to display and input names into the program.

Using a form view requires only a few more steps than using a dialog box. All the hard work is handled by the framework and the MFC CFormView class. Using ClassWizard, you can add a form view to a project using 30 or 40 lines of your own code.

Creating a Dialog Resource for a Form View

Although a form view uses a dialog resource to lay out its controls, a form view isn't really a dialog box; instead, a form view uses the dialog resource as a template when the view is created. For this reason, the CFormView class has special requirements for the dialog resources it uses. Use the properties shown in Table 23.2 for dialog resources used by form views.

TABLE 23.2. PROPERTIES FOR DIALOG RESOURCES USED BY FORM VIEWS.

Property	Value
Style	Child
Border	None
Visible	Unchecked
Titlebar	Unchecked

Other than the values listed in Table 23.2, there are no other limitations for dialog box properties or controls. Any controls you can add to a dialog box can be used in a form view.

Developer Studio makes it easy to add a dialog box resource to your project that has all the properties needed for a form view. Follow these steps:

1. Right-click the tree inside the ResourceView window.

2. Select Insert from the context menu. A dialog box will be displayed containing a tree of resources that can be added to your project.

3. Expand the Dialog tree; a list of dialog box templates is displayed.

4. Select the IDD_FORMVIEW template, and click the New button.

These steps will add a new dialog box resource to the DVTest project. Add list box, pushbutton, and edit controls to the dialog box resource, as shown in Figure 23.3.

FIGURE 23.3.

The dialog resource used as a form view in the DVTest project.

Set the dialog resource and control resource IDs as listed in Table 23.3. The list box should not be automatically sorted by Windows for this example, so clear the Sort attribute for the list box control. Use default properties for all other controls.

TABLE 23.3. PROPERTIES FOR THE CDVTest FORM VIEW DIALOG RESOURCE.

Property	ID
Dialog	IDD_FORMVIEW
Edit control	IDC_EDIT
List Box control	IDC_LIST
Close button	IDC_CLOSE
Apply button	IDC_APPLY

Adding a Form View Class to a Project

Use ClassWizard to add a form view class to a project, much as you would add a dialog box class to a project. After creating the dialog resource, add the form view class using the following steps:

1. Open ClassWizard. Because ClassWizard knows that a new resource has been added, a dialog box prompts you to choose between two options for the new dialog resource. Select the option labeled Create a New Class.

2. Fill in the Add Class dialog box using the values from Table 23.4, then click OK.

TABLE 23.4. SAMPLE VALUES FOR THE ADD CLASS DIALOG BOX.

Control	Value
Name	CFormTest
Base Class	CFormView
File	FormTest.cpp
Dialog ID	IDD_FORMVIEW
Automation	None

Use ClassWizard to add two member variables to the CFormTest class, as shown in Table 23.5.

TABLE 23.5. CONTROL VARIABLES ADDED TO THE CFormTest CLASS.

Control ID	Control Type	Variable Type	Variable Name
IDC_LIST	Control	CListBox	m_lbNames
IDC_EDIT	Control	CEdit	m_edNames

Using CFormView Instead of CView

Because CFormView is a subclass derived from CView, you can substitute it for CView in most cases. As was discussed in Hour 9, a document class is associated with a view class using a CMultiDocTemplate object in MDI programs. You can change the view associated with a particular document by editing the parameters used when the CMultiDocTemplate object is constructed.

Listing 23.1 associates the CFormTest view class with the CDVTestDoc document class. Update the code that creates the document template in the CDVTestApp::InitInstance function, found in the DVTest.cpp source file. You must change only the fourth parameter to the constructor, as shown by the comment.

INPUT

LISTING 23.1. CONSTRUCTING A CMultiDocTemplate OBJECT THAT ASSOCIATES CDVTestDoc AND CFormTest.

```
CMultiDocTemplate* pDocTemplate;
pDocTemplate = new CMultiDocTemplate(
        IDR_DVTESTTYPE,
        RUNTIME_CLASS(CDVTestDoc),
        RUNTIME_CLASS(CChildFrame), // custom MDI child frame
        RUNTIME_CLASS(CFormTest));  // Change this line
AddDocTemplate(pDocTemplate);
```

Because `CFormTest` is now used, the class declaration for `CFormTest` must be included into the `DVTest.cpp` source file. Add the following line after all other `#include` directives at the top of the `DVTest.cpp` source file:

```
#include "FormTest.h"
```

Handling Events and Messages in the Form View Class

A form view must handle a wide variety of messages. Just like any view, it must support several interfaces as part of the Document/View architecture. However, unlike other views, a form view must also handle any controls contained by the view. For example, two events generated by controls must be handled in the `CFormTest` class:

- When the button labeled Apply is pressed, the view should update the document and prepare for a new entry.
- When the button labeled Close is pressed, the view should be closed.

Use ClassWizard to add two message-handling functions for these events, using the values from Table 23.6.

TABLE 23.6. MESSAGE-HANDLING EVENTS ADDED TO THE `CFormTest` CLASS.

Object ID	Message	Function Name
IDC_APPLY	BN_CLICKED	OnApply
IDC_CLOSE	BN_CLICKED	OnClose

The code to handle control events is fairly straightforward. Edit the new functions added to the `CFormTest` class so that they look like the code in Listing 23.2.

INPUT **LISTING 23.2.** `CFormTest` FUNCTIONS USED TO HANDLE CONTROL MESSAGES.

```
void CFormTest::OnApply()
{
    CDVTestDoc* pDoc = (CDVTestDoc*)GetDocument();
    ASSERT_VALID( pDoc );
    CString szName;
    m_edNames.GetWindowText( szName );
    m_edNames.SetWindowText( "" );
    m_edNames.SetFocus();
    if( szName.GetLength() > 0 )
```

continues

23

LISTING 23.2. CONTINUED

```
        {
            int nIndex = pDoc->AddName( szName );
            m_lbNames.InsertString( nIndex, szName );
            m_lbNames.SetCurSel( nIndex );
        }
}
void CFormTest::OnClose()
{
    PostMessage( WM_COMMAND, ID_FILE_CLOSE );
}
```

You must manually add an include statement for the document class. At the top of the
FormTest.cpp file, add the following line just after all the other #include directives:

```
#include "DVTestDoc.h"
```

The OnApply function is split into three main parts:

- The document pointer is retrieved and verified, as in the OnDraw function discussed
  in Hour 9.

- The contents of the edit control are collected and stored in a CString object. After
  the string is collected, the control is cleared and the input focus is returned to the
  edit control. This enables the user to immediately make a new entry.

- If a string was entered, szName will have a length greater than zero. If so, the name
  is added to the document and the list box is updated. The SetCurSel function is
  used to scroll to the new list box item.

The OnClose member function uses the PostMessage function to send an ID_FILE_CLOSE
message to the application. This has the same effect as selecting Close from the File
menu.

Handling OnInitialUpdate

When using a form view, update it during OnInitialUpdate, as the view is initially displayed. In Hour 9, CDVTestView used OnDraw to retrieve the document's contents and
display the items in the view. The OnInitialUpdate function uses similar code, as
shown in Listing 23.3. Before editing the code, add the OnInitialUpdate function to
the CFormTest class using ClassWizard.

LISTING 23.3. USING `OnInitialUpdate` TO RETRIEVE DATA FROM THE DOCUMENT.

INPUT

```
void CFormTest::OnInitialUpdate()
{
    CFormView::OnInitialUpdate();
    CDVTestDoc* pDoc = (CDVTestDoc*)GetDocument();
    ASSERT_VALID(pDoc);
    for( int nIndex = 0; nIndex < pDoc->GetCount(); nIndex++ )
    {
        CString szName = pDoc->GetName( nIndex );
        m_lbNames.AddString( szName );
    }
}
```

When a dialog box is displayed, the dialog resource is used to size the dialog box's window. A form view is not automatically sized this way, which leads to an unexpected display if you aren't aware of this behavior. However, you can resize the view to the exact dimensions of the dialog resource by using the `ResizeParentToFit` function. Add the following two lines of code to the `CFormTest::OnInitialUpdate` member function:

```
ResizeParentToFit( FALSE );
ResizeParentToFit();
```

Nope, it's not a typo; you must call `ResizeParentToFit` twice to make sure that the size is calculated correctly. The first call allows the view to expand and the second call shrinks the view to fit the dialog resource.

Preventing a View Class from Being Resized

Like all views, you can resize a form view in three ways:

- By dragging the view's frame with the mouse
- By pressing the minimize icon
- By pressing the maximize icon

Although the minimize button is handy, the other sizing methods are a problem for form views. Because a form view looks like a dialog box and the control layout is specified in the dialog resource, preventing the user from resizing is a good idea.

The form view class doesn't actually have any control over the minimize and maximize buttons—they belong to the frame, which also controls the capability to change the size of the view by dragging it with a mouse. The `CChildFrame` class is the frame used by default in MDI applications, although you can change the frame class by using a different class name when the document template is created.

To remove the sizable frame and minimize button from the frame class, add two lines of code to the frame class `PreCreateWindow` member function. The `PreCreateWindow` function is called just before the window is created. This enables you to change the style of the window, as shown in Listing 23.4.

INPUT

LISTING 23.4. USING THE `PreCreateWindow` FUNCTION TO CHANGE `CChildFrame` STYLE ATTRIBUTES.

```
BOOL CChildFrame::PreCreateWindow(CREATESTRUCT& cs)
{
    // Mask away the thickframe and maximize button style bits.
    cs.style &= ~WS_THICKFRAME;
    cs.style &= ~WS_MAXIMIZEBOX;
    return CMDIChildWnd::PreCreateWindow(cs);
}
```

The `&=` operator is the C++ bitwise AND operator, which is used to clear or remove a bit that is set in a particular value. The tilde (~) is the C++ inversion operator, used to "flip" the individual bits of a particular value. These two operators are commonly used together to mask off attributes that have been set using the bitwise OR operator. In Listing 23.4, the `WS_THICKFRAME` and `WS_MAXIMIZEBOX` attributes are cleared from the `cs.style` variable.

Compile and run the DVTest project. Figure 23.4 shows DVTest after a few names have been added to the list box.

FIGURE 23.4.

DVTest after adding a form view to the project.

Summary

In this hour you learned about using form views in place of standard views or dialog boxes. Form views enable you to easily use controls in a view, just as they are used in dialog boxes. The DVTest program from Hour 9 was modified to take advantage of form views and multiple views.

Q&A

23

Q How can I change the color of the form view window?

A You can use the WM_CTLCOLOR message, just as with dialog boxes and other controls. The following source code shows how to change the background of a form view to green:

```
HBRUSH CFormTest::OnCtlColor(CDC* pDC, CWnd* pWnd, UINT nCtlColor)
{
    HBRUSH hbr = CFormView::OnCtlColor(pDC, pWnd, nCtlColor);

    if(nCtlColor == CTLCOLOR_DLG)
    {
        hbr = CreateSolidBrush(RGB(0,255,0));
    }
    return hbr;
}
```

Workshop

The Workshop is designed to help you anticipate possible questions, review what you've learned, and begin thinking ahead to putting your knowledge into practice. The answers to the quiz are in Appendix A, "Quiz Answers."

Quiz

1. What are some differences between a form view and a dialog box?
2. What are the special requirements for dialog box resources used in a form view?
3. How do you size the frame of a form view so that it is the same size as its dialog box resource?
4. A dialog box is initialized in the OnInitDialog function. What function is used to initialize a form view?
5. How do you prevent an MDI child window from being resized?
6. What class is used to implement the window frame for MDI child windows?

7. What view class is used to implement form views?

8. What view class enables you to use an edit control as a view?

9. What view class enables your view to have a large virtual area that is seen through a smaller scrolling viewport?

10. What class is used in an MDI application to associate a view class and a document class?

Exercises

1. Because the CChildFrame class was modified to prevent resizing, the instances of the CDisplayView class cannot be resized. Modify DVTest so that display views can be resized and form views can't be resized.

2. Modify the form view in DVTest so that it displays the number of items stored in the document.

HOUR 24

Creating ActiveX Controls

As discussed in Hour 19, "Using ActiveX Controls," ActiveX controls are components that can be used to easily add new functionality to your application. In this hour, you will learn about

- Some of the internal plumbing that is required for an ActiveX control
- The support provided by MFC for ActiveX control development
- How to test ActiveX controls using tools supplied with Visual C++

What Is an ActiveX Control?

NEW TERM The *Component Object Model*, or *COM*, is a specification that defines how software components should cooperate with each other. ActiveX technologies are all built on top of the COM specification.

NEW TERM In COM, an *interface* is a group of related functions that are implemented together. All interfaces are named beginning with I, such as IUnknown, an interface that is supported by all COM objects.

At a minimum, an ActiveX control must be a COM object. The minimum requirement for all COM objects is that they—and hence all ActiveX controls—must support the interface, IUnknown. In addition, an ActiveX control is expected to provide a user interface. The control can be hidden at runtime, but it must provide a design-time user interface so that it can be used by tools such as Visual C++ or Visual Basic. Other than these requirements, you have a great deal of latitude when deciding how a control is to be implemented. Previously, the OLE custom control architecture required support of at least 14 interfaces.

> Support for the IUnknown interface is provided automatically when you use MFC and ActiveX ControlWizard to build your control.

Reducing the number of required interfaces enables ActiveX controls to be much smaller than the older OLE controls. It also makes it feasible to use ActiveX controls to implement functionality where the size of the control is an important factor. Web pages can be more intelligent when a control is downloaded and activated to your browser. For example, Microsoft's Internet Explorer has support for downloading ActiveX controls from a Web page. Although this opens a lot of exciting functionality, the size of the control to be downloaded must be kept as small as possible.

ActiveX Control Properties, Events, and Methods

Interaction with an ActiveX control takes place via properties, events, and methods. As discussed in Hour 19, the host window for an ActiveX control is known as its container.

Properties

NEW TERM   A *property* is an attribute associated with the control. Properties are exposed by ActiveX controls, as well as by the client where the control is located. There are four basic types of properties:

- *Ambient properties* are provided to the control by the container. The control uses these properties in order to "fit in" properly. Commonly used ambient properties include the container's background color, default font, and foreground color.

- *Extended properties* are implemented by the container but appear to be generated by the control. For example, the tab order of various controls in a container is an extended property.

- *Stock properties* are control properties implemented by the ActiveX control development kit. Examples of stock properties are the control font, the caption text, and the foreground and background colors.

- *Custom properties* are control properties that you implement.

Events

An event is used to send a notification message to the control's container. Typically, events are used to notify the container when mouse clicks or other events take place. There are two basic types of events:

- *Stock events* are implemented by the ActiveX control development kit and are invoked just like a function call, such as FireError.

- *Custom events* are implemented by you, although the MFC class library and ClassWizard handle much of the work for you.

Methods

New Term   A *method* is an exposed function that can be applied to a control via the IDispatch interface. Methods are exposed through a technique known as *automation*. Automation is a way of enabling a COM object to be controlled by another party through the IDispatch interface.

Because ActiveX controls use automation, all sorts of programs—even those built using scripting languages such as JScript and VBScript—have access to their method functions.

Creating an ActiveX Control

New Term   *Subclassing* is a method of borrowing functionality from an existing window or control. By subclassing an existing window or control, you can concentrate on adding only the new features offered by your control. The control from which the functionality is borrowed is known as the *superclass*.

As an example of creating an ActiveX control, you will now create an ActiveX control named OleEdit that subclasses the existing Windows edit control. The OleEdit control is similar to the basic Windows edit control, except that it exposes properties that allow it to accept only numbers, letters, or a combination of both.

The control works by performing extra processing when the WM_CHAR message is received by the control. Windows sends WM_CHAR to notify the edit control that the user has pressed a key on the keyboard. Ordinarily, the edit control would simply add the new character to the edit control. When the WM_CHAR message is received by the OleEdit control, it is processed as shown in Figure 24.1.

24

FIGURE 24.1.

Handling WM_CHAR
in OleEdit.

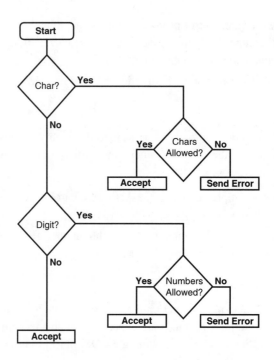

The example will also expose additional properties that can be changed. The property
flags m_fTextAllowed and m_fNumbersAllowed are exposed by the OleEdit control's
container.

Creating an ActiveX Control Project

To begin creating the OleEdit control, use the ActiveX ControlWizard. Using ActiveX
ControlWizard to build a control is very much like using AppWizard to build applications. To start ActiveX ControlWizard and create the OleEdit control, follow these steps:

1. Select File | New. The New dialog box is displayed.

2. Select the Projects tab. A list of project types is displayed.

3. To create an ActiveX control, select MFC ActiveX ControlWizard as the project
   type.

4. Specify OleEdit as the project name; a default location for your project will automatically be provided for the location.

5. Make sure the Create New Workspace radio button is selected, and click OK to
   create the project.

6. The initial page from the ActiveX ControlWizard is shown in Figure 24.2. This page enables you to specify the basic characteristics of the project, such as the number of controls handled by this server, whether help files should be generated, and so on. Accept all the default options presented on this page by clicking the Next button.

FIGURE 24.2.

The first page of ActiveX ControlWizard.

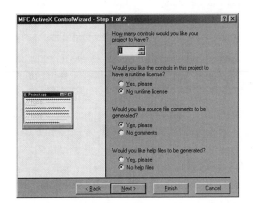

7. The second ActiveX ControlWizard page is shown in Figure 24.3. This page lets you change the names associated with the control and its OLE interfaces, as well as define properties for the control. There is also a drop-down list that enables you to specify a base class for the control. Select Edit from the drop-down list to make the OleEdit control a subclass of the standard edit control.

FIGURE 24.3.

The second page of ActiveX ControlWizard.

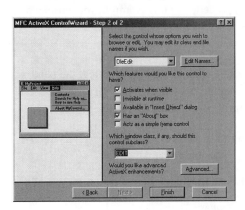

8. Click the Finish button. As with other projects built using Visual C++ wizards, a list of the files to be created is displayed. Click OK, and the skeleton project is created.

MFC Support for ActiveX Controls

A set of MFC classes is used as a framework for all ActiveX controls built using ActiveX ControlWizard. The wizard automatically creates three classes that are specific to your project, using these three classes as base classes:

- `COleControlModule` is the class that manages the ActiveX control module. This class plays a role similar to the `CWinApp` class used in applications built using AppWizard. For the OleEdit project, the derived class is named `COleEditApp`.

- `COleControl` is the base class that represents the actual control window. This class is derived from `CWnd` and includes extra ActiveX functionality for communicating with containers. For the OleEdit project, the derived class is named `CTestCtrl`.

- `COlePropertyPage` is the base class used to manage the property page for the control. For the OleEdit project, the derived class is named `CTestPropPage`.

Drawing the Control

All visible OLE controls must be capable of drawing themselves. Even controls that aren't visible when active should draw something as an aid during program development. The OleEdit control is visible at runtime, and it should appear to be a standard edit control.

> You might think that because OleEdit is subclassed from the standard edit control, it should be able to draw itself. Unfortunately, very few controls actually draw themselves properly; the edit control is not one that handles drawing properly. For most controls, you must be prepared to handle the drawing yourself.

When an ActiveX control project is initially created, the control's `OnDraw` function draws an ellipse inside the bounding rectangle. This is extremely useful if you happen to be creating an ellipse control. However, because OleEdit must look like an edit control, you must change the `OnDraw` function. The changes to `OnDraw` required for the OleEdit control are provided in Listing 24.1.

INPUT   LISTING 24.1. THE `OnDraw` FUNCTION USED BY `COleEditCtrl`.

```
void COleEditCtrl::OnDraw(
CDC* pdc, const CRect& rcBounds, const CRect& rcInvalid)
{
    COLORREF  clrBackground = TranslateColor(GetBackColor());
    CBrush*   pOldBrush;
    CBrush    brBackground( clrBackground );
```

```
    pdc->FillRect( rcBounds, &brBackground );
    pOldBrush = pdc->SelectObject( &brBackground );
    pdc->SelectObject( pOldBrush );
    DoSuperclassPaint(pdc, rcBounds);
    CRect rc(rcBounds);
    pdc->DrawEdge( rc, EDGE_SUNKEN, BF_RECT );
}
```

The code provided in Listing 24.1 does three things. First, it fills the control's bounding rectangle with the ambient background color. Next, it calls DoSuperclassPaint to give the edit control a chance to attempt to draw itself properly. Finally, it calls DrawEdge to draw a three-dimensional edge along the control's bounding rectangle.

Defining Properties

24

Most ActiveX controls implement properties. When exposing a property for your control, you should use a stock property whenever possible. This is a good idea for two reasons:

- Your control will be easier to use because stock properties fit into a commonly used format. For example, the Font property is very easy to manipulate using Visual Basic and Delphi.
- Your control will also be easier to create because Visual C++ enables you to add a stock property in just a few mouse clicks.

OleEdit uses four properties: the Font and Text stock properties and the fTextAllowed and fNumbersAllowed custom properties.

Using ClassWizard, add the stock properties for the OleEdit control. Select the Automation tab, and click the Add Property button. Fill in the dialog box using the values provided in Table 24.1.

TABLE 24.1. STOCK PROPERTIES FOR THE OLEEDIT CONTROL.

External Name	Implementation
Font	Stock
Text	Stock

Use ClassWizard to add a custom property name fNumbersAllowed to the OleEdit project. Click the Add Property button and use the values provided in Table 24.2.

TABLE 24.2. THE fNumbersAllowed CUSTOM PROPERTY FOR THE OLEEDIT CONTROL.

Control	Value
External name	fNumbersAllowed
Type	BOOL
Member variable name	m_fNumbersAllowed
Notification function	OnFNumbersAllowedChanged
Implementation	Member variable

Use ClassWizard to add the fTextAllowed property, following the steps used to add the previous properties. Use the values provided in Table 24.3.

TABLE 24.3. THE fTextAllowed CUSTOM PROPERTY FOR THE OLEEDIT CONTROL.

Control	Value
External name	fTextAllowed
Type	BOOL
Variable name	m_fTextAllowed
Notification function	OnFTextAllowedChanged
Implementation	Member variable

Modify, the COleEditCtrl class constructor to contain code that initializes the custom properties added in the previous steps. The modified constructor is shown in Listing 24.2.

INPUT   **LISTING 24.2.** MODIFICATIONS TO THE COleEditCtrl CONSTRUCTOR.

```
COleEditCtrl::COleEditCtrl()
{
    InitializeIIDs(&IID_DOleEdit, &IID_DOleEditEvents);
    m_fTextAllowed = TRUE;
    m_fNumbersAllowed = TRUE;
}
```

Every control created using ControlWizard includes a default property page. You modify the OleEdit property page by adding two check boxes that control the states of the m_fTextAllowed and m_fNumbersAllowed flags. Open the IDD_PROPPAGE_OLEEDIT dialog box resource and add two check box controls, as shown in Figure 24.4.

FIGURE 24.4.

The property page used in OleEdit.

Table 24.4 lists the properties for the check box controls. All properties that aren't listed should be set to the default values.

TABLE 24.4. PROPERTY VALUES FOR CHECK BOX CONTROLS IN THE OLEEDIT PROPERTY PAGE.

Control	Resource ID	Caption
Numbers check box	IDC_CHECK_NUMBERS	&Numbers Allowed
Text check box	IDC_CHECK_TEXT	&Text Allowed

Use ClassWizard to associate COleEditPropPage member variables with the controls, using the values shown in Table 24.5.

TABLE 24.5. VALUES FOR NEW MEMBER VARIABLES IN COleEditPropPage.

Control ID	Variable Name	Category	Type	Property Name
IDC_CHECK_NUMBERS	m_fNumbersAllowed	Value	BOOL	fNumbersAllowed
IDC_CHECK_TEXT	m_fTextAllowed	Value	BOOL	fTextAllowed

ClassWizard uses the optional Property Name field to generate source code that exchanges the values from the property sheet to the control class. The DDP and DDX macros are used to transfer and validate property page data. The code used to transfer the value of the IDC_CHECK_TEXT control looks like this:

```
//{{AFX_DATA_MAP(COleEditPropPage)
DDP_Check(pDX, IDC_CHECK_TEXT, m_fTextAllowed, _T("fTextAllowed"));
DDX_Check(pDX, IDC_CHECK_TEXT, m_fTextAllowed;
//}}AFX_DATA_MAP
DDP_PostProcessing(pDX);
```

Inside the control class, you must collect the values from the property page during DoPropExchange, as shown in Listing 24.3.

24

LISTING 24.3. COLLECTING PROPERTY PAGE DATA DURING DoPropExchange.

```
void COleEditCtrl::DoPropExchange(CPropExchange* pPX)
{
    ExchangeVersion(pPX, MAKELONG(_wVerMinor, _wVerMajor));
    COleControl::DoPropExchange(pPX);

    PX_Bool(pPX, _T("fNumbersAllowed"), m_fNumbersAllowed );
    PX_Bool(pPX, _T("fTextAllowed"), m_fTextAllowed );
}
```

The OleEdit control supports the stock font property. An easy way to give the control access to all the available fonts is to add the standard font property page to the control. The property pages associated with an ActiveX control are grouped together between the BEGIN_PROPPAGEIDS and END_PROPPAGEIDS macros in the control class implementation file.

Listing 24.4 shows how the standard font property page is added to the control using the PROPPAGEID macro. Remember to change the second parameter passed to the BEGIN_PROPPAGEIDS macro, the number of property pages used by the control object. Locate the existing BEGIN_PROPPAGEIDS macro in the OleEditCtl.cpp file, and change that section of the file so that it looks like the code in Listing 24.4.

LISTING 24.4. ADDING THE STANDARD FONT PROPERTY PAGE TO OLEEDIT.

```
BEGIN_PROPPAGEIDS(COleEditCtrl, 2)   // changed
  PROPPAGEID(COleEditPropPage::guid)
  PROPPAGEID(CLSID_CFontPropPage)        // changed
END_PROPPAGEIDS(COleEditCtrl)
```

As you will see when you test the control later in the hour, adding the font property page, along with exposing the stock font property, enables a user to easily change the control font. The only code that is written to allow the user to change the control's font is in Listing 24.4.

Handling Character Input in the Sample Control

As discussed earlier, OleEdit uses exposed properties to determine whether characters entered on the keyboard are stored in the edit control. If an invalid character is input, an Error event is fired to the control's container. The message sent to the control as characters are input to the control is WM_CHAR. Using ClassWizard, add a message-handling function to the COleEditCtrl class, using the values from Table 24.6.

TABLE 24.6. HANDLING THE WM_CHAR MESSAGE IN COleEditCtrl.

Class Name	Object ID	Message	Function
COleEditCtrl	COleEditCtrl	WM_CHAR	OnChar

The source code for the `COleEditCtrl::OnChar` function is provided in Listing 24.5.

INPUT **LISTING 24.5.** HANDLING THE WM_CHAR MESSAGE IN COleEditCtrl::OnChar.

```
void COleEditCtrl::OnChar(UINT nChar, UINT nRepCnt, UINT nFlags)
{
    if(_istdigit(nChar) )
    {
        if( m_fNumbersAllowed == FALSE )
        {
            FireError( CTL_E_INVALIDPROPERTYVALUE,
                    _T("Numbers not allowed") );
        }
        else
        {
            COleControl::OnChar(nChar, nRepCnt, nFlags);
        }
    }
    else if( _istalpha(nChar) )
    {
        if( m_fTextAllowed == FALSE )
        {
            FireError( CTL_E_INVALIDPROPERTYVALUE,
                    _T("Characters not allowed") );
        }
        else
        {
            COleControl::OnChar(nChar, nRepCnt, nFlags);
        }
    }
    else
        COleControl::OnChar (nChar, nRepCnt, nFlags);
}
```

The `OnChar` handler tests for valid characters based on the property flags `m_fTextAllowed` and `m_fNumbersAllowed`. Valid characters are passed to `COleControl::OnChar`, the base class handler for WM_CHAR. If an invalid character is detected, an `Error` event is fired to the control's container.

Modifying the Control's Bitmap

When an ActiveX control is used in a tool such as Developer Studio, Visual Basic, or the ActiveX control test container, a bitmap associated with the control is displayed to the user. In Developer Studio, the bitmap is added to the control palette used to design dialog box resources. In the test container, a toolbar button displaying the bitmap is added to the container's toolbar.

Open the IDB_OLEEDIT bitmap resource and edit the bitmap image as shown in Figure 24.5. Save the bitmap and compile the OleEdit project.

FIGURE 24.5.

The OleEdit bitmap resource.

> To ensure that the text fits properly in the bitmap, use a regular (non-bold) 8-point Arial font.

Build the OleEdit project. As part of the build process, the control will be registered with the operating system. In the next section, you will learn how to test your control.

Testing an ActiveX Control

After following the steps in the previous sections, you are in possession of an OleEdit ActiveX control. However, because the control is a component rather than an executable program, it can't be run as an EXE. Testing an ActiveX control requires a few extra steps, which are discussed in this section.

Choosing a Test Container for Your Control

Every ActiveX control requires a control container. The simplest control container is the ActiveX control test container included with Developer Studio and the Win32 SDK. Other ActiveX control containers include Microsoft Access and Visual Basic. In this section, you will test the OleEdit control with the ActiveX Control Test Container, which is included with Developer Studio.

Using the ActiveX Control Test Container

In order to launch the OleEdit control in the Developer Studio debugger, you must specify the application to be used to load the control. You can do this by following these steps:

1. Select Settings from the Project menu in Developer Studio. The Project Setting dialog box is displayed.

2. Click the Debug tab.

3. A small button with a right-arrow icon is located next to the Executable for Debug Session edit control. Click this button and choose ActiveX Control Test Container from the menu that is displayed.

4. Click OK to dismiss the dialog box and save your changes.

After you have made these changes, you can use the Developer Studio debugger to launch the test container. Click the Go icon in the toolbar or otherwise start a debug session to display the test container, as shown in Figure 24.6.

FIGURE 24.6.

The ActiveX control test container.

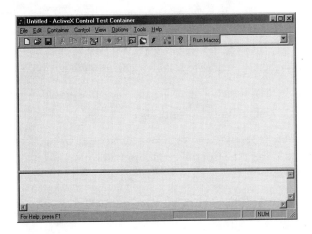

24

You can also launch the ActiveX control test container by selecting its menu item from the Tools menu. This doesn't start your control inside the Visual C++ debugger.

When an ActiveX control created by ControlWizard is compiled, the control is automatically registered. To display a list of all registered controls, select Insert New Control from the Edit menu. A dialog box containing all available ActiveX controls is displayed. Select the OleEdit edit control, and click OK. The OleEdit control is inserted into the test container, as shown in Figure 24.7.

FIGURE 24.7.

The ActiveX control test container and the OleEdit control.

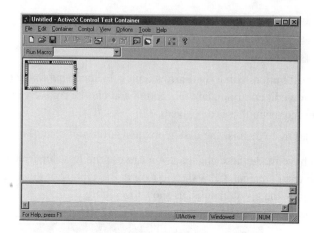

Testing Properties and Methods

You can use the test container to test your control in two ways:

- Through an Automation interface that lists all exposed properties and methods
- Through your control's property sheet

To access all the properties and methods implemented by an ActiveX control, select Invoke Methods from the Control menu. An Invoke Method dialog box is displayed, as shown in Figure 24.8.

FIGURE 24.8.

Accessing the properties and methods exposed by OleEdit.

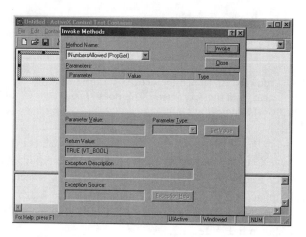

Properties are accessed by calling the underlying methods that are used to implement the property. Methods that are used to set properties have PropPut listed after the property name. Methods used to retrieve properties have PropGet listed after the property name.

To display the list of methods exposed by the control, click the drop-down list. Every method can be accessed through this dialog box. To invoke a particular method, select the method name from the drop-down list and click Invoke.

A slightly easier way to use the interface is provided through the control's property sheet. You can use the test container to invoke the control's property sheet by selecting Properties from the Edit menu. The property sheet for OleEdit is shown in Figure 24.9.

FIGURE 24.9.

The property sheet used by OleEdit.

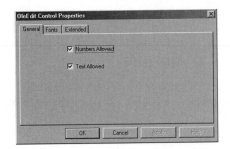

Summary

In this hour you learned how to create and test ActiveX controls. ActiveX controls are smaller and simpler versions of OLE custom controls. Developer Studio helps to simplify the task of creating an ActiveX control. The ActiveX ControlWizard is very similar to AppWizard and guides you through the steps required to create a skeleton version of your control.

Q&A

Q If I test my ActiveX control in the test container, is it reasonable to assume that it will work in all control containers?

A You might think so, but in reality you should test your control in as many containers as you can find. The test container is useful for performing basic tests on your control. You should also test your control in whatever environment it will be used. For example, if your control will be used in Visual Basic programs, you should test your control using VB as a container.

Q Why does ControlWizard offer the Invisible at Runtime option? What use is an invisible control?

A There actually are a large number of controls that don't have a need for a user interface. For example, an ActiveX control that performs protocol conversion for data communications might never be presented to the user; it can just perform work for its container. By offering this option, the control is easier to develop because the control doesn't need to handle user-interface issues. The control is also easier to use because it will hide itself automatically.

Workshop

The Workshop is designed to help you anticipate possible questions, review what you've learned, and begin thinking ahead to putting your knowledge into practice. The answers to the quiz are in Appendix A, "Quiz Answers."

Quiz

1. What is an ActiveX interface?
2. What interface must be supported by an ActiveX control?
3. What are some examples of ActiveX control containers?
4. What four types of properties are supported by an ActiveX control?
5. What are the two types of events generated by ActiveX controls?
6. What macros are used to transfer data to and from property pages in an ActiveX control?
7. What MFC base classes provide support for ActiveX controls?
8. What type of properties are supplied to the ActiveX control by its container?
9. What is subclassing?
10. What function is called by an ActiveX control to request that the subclassed control repaint itself?

Exercises

1. Change the OleEdit project so that hexadecimal numbers can be entered when the Numbers Only flag is set.
2. Change the OleEdit project so that only letters, numbers, and backspaces can be entered into the control.

APPENDIX A

Quiz Answers

This appendix lists the answers to the quiz questions in the Workshop sections at the end of each hour.

Hour 1, "Using Visual C++ 6"

1. A library is a collection of reusable source code or compiled code that can be used in a program. The MFC class library and the standard C++ library are examples of commonly used libraries.

2. You build a project by using one of these steps:
   - Pressing F7 on the keyboard
   - Clicking the Build button on the toolbar
   - Selecting Build|Build from the main menu

3. A wizard is a tool similar to a dialog box that guides you through a series of steps.

4. AppWizard, ClassWizard, and ControlWizard

5. Press the F1 function key.

6. ClassView, FileView, and ResourceView

7. `OnDraw`

8. The F7 function key

9. Ctrl+Z

10. Undo reverses an action; Redo reverses an Undo.

Hour 2, "Writing Simple C++ Programs"

1. The `cout iostream` object is used to display output to a console-mode window. The `cin iostream` object is used to collect input from the keyboard.

2. When including project-specific files that are located in the project directory, use quotes around the header filename, as in the following:

   ```
   #include "myfile.h"
   ```

   When including library files that are located in a standard location, use angle brackets around the filename, like this:

   ```
   #include <myfile.h>
   ```

3. Character values are stored in variables that have the `char` type.

4. A C++ namespace provides a container for a set of names. This prevents identical names in two parts of your application from conflicting with each other.

5. To declare multiple variables on one line, separate the variable names with a comma, like this:

   ```
   int nFoo, nBar, nBaz;
   ```

6. Type safety refers to the capability of a C++ compiler to enforce rules that ensure that variables and functions are used as they are intended. This helps the compiler detect a large number of common errors.

7. The floating-point variable types are `float`, `double`, and `long double`.

8. The C++ assignment operator is the equals sign, =, as in `nFoo = 5;`.

9. Integer values are normally stored in variables that have the `int` type. To save space, smaller values may be stored in the `char` and `short int` types.

10. If you know that a value will not be negative, you can double the maximum value stored in the variable by declaring it as `unsigned`.

Hour 3, "Functions, Structures, and Classes"

1. A function is a group of computer instructions that perform a well-defined task.
2. The function's name, return value, parameter list, and function body
3. Classes are exactly like structures, except that members of a class cannot be accessed from outside the class by default.
4. The constructor
5. The destructor
6. 42
7. The * symbol is used for multiplication.
8. The / symbol is used for division.

Hour 4, "Using Dialog Boxes"

1. A modal dialog box prevents the user from interacting with the program until the dialog box is dismissed. A modeless dialog box does not prevent the user from interacting with the program.
2. `WM_INITDIALOG`
3. `.h`
4. `.cpp`
5. The warning icon, `MB_ICONEXCLAMATION`
6. The stop sign icon, `MB_ICONSTOP`
7. `CDialog`
8. `DoModal`
9. `IDYES`
10. `IDNO`

Hour 5, "Button Controls"

1. A Cancel button is used to close the dialog box and discard any changes that have been made. A Close button is used to close the dialog box and keep any changes that have been made.
2. An OK button is used to close the dialog box and keep any changes that have been made. An Apply button keeps changes that have been made but does not close the

dialog box; this button is often used when the Apply button is used to update the application that displays the dialog box.

3. CButton
4. Check boxes, radio buttons, pushbuttons, group boxes, and owner-drawn buttons.
5. Clear the Tab Stop property for the control.
6. Enable
7. ShowWindow
8. The default label is selected when no case labels match the switch expression.
9. The = operator is used for assignment. The == operator is used to test for equality.
10. SetWindowText

Hour 6, "Using Edit Controls"

1. CEdit
2. An MLE is a multiline edit control and accepts multiple lines of text as input. An SLE is a single-line edit control and accepts single lines of text as input.
3. A DDV routine is used to validate data input stored in a control. A DDX routine is used to transfer data to or from a control.
4. UpdateData
5. GetWindowText
6. SetWindowText
7. Password
8. Ctrl+V
9. Ctrl+C
10. Ctrl+X

Hour 7, "Using List Box and Combo Box Controls"

1. CListBox
2. LBN_DBLCLCK
3. AddString and InsertString
4. GetCount
5. GetCurSel

6. Single-selection, multiple-selection, and extended-selection

7. `for`, `while`, and `do-while`

8. `CComboBox`

9. `InsertString`

10. Simple, drop-down, and drop list

Hour 8, "Messages and Event-Driven Programming"

1. The default window procedure is a special function supplied by Windows that handles messages not handled by the application.

2. Messages are physical chunks of data and are easily prioritized. They are not processor or language dependent.

3. When the mouse cursor passes over a window, the window receives the `WM_MOUSEMOVE` and `WM_NCMOUSEMOVE` messages.

4. A message map is used to associate a message with a function used to process that message.

5. `CObject` is the base class for most MFC classes.

6. The `ASSERT` macro is used to test an expression that is not needed when the program is compiled for release mode. The `VERIFY` macro is used to test an expression that is used when the program is compiled for release mode. When compiled for release mode, the `ASSERT` macro and the expression contained inside it will be removed; the `VERIFY` macro is also removed, but its contained expression is compiled.

7. `WM_LBUTTONDOWN`

8. The message map entries reserved for use by ClassWizard begin with `//{{AFX_MSG_MAP` and end with `//}}AFX_MSG_MAP`.

Hour 9, "The Document/View Architecture"

1. A pointer that points to one variable can be changed to point to another variable; references must be bound to a single variable for their lifetime. A reference to a class uses `.` to access a member, a pointer to a class uses the `->` operator.

2. Passing a pointer to an object rather than the object itself is almost always more efficient. Passing a pointer parameter is a 32-bit variable; passing an object such as

a class instance requires that a copy be made of the instance—and not only must the copy be made, it must be destroyed after the copy is no longer needed.

3. The `new` keyword is used to dynamically allocate memory.

4. The `delete` keyword is used to release memory allocated with `new`.

5. Classes derived from `CView` are responsible for the user interface.

6. The four classes are
   - Document classes derived from `CDocument`
   - View classes derived from `CView`
   - Frame classes derived from `CFrameWnd`
   - Application classes derived from `CWinApp`

7. The document class is responsible for an application's data.

8. The `GetDocument` function returns a pointer to the document associated with a view.

9. A document class uses `UpdateAllViews` to notify views associated with the document that their user interfaces might need to be updated.

Hour 10, "Menus"

1. The `CMenu` class

2. The `WM_CONTEXTMENU` message

3. An ellipsis (...) after the menu item

4. A letter that is used to represent the menu item, such as x in Exit

5. A keyboard shortcut to a message-handling function

6. A right arrow

7. To create a mnemonic, place an ampersand in front of the mnemonic character.

8. `WM_COMMAND`

9. `IDR_MAINFRAME`

10. The Separator property

Hour 11, "Device Contexts"

1. An information context cannot be used for output.

2. `SelectStockObject`

3. Approximately 1440

4. A pen

5. A brush

6. Use the `GetTextMetrics` function.

7. `RGB` is used to create a `COLORREF` value.

8. `CDC`

9. If `SelectObject` returns `NULL`, the call failed.

10. `MM_TEXT`

Hour 12, "Using Pens and Brushes"

1. Width, color, and style

2. Cosmetic and geometric

3. `CPen`

4. `BLACK_PEN`, `WHITE_PEN`, and `NULL_PEN`

5. `PS_SOLID`, `PS_DASH`, `PS_DOT`, `PS_DASHDOT`, `PS_DASHDOTDOT`, `PS_NULL`, `PS_INSIDEFRAME`, and `PS_ALTERNATE`

6. `PS_SOLID`, `PS_DASH`, `PS_DOT`, `PS_DASHDOT`, `PS_DASHDOTDOT`, `PS_NULL`, and `PS_INSIDEFRAME`

7. Solid, hatch, pattern, and stock

8. `BLACK_BRUSH`, `DKGRAY_BRUSH`, `GRAY_BRUSH`, `HOLLOW_BRUSH`, `LTGRAY_BRUSH`, `NULL_BRUSH`, and `WHITE_BRUSH`

9. `CBrush`

10. `Ellipse`

Hour 13, "Fonts"

1. Serif fonts include Courier, Garamond, and Times Roman; sans-serif fonts include Arial, Tahoma, and MS Sans Serif.

2. `ANSI_FIXED_FONT`, `ANSI_VAR_FONT`, `DEVICE_DEFAULT_FONT`, `DEFAULT_GUI_FONT`, `OEM_FIXED_FONT`, and `SYSTEM_FONT`

3. The font escapement is the angle in tenths of a degree that a line of text forms with the bottom of the page.

4. `CFont`

A

5. Decorative, Modern, Roman, Script, Swiss, and Dontcare
6. `DEFAULT_PITCH`, `FIXED_PITCH`, and `VARIABLE_PITCH`
7. `SetFont`

Hour 14, "Icons and Cursors"

1. `SetIcon`
2. The hotspot
3. `SetCapture`
4. `SetCursor`
5. `WM_SETCURSOR`
6. 16×16
7. `BeginWaitCursor`

Hour 15, "Spin, Progress, and Slider Controls"

1. The Orientation property can be set to either horizontal (left-right) or vertical (up-down).
2. Auto-buddy
3. The `CSpinButtonCtrl::SetRange` member function is used to set the minimum and maximum limits for an up-down control.
4. The control tab order determines which control is paired with the up-down control. The up-down control must follow the buddy control in the tab order.
5. Tick marks
6. The `CSliderCtrl::SetRange` member function is used to set the minimum and maximum limits for an up-down control.
7. The `CProgressCtrl::SetRange` member function is used to set the minimum and maximum limits for an up-down control.

Hour 16, "Using Bitmaps and Image Lists"

1. Masked and unmasked. Masked image lists include a mask used to draw the image transparently.

2. If items are often added to the image list, the grow-by parameter reduces the number of costly internal resize operations performed by the image list.

3. A transparent image is an image that allows part of the background surface to be visible.

4. The color mask is used to determine the color in the bitmap that is treated as the transparent color. The image list uses this information to create a mask for the image.

5. ILD_TRANSPARENT

6. The ILD_BLENDxx styles are used to combine the image with the system highlight color.

7. You are always responsible for destroying the bitmap or icon used as a source for the image stored in the image list. The image list will keep a copy of the image internally.

8. An overlapped image is made up of two combined image list items.

9. CBitmap

10. BitBlt

Hour 17, "List View Controls"

1. There are four list view styles: Icon, Small Icon, Report, and List.

2. Icon view uses a 32×32 icon. Small icon view uses a 16×16 icon.

3. SetWindowLong

4. First, you must initialize the LV_COLUMN structure, then call CListCtrl's InsertColumn member function.

5. Call CListCtrl's SetItem text member function.

6. -1

7. CListCtrl

8. No

9. The report view

10. LV_ITEM

Hour 18, "Tree Views"

1. TVN_BEGINLABELEDIT and TVN_ENDLABELEDIT

2. Edit labels

A

3. The first image is displayed when the tree view item is in its normal state. The second image is displayed when the item is selected.

4. `CTreeCtrl::DeleteAllItems()`

5. The properties for any view can be changed in the `PreCreateWindow` function.

6. The `TVS_HASLINES` is equivalent to the Has Lines property; `TVS_LINESATROOT` is the same as the Lines at Root property, `TVS_BUTTONS` is the same as the Has Buttons property, and the `TVS_EDITLABELS` style is equivalent to the Edit Labels property.

7. Unlike the list view control, where items are referred to by an index, items in a tree view control are referred to through an `HTREEITEM` handle.

8. Images stored in a tree view control can be any size.

9. Use the `TVI_FIRST` symbol when calling `CTreeCtrl::InsertItem`:

   `m_tree.InsertItem( szLabel, 1, 1, hParent, TVI_FIRST );`

Hour 19, "Using ActiveX Controls"

1. In the Components and Controls Gallery

2. Visual FoxPro, Visual Basic, Access, and Delphi are just a few development tools that support ActiveX controls.

3. Examples of events fired from ActiveX controls include mouse clicks, pressed buttons, and expiring timers.

4. Examples of properties exposed by ActiveX controls are the font and background color used by a control.

5. A grid control, such as the Microsoft Hierarchical FlexGrid

6. False

7. In AppWizard step two, the ActiveX Controls check box must be selected.

8. A function that is exposed by the control and called by the control's container

9. False

Hour 20, "Dynamic HTML"

1. `CHtmlView`

2. `Navigate` and `Navigate2`

3. `GoBack`

4. `GoHome`

5. LoadFromResource

6. GoForward

7. onmouseover

8. onmouseout

9. Right-click the HTML text in the editor, and choose Properties from the shortcut menu.

Hour 21, "Printing"

1. Call the GetDeviceCaps function and ask for RASTERCAPS information. Check the RC_BITBLT bit in the result. (See Listing 21.2.)

2. The five MFC view functions that are most commonly overridden for printing are

   - OnPreparePrinting
   - OnBeginPrinting
   - OnPrepareDC
   - OnPrint
   - OnEndPrinting

3. These functions are called once for each print job:

   - OnPreparePrinting
   - OnBeginPrinting
   - OnEndPrinting

   These functions are called once for each printed page:

   - OnPrepareDC
   - OnPrint

4. CPrintInfo

5. OnBeginPrinting

6. About 1,440

7. Set the CPrintInfo::m_bContinue member variable to TRUE

8. The positive direction is up—the bottom of the page is usually a large negative number.

9. The positive direction is to the right.

10. OnEndPrinting

A

Hour 22, "Using MFC to Save Program Data"

1. Persistence is the capability of an object to remember its state between executions.

2. Serialization is the act of storing the state of an object for the purpose of loading it at another time.

3. Serialization is the act of storing the state of a persistent object to an archive; deserialization is the act of reading data from an archive and re-creating a persistent object.

4. CArchive

5. Serialize

6. SerializeElements

Hour 23, "Form Views"

1. A form view is always modeless, whereas a dialog box can be either modal or modeless. A form view fits into the Document/View architecture and receives view messages from the MFC framework; a dialog box does not.

2. A dialog box resource used in a form view must have the following attributes:
   - Style: Child
   - Border: None
   - Visible: Unchecked
   - Titlebar: Unchecked

3. You must call ResizeParentToFit twice during OnInitialUpdate:
```
ResizeParentToFit( FALSE );
ResizeParentToFit( );
```

4. OnInitialUpdate and OnUpdate

5. To prevent an MDI child window from being resized, you must change the style of the frame that contains the form window. By default, this is the CChildFrame class. Masking off the WS_THICKFRAME style bits during PreCreateWindow will create a frame window that cannot be resized. If you make this modification, you might also want to mask off the WS_MAXIMIZEBOX style bit; this will disable the Maximize button on the form view.

6. CChildFrame

7. CFormView

8. CEditView

9. `CScrollView`

10. `CMultiDocTemplate`

Hour 24, "Creating ActiveX Controls"

1. An ActiveX interface is a group of related functions that are grouped together.

2. `IUnknown`

3. The ActiveX Control Test Container, Visual Basic, Internet Explorer, Access, Word, Excel, PowerPoint, and many others.

4. Ambient, Extended, Stock, and Custom

5. Stock and Custom

6. `DDP` and `DDX`

7. `COleCtrl`, `COleControlModule`, and `COlePropertyPage`

8. Ambient properties

9. Subclassing is a method of borrowing functionality from another window or control.

10. `DoSuperclassPaint`

A

Appendix B

The Developer Studio IDE

This appendix covers some basic information about the Developer Studio Integrated Development Environment.

Developer Studio is a one-stop solution for a Windows Developer using Visual C++. Developer Studio includes test and resource editors, a C++ compiler, an integrated debugger, and online help that are all integrated into an easy-to-use tool.

Using Developer Studio's Dockable Windows

Many of the views displayed by Developer Studio are dockable, which means they can be attached to the edge of the Developer Studio workspace where they remain until undocked. The project workspace window is an example of a dockable view.

To undock a dockable window, double-click the window's edge. To dock a floating window, move it to the edge of the workspace. If it is a dockable window, it docks itself. If you want to move a dockable window close to the edge of a workspace without docking, press the Ctrl key on the keyboard when you move the window.

What Is the Developer Studio Editor?

Developer Studio includes a sophisticated editor as one of its tools. The editor is integrated with the other parts of Developer Studio; files are edited in a Developer Studio child window.

You use the Developer Studio editor to edit C++ source files that will be compiled into Windows programs. The editor supplied with Developer Studio is similar to a word processor, but instead of fancy text-formatting features, it has features that help make writing source code easy.

Why Use the Developer Studio Editor?

You can use almost any editor to write C++ source code, but there are several reasons to consider using the editor integrated with Developer Studio. The editor includes many features that are found in specialized programming editors.

- Automatic syntax highlighting colors keywords, comments, and other source code in different colors.
- Automatic "smart" indenting helps line up your code into easy-to-read columns.
- Auto-Completion automatically displays a menu of items to help you finish C++ statements.
- Parameter Help displays the parameters for Windows functions as you type.
- Emulation for keystrokes used by other editors helps if you are familiar with editors such as Brief and Epsilon.
- Integrated keyword help enables you to get help on any keyword, MFC class, or Windows function just by pressing F1.
- Drag-and-drop editing enables you to easily move text by dragging it with the mouse.
- Integration with the compiler's error output helps you step through the list of errors reported by the compiler and positions the cursor at every error. This enables you to make corrections easily without leaving Developer Studio.

Using the Developer Studio Editor

The easiest way to learn about the Developer Studio editor is to edit a file and run through a few common actions, such as creating a new source file, saving and loading files, and using a few keyboard commands.

Editing a New Source File

To edit a new source file, click the New Text File icon on the toolbar. The New Text File icon looks like a blank piece of paper with a yellow highlight in one corner. You can also open a new source file using the menu by following these steps:

1. Select New from the File menu. This displays the New dialog box, which enables you to create a new text file, project, or other type of file.

2. Select the Files tab. Several different types of files will be displayed. Select the C++ Source File icon in the list box.

3. Click OK to close the New dialog box and open the new file for editing.

Each of the preceding methods creates an empty source file ready for editing. Type the source code from Listing B.1 into the new file.

INPUT   **LISTING B.1.** A MINIMAL C++ PROGRAM.

```
// This is a comment
int main()
{
    return 0;
}
```

B

The source code in Listing B.1 is a legal C++ program, although it doesn't actually do anything. As you typed the source code into the editor, the colors for some of the words should have changed. This is called syntax highlighting, and it's one of the features of Developer Studio's editor.

The first line in Listing B.1 begins with //, which is used to mark the beginning of a single-line comment in a C++ program. By default, comments are colored green by the Developer Studio editor. In contrast, `int` and `return` are colored blue to indicate they are C++ keywords.

Another editor feature is called *smart indenting*. This feature automatically arranges your text as you type, applying formatting rules to your text as each word or line is entered into the editor. For example, enter the source code from Listing B.2 into the text editor. Press Return at the end of each line, but do not add any spaces or tabs. As each line is typed, the editor rearranges the text into a standard format for you.

LISTING B.2. A SIMPLE C++ CLASS DECLARATION.

```cpp
class CFoo
{
    int nFoo;
    int nBar;
public:
    CFoo();
}
```

The source code provided in this book follows the same formatting convention used by the Developer Studio editor. Although some coding styles might be more compact, this style is very easy to read.

Saving a Source File

To save the contents of the editor, click the Save icon on the toolbar. The Save icon looks like a small floppy disk. You can also press Ctrl+S or select Save from the File menu.

When you update an existing source file you don't see a dialog box, and no further action is needed on your part. The existing file is updated using the current contents of the editor. If you save a new file, you see the Save As dialog box, and you must choose a location and filename for the new source file. Save the contents of Listing B.2 in the C:\ directory using the name CFoo.cpp. After saving the file, close CFoo.cpp by selecting Close from the File menu.

To save a file under a new name, select Save As from the File menu or press F12. Enter the new path and filename using the Save As dialog box as described previously.

Opening an Existing Source File

To open an existing source file, click the Open icon on the toolbar. The Open icon looks like a folder that is partially open. You can also press Ctrl+O or select Open from the File menu. Any of these methods brings up the File Open dialog box.

To open the CFoo.cpp file for editing, pop up the File Open dialog box and navigate to the C:\ directory. Select the CFoo.cpp file and click the button labeled Open. The CFoo.cpp file is loaded into the editor.

Using Editor Commands

As discussed in the first hour, a large set of editing commands is available from the keyboard. Although most editor commands are also available from the menu or toolbar, the following commands are frequently used from the keyboard:

- Undo, which reverses the previous editor action, is performed by pressing Ctrl+Z on the keyboard. The number of undo steps that can be performed is configurable in the Options dialog box.

- Redo, which is used to reverse an undo, is performed by pressing Ctrl+Y.

- LineCut, which removes or "cuts" the current line and places it on the Clipboard, is performed by pressing Ctrl+L.

- Cut removes any marked text from the editor and places it on the Clipboard. This command is performed by pressing Ctrl+X.

- Copy copies any marked text to the Clipboard but unlike the Cut command, does not remove the text from the editor. If no text is marked, the current line is copied. This command is performed by pressing Ctrl+C.

- Paste copies the Clipboard contents into the editor at the insertion point. This command is performed by pressing Ctrl+V.

This is only a small list of the available keyboard commands. To see a complete list, select Keyboard from the Help menu.

What Is the Microsoft Developer Network Library?

The Microsoft Developer Network (MSDN) library is the online help system integrated into Developer Studio. A similar version of the MSDN library is offered as a separate product. Usually, the indexes used by the MSDN library are copied to your hard disk, and the actual database remains on the CD. This spares a great deal of hard disk space. If you would like to speed up the MSDN library, run the setup program located on the first MSDN library CD, and install the library contents to a local hard drive.

B

Why Use the MSDN Library?

Because Visual C++ is not sold with a documentation set, the MSDN library is the only documentation that is included with the product. Although the online documentation is also available from Microsoft in book form, it costs you extra.

The MSDN library has several advantages over hard-copy documentation.

- It is fully searchable. There's a saying, "You can't search dead wood," and it applies perfectly to the difference between hard-copy documentation and Developer Studio's MSDN library. Suppose you're having a problem with a list box control. In a few seconds you can search the entire documentation set, including the MSDN library if you have it, and immediately begin looking up relevant information.

- You get context-sensitive help that brings up the MSDN library when you press the F1 key. When is the last time you pressed F1 and had a book fall off the bookshelf and open to the correct page?

- MSDN library is completely integrated into Developer Studio. One of the tabs in the project workspace window displays the MSDN library table of contents. The current topic is displayed in a Developer Studio child window.

- Last, but not least, you can always print out a hard copy when needed, and you don't even need a copying machine.

Getting Context-Sensitive Help

To get context-sensitive help from the MSDN library, press F1. You select a topic based on the current window and cursor position, and the MSDN library viewer will be launched. If you press F1 while editing a source file, help is provided for the word under the cursor. If there is more than one possible help topic, you see a list of choices.

Open a new document for editing, as described earlier in this chapter, and enter the source code provided in Listing B.3.

INPUT   **LISTING B.3.** TESTING THE MSDN LIBRARY'S CONTEXT-SENSITIVE HELP.

```
int main()
{
    return 0;
}
```

Every word in this example has a help topic. To get context-sensitive help, move the cursor to any word in Listing B.3 and press F1.

Searching for Help Using a Keyword

To search the MSDN library keyword list, click the Search tab in the MSDN viewer. The Search tab enables you to create a query in order to find a topic. You can use a query to search the entire contents, a subset of the contents, or the results of the last query. The last option is useful when you're narrowing the scope of a search. You can apply the query to the entire contents of MSDN library or to only the titles of each topic.

A query can be as simple as a single word, or it can be used to look for words that are adjacent or close to each other. You can use the AND, OR, NEAR, and NOT operators to create queries. Operators aren't required to be capitalized, although it helps to set off the operator from your search items. For example, to find all the topics where the words *dialog* and *tab* are close to each other, use the following query:

```
dialog NEAR tab
```

To look for topics where the word *main* is found but exclude any topics that contain the word *WinMain*, use the following query:

```
main NOT WinMain
```

Browsing Through the Contents Window

A third way to use the MSDN library is to browse through the contents listing under the Contents tab. The contents pane displays the titles for every available topic, arranged in an easy-to-use tree view.

When the MSDN library contents tree is completely collapsed, the contents pane displays the titles for the top level of the available topics. The titles displayed at the top level are somewhat like the titles of a series of books; the icon even looks like a book. When the book icon is closed, there is a plus sign next to the book title, indicating that the book can be opened to display its contents. Clicking the plus sign opens the book icon and expands the contents tree to display the contents of the open book. Topics are represented by icons that look like a page of text. To display the selected topic, click the topic icon; the MSDN library topic window opens. Clicking the plus sign also changes the plus sign to a minus, which you can click to close the book.

B

INDEX

Microsoft Foundation Class Hierarchy - Version 6.0

CObject

Classes Not Derived from CObject

Graphical Drawing

CDC
- CClientDC
- CMetaFileDC
- CPaintDC
- CWindowDC

Control Support

- CDockState
- CImageList

Graphical Drawing Objects

CGdiObject
- CBitmap
- CBrush
- CFont
- CPalette
- CPen
- CRgn

Menus

- CMenu

Command Line

- CCommandLineInfo

ODBC Database Support

- CDatabase
- CRecordset

user recordsets

- CLongBinary

DAO Database Support

- CDaoDatabase
- CDaoQueryDef
- CDaoRecordset
- CDaoTableDef
- CDaoWorkspace

Synchronization

CSyncObject
- CCriticalSection
- CEvent
- CMutex
- CSemaphore

Arrays

- CArray(Template)
- CByteArray
- CDWordArray
- CObArray
- CPtrArray
- CStringArray
- CUintArray
- CWordArray

— arrays of user types

Lists

- CList (Template)
- CPtrList
- CObList
- CStringList

— lists of user types

Maps

- CMap (Template)
- CMapWordToPtr
- CMapPtrToWord
- CMapPtrToPtr
- CMapWordToOb
- CMapStringToPtr
- CMapStringToOb
- CMapStringToString

— maps of user types

Internet Services

- CInternetSession
- CInternetConnection
  - CFtpConnection
  - CGopherConnection
  - CHttpConnection
- CFileFind
  - CFtpFileFind
  - CGopherFileFind
- CGopherLocator

Windows Sockets

- CAsyncSocket
  - CSocket

Internet Server API

- CHtmlStream
- CHttpFilter
- CHttpFilterContext
- CHttpServer
- CHttpServerContext

Runtime Object Model Support

- CArchive
- CDumpContext
- CRuntimeClass

Simple Value Types

- CPoint
- CRect
- CSize
- CString
- CTime
- CTimeSpan

Structures

- CCreateContext
- CMemoryState
- COleSafeArray
- CPrintInfo

Support Classes

- CCmdUI
  - COleCmdUI
- CDaoFieldExchange
- CDataExchange
- CDBVariant
- CFieldExchange
- COleDataObject
- COleDispatchDriver
- CPropExchange
- CRectTracker
- CWaitCursor

Typed Template Collections

- CTypedPtrArray
- CTypedPtrList
- CTypedPtrMap

OLE Type Wrappers

- CFontHolder
- CPictureHolder

OLE Automation Types

- COleCurrency
- COleDateTime
- COleDateTimeSpan
- COleVariant

Synchronization

- CMultiLock
- CSingleLock